LATIN AMERICA

and the

CARIBBEAN

A Continental Overview
of Environmental Issues

THE WORLD'S ENVIRONMENTS

KEVIN HILLSTROM AND
LAURIE COLLIER HILLSTROM, SERIES EDITORS

Global warming, rain forest destruction, mass extinction, overpopulation—the environmental problems facing our planet are immense and complex.

ABC-CLIO's series The World's Environments offers students and general readers a handle on the key issues, events, and people.

The six titles in the series examine the unique—and common—problems facing the environments of every continent on Earth and the ingenious ways local people are attempting to address them. Titles in this series:

Africa and the Middle East

Asia

Australia, Oceania, and Antarctica

Europe

Latin America and the Caribbean

North America

LATIN
AMERICA
and the
CARIBBEAN

A Continental Overview
of Environmental Issues

KEVIN HILLSTROM
LAURIE COLLIER HILLSTROM

A B C ☰ C L I O

Santa Barbara, California
Denver, Colorado   Oxford, England

Library of Congress Cataloging-in-Publication Data
Hillstrom, Kevin, 1963–
    Latin America and the Caribbean : a continental overview of
environmental issues / Kevin Hillstrom, Laurie Collier Hillstrom.
        p. cm. — (The world's environments)
    Includes bibliographical references and index.

    ISBN 1-57607-690-3 (acid-free paper); 1-57607-691-1 (eBook)
    1. Latin America—Environmental conditions. 2. Environmental
degradation—Latin America. 3. Environmental protection—Latin America.
4. Conservation of natural resources—Latin America. 5. Caribbean
Area—Environmental conditions. 6. Environmental degradation—Caribbean
Area. 7. Environmental protection—Caribbean Area. 8. Conservation of
natural resources—Caribbean Area. I. Hillstrom, Laurie Collier, 1965–
II. Title III. Series: Hillstrom, Kevin, 1963– . World's environments.

GE160.L29H55 2003
363.7'0098—dc22   2003017182

08 07 06 05 04   10 9 8 7 6 5 4 3 2 1

This book is also available on the World Wide Web as an eBook.
Visit http://www.abc-clio.com for details.

ABC-CLIO, Inc.
130 Cremona Drive, P.O. Box 1911
Santa Barbara, California 93116-1911

This book is printed on acid-free paper. ∞
Manufactured in the United States of America

Contents

List of
Tables and Figures

Introduction

THE WORLD'S ENVIRONMENTS

As the nations of the world enter the twenty-first century, they confront a host of environmental issues that demand attention. Some of these issues—pollution of freshwater and marine resources, degradation of wildlife habitat, escalating human population densities that place crushing demands on finite environmental resources—have troubled the world for generations, and they continue to defy easy solutions. Other issues—global climate change, the potential risks and rewards of genetically modified crops and other organisms, unsustainable consumption of freshwater resources—are of more recent vintage. Together, these issues pose a formidable challenge to our hopes of building a prosperous world community in the new millennium, especially since environmental protection remains a low priority in many countries. But despite an abundance of troubling environmental indicators, positive steps are being taken at the local, regional, national, and international levels to implement new models of environmental stewardship that strike an appropriate balance between economic advancement and resource protection. In some places, these efforts have achieved striking success. There is reason to hope that this new vision of environmental sustainability will take root all around the globe in the coming years.

The World's Environments series is a general reference resource that provides a comprehensive assessment of our progress to date in meeting the numerous environmental challenges of the twenty-first century. It offers detailed, current information on vital environmental trends and issues facing nations around the globe. The series consists of six volumes, each of which addresses conservation issues and the state of the environment in a specific region of the world: individual volumes for *Asia, Europe,* and *North America,* published in spring 2003, will be joined by *Africa and the Middle East; Australia, Oceania, and Antarctica;* and *Latin America and the Caribbean* in the fall of the same year.

Each volume of The World's Environments includes coverage of issues unique to that region of the world in such realms as habitat destruction, water pollution, depletion of natural resources, energy consumption, and development. In addition, each volume provides an overview of the region's response to environmental matters of worldwide concern, such as global warming. Information on these complex issues is presented in a manner that is informative, interesting, and understandable to a general readership. Moreover, each book in the series has been produced with an emphasis on objectivity and utilization of the latest environmental data from government agencies, nongovernmental organizations (NGOs), and international environmental research agencies, such as the various research branches of the United Nations.

Organization

Each of the six volumes of The World's Environments consists of ten chapters devoted to the following major environmental issues:

Population and Land Use. This chapter includes continental population trends, socioeconomic background of the populace, prevailing consumption patterns, and development and sprawl issues.

Biodiversity. This chapter reports on the status of flora and fauna and the habitat upon which they depend for survival. Areas of coverage include the impact of alien species on native plants and animals, the consequences of deforestation and other forms of habitat degradation, and the effects of the international wildlife trade.

Parks, Preserves, and Protected Areas. This chapter describes the size, status, and biological richness of area park systems, preserves, and wilderness areas and their importance to regional biodiversity.

Forests. Issues covered in this chapter include the extent and status of forest resources, the importance of forestland as habitat, and prevailing forest management practices.

Agriculture. This chapter is devoted to dominant farming practices and their impact on local, regional, and national ecosystems. Subjects of special significance in this chapter include levels of freshwater consumption for irrigation, farming policies, reliance on and attitudes toward genetically modified foods, and ranching.

Freshwater. This chapter provides detailed coverage of the ecological health of rivers, lakes, and groundwater resources, extending special attention to pollution and consumption issues.

Oceans and Coastal Areas. This chapter explores the ecological health of continental marine areas. Principal areas of coverage include the current state of (and projected outlook for) area fisheries, coral reef conservation, coastal habitat loss from development and erosion, and water quality trends in estuaries and other coastal regions.

Energy and Transportation. This chapter assesses historic and emerging trends in regional energy use and transportation, with an emphasis on the environmental and economic benefits and drawbacks associated with energy sources ranging from fossil fuels to nuclear power to renewable technologies.

Air Quality and the Atmosphere. This chapter reports on the current state of and future outlook for air quality in the region under discussion. Areas of discussion include emissions responsible for air pollution problems like acid rain and smog, as well as analysis of regional contributions to global warming and ozone loss.

Environmental Activism. This chapter provides a summary of the history of environmental activism in the region under discussion.

In addition, each volume of The World's Environments contains sidebars that provide readers with information on key individuals, organizations, projects, events, and controversies associated with specific environmental issues. By focusing attention on specific environmental "flashpoints"—the status of a single threatened species, the future of a specific wilderness area targeted for oil exploration, the struggles of a single village to adopt environmentally sustainable farming practices—many of these sidebars also shed light on larger environmental issues. The text of each volume is followed by an appendix of environmental and developmental agencies and organizations on the World Wide Web. Finally, each volume includes a general index containing citations to issues, events, and people discussed in the book, as well as supplemental tables, graphs, charts, maps, and photographs.

Coverage by Geographic Region

Each of the six volumes of The World's Environments focuses on a single region of the world: Africa and the Middle East; Asia; Australia, Oceania, and Antarctica; Europe; Latin America; and North America. In most instances, the arrangement of coverage within these volumes was obvious, in accordance with widely recognized geographic divisions. But placement of a few countries was more problematic. Mexico, for instance, is recognized both as part of North America and as the northernmost state in Latin America. Moreover, some international environmental research agencies (both governmental and nongovernmental) place data on Mexico under the North American umbrella, while others classify it among Central American and Caribbean nations. We ultimately decided to place Mexico in the Latin America volume, which covers Central and South America, in recognition of its significant social, economic, climatic, and environmental commonalities with those regions.

Similarly, environmental data on the vast Russian Federation, which sprawls over northern reaches of both Europe and Asia, is sometimes found in resources on Asia, and at other times in assessments of Europe's environment. Since most of Russia's population is located in the western end of its territory, we decided to cover the country's environmental issues in The World's Environments *Europe* volume, though occasional references to environmental conditions in the Russian Far East do appear in the Asia volume.

Finally, we decided to expand coverage in the Africa volume to cover environmental issues of the Middle East—also sometimes known as West Asia. This decision was made partly out of a recognition that the nations of Africa and the Middle East share many of the same environmental challenges—extremely limited freshwater supplies, for instance—and partly because of the space required in the Asia volume to fully explicate the multitude of grave environmental problems confronting Asia's central, southern, and eastern reaches. Coverage of other nations that straddle continental boundaries—such as the countries of the Caucasus region—are also concentrated in one volume, though references to some nations may appear elsewhere in the series.

Following is an internal breakdown of the volume-by-volume coverage for The World's Environments. This is followed in turn by overview maps for the current volume, showing country locations and key cities and indicating physical features.

Africa and the Middle East

Middle East and North Africa:

Algeria
Bahrain
Cyprus
Egypt
Gaza
Iraq
Israel
Jordan
Kuwait
Lebanon
Libya
Morocco
Oman
Qatar
Saudi Arabia
Syrian Arab Republic
Tunisia
Turkey
United Arab Emirates
West Bank
Yemen

Sub-Saharan Africa:

Angola
Benin
Botswana
Burkina Faso
Burundi
Cameroon
Central African Republic
Chad
Congo, Republic of the
Congo, Democratic Republic of
 (Zaire)

Côte d'Ivoire
Equatorial Guinea
Eritrea
Ethiopia
Gabon
Gambia
Ghana
Guinea
Guinea-Bissau
Kenya
Lesotho
Liberia
Madagascar
Malawi
Mali
Mauritania
Mozambique
Namibia
Niger
Nigeria
Rwanda
Senegal
Sierra Leone
Somalia
South Africa
Sudan
Tanzania
Togo
Uganda
Zambia
Zimbabwe

Asia

Afghanistan
Armenia
Azerbaijan

Bangladesh
Bhutan
Cambodia
China
Georgia
India
Indonesia
Iran
Japan
Kazakhstan
Korea, Democratic People's
   Republic of (North)
Korea, Republic of (South)
Kyrgyzstan
Lao People's Democratic Republic
Malaysia
Mongolia
Myanmar (Burma)
Nepal
Pakistan
Philippines
Singapore
Sri Lanka
Tajikistan
Thailand
Turkmenistan
Uzbekistan
Vietnam

Australia, Oceania, and Antarctica
Australia
Cook Islands
Fiji
French Polynesia
Guam
Kiribati

Nauru
New Caledonia
Northern Mariana Islands
Marshall Islands
Federated States of Micronesia
New Guinea
New Zealand
Palau
Papua New Guinea
Pitcairn Island
Samoa
Solomon Islands
Tonga
Tuvalu
Vanuatu
Wallis and Futuna
Various territories
*(Note: Antarctica is discussed in a
   stand-alone chapter)*

Europe
Albania
Austria
Belarus
Belgium
Bosnia and Herzegovina
Bulgaria
Croatia
Czech Republic
Denmark
Estonia
Finland
France
Germany
Greece
Hungary

Iceland

Ireland

Italy

Latvia

Lithuania

Republic of Macedonia

Moldova

Netherlands

Norway

Poland

Portugal

Romania

Russian Federation

Slovakia

Slovenia

Spain

Sweden

Switzerland

Ukraine

United Kingdom

Yugoslavia

**Latin America
and the Caribbean**

Argentina

Belize

Bolivia

Brazil

Caribbean territories

Chile

Colombia

Costa Rica

Cuba

Dominican Republic

Ecuador

El Salvador

Guatemala

Guyana

Haiti

Honduras

Jamaica

Mexico

Nicaragua

Panama

Paraguay

Peru

Suriname

Trinidad and Tobago

Uruguay

Venezuela

North America

Canada

United States

CARIBBEAN
SEA

ATLANTIC
OCEAN

Magdalena River

LLANOS
Orinoco River
La Gran
Sabana

Guaviare River

EQUATOR

Negro River

Putumayo River
Japurá River
Branca River
Amazon River

Amazon River

A
N
D
E
S

Marañón River
Ucayali River
Juruá River
Purus River
Tapajós River
Xingu River
Araguaia River
Tocantins River

Lake Titicaca

MATO
GROSSO

São Francisco River
SERRA DO ESPINHAÇO

Lake Poopó

ALTIPLANO

ATACAMA DESERT

CHACO
Paraguai River
Paraná River

TROPIC OF CAPRICORN

GRAN
Bermejo River

SERRA DO MAR

PACIFIC
OCEAN

Salinas Grande
Paraná River
Uruguay River

LAS
PAMPAS

Colorado River

ATLANTIC
OCEAN

Negro River

PATAGONIA

Falkland Islands

Strait of
Magellan

Elevation (meters)
0–200
200–500
500–1,000
1,000–2,000
2,000–3,000
3,000–4,000
4,000–5,000
5,000–6,000

0   300   600 900 km

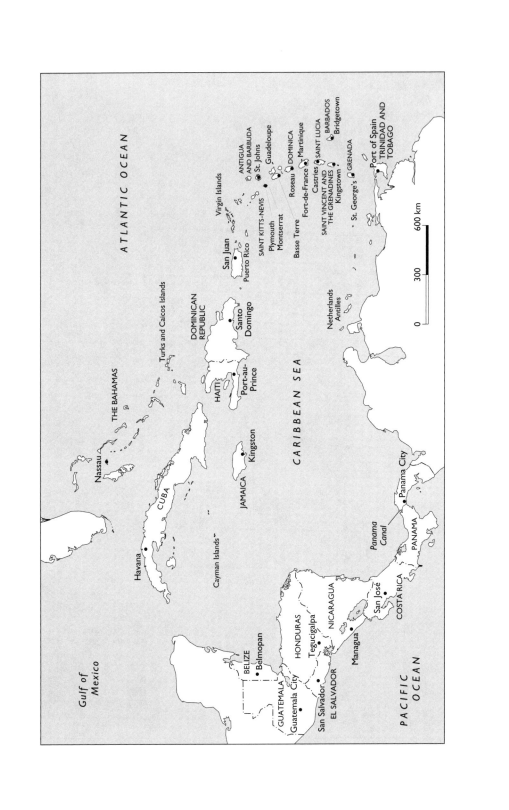

Gulf of Mexico

ATLANTIC OCEAN

Havana

THE BAHAMAS

Nassau

CUBA

Cayman Islands

JAMAICA
Kingston

Turks and Caicos Islands

DOMINICAN REPUBLIC

Santo Domingo

HAITI
Port-au-Prince

Virgin Islands

San Juan
Puerto Rico

SAINT KITTS-NEVIS

ANTIGUA AND BARBUDA
St. Johns

Guadeloupe
Basse Terre

Plymouth
Montserrat

DOMINICA
Roseau

Fort-de-France
Martinique

Castries
SAINT LUCIA

BARBADOS
Bridgetown

SAINT VINCENT AND THE GRENADINES
Kingstown

St. George's
GRENADA

Port of Spain
TRINIDAD AND TOBAGO

Netherlands Antilles

CARIBBEAN SEA

BELIZE
Belmopan

GUATEMALA
Guatemala City

San Salvador
EL SALVADOR

HONDURAS
Tegucigalpa

NICARAGUA

Managua

COSTA RICA
San José

Panama Canal
Panama City
PANAMA

PACIFIC OCEAN

0   300   600 km

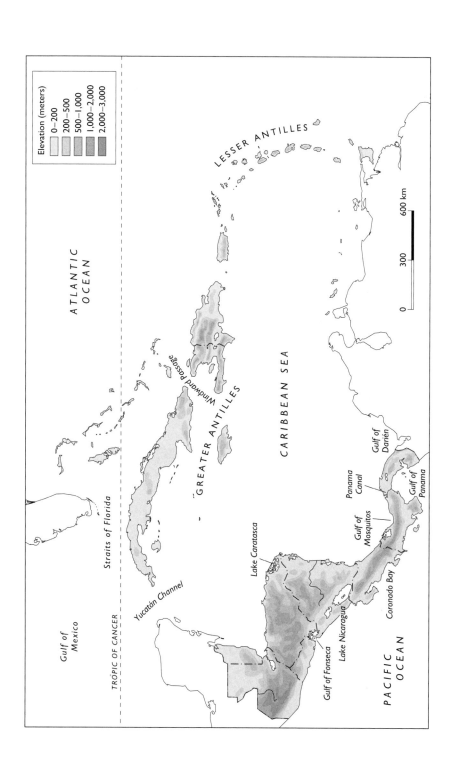

Elevation (meters)

0–200
200–500
500–1,000
1,000–2,000
2,000–3,000

ATLANTIC OCEAN

Gulf of Mexico

TROPIC OF CANCER

Straits of Florida

Yucatán Channel

GREATER ANTILLES

Windward Passage

LESSER ANTILLES

CARIBBEAN SEA

Lake Caratasca

Gulf of Fonseca

Lake Nicaragua

Coronado Bay

Gulf of Mosquitos

Panama Canal

Gulf of Panama

Gulf of Darién

PACIFIC OCEAN

0   300   600 km

Acknowledgments

The authors are indebted to many members of the ABC-CLIO family for their fine work on this series. Special thanks are due to Vicky Speck, Gina Zondorak, and Kevin Downing. We would also like to extend special thanks to our advisory board members, whose painstaking reviews played a significant role in shaping the final content of each volume, and to the contributors who lent their expertise and talent to this project.

Biographical Notes

Authors

KEVIN HILLSTROM and **LAURIE HILLSTROM** have written and edited award-winning reference books on a wide range of subjects, including American history, international environmental issues, environmental activism, outdoor travel, and business and industry. Works produced by the Hillstroms include *Environmental Leaders 1* and *2* (1997 and 2000), the four-volume *American Civil War Reference Library* (2000), the four-volume *Vietnam War Reference Library* (2000), *Paddling Michigan* (2001), *Encyclopedia of Small Business, 2d ed.* (2001), and *The Vietnam Experience: A Concise Encyclopedia of American Literature, Films, and Songs* (1998).

Advisory Board

J. DAVID ALLAN received his B.Sc. (1966) from the University of British Columbia and his Ph.D. (1971) from the University of Michigan. He served on the Zoology faculty of the University of Maryland until 1990, when he moved to the University of Michigan, where he currently is Professor of Conservation Biology and Ecosystem Management in the School of Natural Resources and Environment. Dr. Allan specializes in the ecology and conservation of rivers. He is the author of *Stream Ecology* (1995) and coauthor (with C. E. Cushing) of *Streams: Their Ecology and Life* (2001). He has published extensively on topics in community ecology and the influence of land use on the ecological integrity of rivers. He serves or has served on committees for the North American Benthological Society, Ecological Society of America, and the American Society of Limnology and Oceanography. He serves or has served on the editorial board of the scientific journals *Freshwater Biology* and *Journal of the North American Benthological Society* and on scientific advisory committees for the American Rivers and Nature Conservancy organizations.

DAVID LEONARD DOWNIE is Director of Education Partnerships for the Earth Institute at Columbia University, where he has conducted research and taught courses on international environmental politics since 1994. Educated at Duke

University and the University of North Carolina, Dr. Downie is author of numerous scholarly publications on the Stockholm Convention, the Montreal Protocol, the United Nations Environment Program, and other topics in global environmental politics. From 1994 to 1999, Dr. Downie served as Director of Environmental Policy Studies at the School of International and Public Affairs at Columbia University.

CHRIS MAGIN was educated at Cambridge University in Cambridge, England. He took an undergraduate degree in Natural Sciences and a Ph.d. in Zoology, conducting fieldwork on hyraxes in Serengeti National Park in Tanzania. Since then he has been a professional conservationist, employed by various international organizations, mainly in Africa and Asia. He currently works for Flora and Fauna International. His special areas of interest are desert ungulates, ornithology, and protected area management.

JEFFREY A. McNEELY is chief scientist at IUCN–The World Conservation Union, where he has worked since 1980. Prior to going to IUCN, he spent three years in Indonesia, two years in Nepal, and seven years in Thailand working on various biodiversity-related topics. He has published more than thirty books, including *A Threat to Life: The Impact of Climate Change on Japan's Biodiversity* (2000); *The Great Reshuffling: The Human Dimensions of Invasive Alien Species* (2001); and *Ecoagriculture: Strategies to Feed the World and Save Wild Biodiversity* (2003). He is currently writing a book on war and biodiversity. He was secretary general of the 1992 World Congress on Protected Areas (Caracas, Venezuela) and has been deeply involved in the development of the Convention on Biological Diversity. He is on the editorial board of seven international journals.

CARMEN REVENGA is a senior associate with the Information Program at the World Resources Institute. Her current work focuses on water resources, global fisheries, and species conservation. She specializes in environmental indicators that measure the condition of ecosystems at the global and regional level and is also part of WRI's Global Forest Watch team, coordinating forest monitoring activities with Global Forest Watch partners in Chile. Ms. Revenga is lead author of the WRI report *Pilot Analysis of Global Ecosystems: Freshwater Systems* (2000) and a contributing author to the WRI's *Pilot Analysis of Global Ecosystems: Coastal Ecosystems* (2001). These two reports assess the condition of freshwater and coastal ecosystems as well as their capacity to continue to provide goods and services on which humans depend. Ms. Revenga is also the lead author of *Watersheds of the World: Ecological Value and Vulnerability* (1998), which is the first analysis of a wide range of global data at the watershed level. Before joining WRI in 1997, she worked as an environmental scientist with Science and Policy Associates, Inc., an environmental consulting firm in Washington, D.C. Her work covered topics in sustainable forestry and climate change.

ROBIN WHITE is a senior associate with the World Resources Institute, an environmental think tank based in Washington, D.C. Her focus at WRI has been on the development of environmental indicators and statistics for use in the *World Resources Report* and in global ecosystems analysis. She was the lead author of the WRI report *Pilot Analysis of Global Ecosystems: Grassland Ecosystems* (2000), which analyzes quantitative information on the condition of the world's grasslands. Her current work focuses on developing an ecosystem goods and services approach to the analysis of the world's drylands. A recent publication regarding this work is WRI's Information Policy Brief, *An Ecosystem Approach to Drylands: Building Support for New Development Policies*. Ms. White completed her Ph.D. in geography at the University of Wisconsin, Madison, with a minor in wildlife ecology. Before joining WRI in 1996, she was a policy analyst with the U.S. Congress, Office of Technology Assessment.

Contributors

RAFIS ABAZOV is a visiting scholar at the Harriman Institute at Columbia University. He graduated from the Kyrgyz National University (1989) and earned his Ph.D. in Political Science in Moscow, Russia (1994). He worked as a regional analyst for a variety of Moscow-based news agencies and newspapers, and as an independent consultant, contributing annual reports to Freedom House's annual *Nations in Transit* report. Rafis Abazov has authored three books and contributed articles to a wide range of publications, including *Eurasian Studies, Central Asian Survey,* and *International Journal of Central Asian Studies.* He has also contributed to the *Encyclopedia of Nationalism* (2001), *Encyclopedia of Modern Asia* (2002), *Encyclopedia of Modern Economies* (2002), and the *Encyclopedia of the Developing World* (forthcoming, 2004).

C. BRAD FAUGHT, PH.D., is a journalist and historian. He is the author of many academic, magazine, and newspaper works. He recently contributed a series of entries to the *Grolier Encyclopedia of the Victoirian Era* (2003) and is the author of *The Oxford Movement: A Thematic History of the Tractarians and Their Times* (2003).

KATHRYN MILES received her Ph.D. in literature from the University of Delaware and is currently an assistant professor of English and environmental studies at Unity College. She has worked as a freelance environmental writer for several newspapers and magazines and has published on British modernism in academic journals. She is a member of ASLE (Association for the Study of Literature and the Environment), NAAGE (North American Alliance of Green Education), and the Virginia Woolf Society.

KIRSTEN SILVIUS, born and raised in Venezuela, received her B.A. degree from Bowdoin College in Brunswick, Maine, and both her M.S. and Ph.D. degrees in ecology from the University of Florida at Gainesville. Currently she is an adjunct professor at the State University of New York's School of Environmental Science and Forestry in Syracuse and since 1989 has also been a Research Associate with the Wildlife Conservation Society. Her research focuses on two main areas: seed dispersal and seed predation processes by birds, mammals, and insects in tropical forests; and wildlife use by indigenous peoples in South America. She is editor of the upcoming book *People in Nature: Wildlife Conservation in South and Central America.* In addition to publications in peer-reviewed scientific journals, she has also written many popular articles for *Wildlife Conservation Magazine.*

RONALD YOUNG is professor of history at Georgia Southern University in Statesboro, Georgia. His areas of specialty include Latin American social history of the nineteenth and twentieth centuries; Latin America's colonial era; the history of urbanization and transportation in Latin America; and studies of Venezuela, Argentina, Brazil, and Mexico.

Population and Land Use

Across Latin America and the Caribbean, various indicators of economic development, human development, and environmental health provide a mixed picture of the region's present status and future outlook. Positive developments include general improvement in education and women's rights, and a notable transition away from authoritarian regimes toward more democratically oriented governments. But many nations are still prone to economic and political turmoil, and desperate poverty continues to stalk the land, casting its shadow over rural communities and city slums alike. In addition, Latin America and the Caribbean are struggling to rein in widespread patterns of land use and exploitation that are clearly unsustainable over the long term, both for economic prosperity and ecosystem health. "Generally speaking, the causes of the increasing air, land and water pollution being experienced by the region, and the health consequences of this, are to be sought in agriculture and unplanned urbanization" (UN Economic Commission for Latin America and the Caribbean and UN Environment Programme 2001).

Population Trends in Latin America
The combined population of Central America (including Mexico), South America, and Caribbean states in mid-2002 was approximately 531 million, an increase of more than 75 percent from 1972, when the regional population was estimated at 299 million—and a jump of more than 500 percent from 1930, when the region held only 100 million people (Population Reference Bureau 2002; UN Centre for Human Settlements 2001). The most heavily populated subregion is South America, which had approximately 354 million inhabitants in mid-2002. Brazil alone accounts for nearly half of this total, with 174 million people; other South American nations with large

populations include Colombia (44 million) and Argentina (37 million). Central America accounts for another 140 million people—with nearly 102 million located in Mexico—and the island states of the Caribbean contribute approximately 37 million. The most populated country in the latter region is Cuba, with about 11 million people (Population Reference Bureau 2002). Altogether, Brazil and Mexico contain more than half of the people in the entire Latin American sector.

Within Latin America, population density varies enormously from country to country and within states and geographic regions of individual countries. In Central America, for example, El Salvador, the smallest and most densely populated country in the region, has a density almost thirty times greater than that of Belize, Central America's least populated country (UN Development Programme 2002).

Populations in Latin America are growing at a faster clip than in most other parts of the world, despite a significant downturn in the region's annual population growth rate, from 2.48 percent in 1972 to 1.52 percent by 2000. Immigration to the United States and other countries is partially responsible for this decline, but a far greater factor is the smaller size of Latin American families at the close of the twentieth century. Whereas the fertility rate for the average Latin American woman was 5.6 children in 1970, that statistic dropped to only 2.7 children in 1999. Improved access to family planning and health care resources are the primary drivers of this change in birth patterns (UN Population Division 2001). Health care advances also have enabled Latin America to slice its child mortality rate by more than half in the last three decades of the twentieth century (World Bank 2002).

Latin American people are, on the average, living significantly longer than they were even three decades ago. In 1970 the average life expectancy was a little under sixty-six years, although there was considerable variation between nations. Thirty years later, life expectancy was more than seventy-two years. Today, the highest life expectancies can be found in the Caribbean (74 years) and in South America (73.5 years)—but again, major differences exist between countries in this regard. For example, life expectancy in Cuba and Puerto Rico is fully twenty years greater than in Haiti, a country that has long been racked by crushing levels of impoverishment, violence, and government corruption. (Haiti also has the highest infant mortality rate in the Western Hemisphere.) In South America, meanwhile, residents of Venezuela and Colombia live, on the average, a full decade longer than residents of Bolivia.

A Rapidly Urbanizing Region

Most of Latin America's population is concentrated on the Pacific seaboard—home to 70 percent of the total population and, not coincidentally, the bulk of

São Paulo, Brazil PHOTODISC, INC.

the region's economic activity—and in urban areas. In fact, Latin America and the Caribbean is the most urbanized region in the developing world. It houses only 8.4 percent of the world population but accounts for some 15 percent of all human beings living in settlements of more than 1 million inhabitants (UN Economic Commission for Latin America and the Caribbean and UN Environment Programme 2001).

Half a century ago, Latin America's population was evenly divided between urban and rural communities. Today, between 70 and 75 percent of Latin America's population is urban, a percentage that is roughly equivalent to that of developed countries in North America and Europe. Two of the four largest cities in the world—Mexico City (18.1 million people in 2001—with another 12 million in the larger metropolitan area) and São Paulo (17.8 million)—are in Latin America, as are three other "megacities" containing more than 8 million residents (Buenos Aires, Rio de Janeiro, and Lima). If the present trend holds, Latin America will be the most urbanized region in the entire world within two decades, with approximately 360 million urban residents, four metropolitan areas of more than 10 million people, and nearly 30 percent of the total population contained in cities with a million or more people (UN Centre for Human Settlements 2001; UN Population Division 2001).

Latin America's dramatic swing toward urbanization is, in essence, the end result of people's basic aspirations to build better lives for themselves and their families. "The reasons people migrate to cities are clear: economic opportunity born of greater economic productivity in the cities; and a better life than in the country as a result of access to health care and other services. Much is made of the squalid and violent conditions of the shantytowns that sprawl across the region, but life expectancy levels for urban dwellers far exceed those for rural areas, as do education levels and most other standard-of-living measures" (Vourvoulias 1999). Nonetheless, the increased educational, employment, and civil participation benefits that accompany migration to cities are by no means made available to all newcomers, and Latin America's swelling urban centers are bedeviled by problems—ranging from air and water pollution to proliferating slums and their attendant health and crime miseries—that are becoming more acute with each passing day. For example, the amount of solid waste generated in Latin American countries has doubled over the past thirty years, and its composition has become increasingly weighted toward nonbiodegradable and toxic materials. But the region's cities currently lack the infrastructure to handle this increase, and they lack sufficient funds to make necessary upgrades to their waste disposal programs (UN Environment Programme 2000).

In many areas, the rapid growth of urban populations and resultant spillage of people, homes, and businesses onto previously undeveloped lands has taken on a fearsome momentum all its own, with municipalities falling far behind in providing basic infrastructure elements such as housing, water, sewer, electricity, streets, schools, and effective law enforcement. For example, in Amazonia—the Amazon rain forest and basin that covers much of equatorial South America—it has been estimated that 60 to 80 percent of the growth in urban centers "has occurred in self-built shantytowns located mainly on the periphery of existing towns and cities, well beyond the reach of established utility and public transport lines. This rapid growth has increased traffic congestion, and air quality has perceptibly deteriorated in all metropolitan centers. As accessible and suitable vacant lands fill in, ecologically unstable but unoccupied areas are eventually taken over by squatters, especially areas prone to flooding" (Browder and Godfrey 1997).

Indeed, the impact of urbanization on Amazonia, the crown jewel of Latin America's natural treasures, has been considerable over the last thirty to forty years.

Far from the lethargic and insular Amazon river town depicted by anthropologists only a generation ago, the current focal point of regional settlement is the volatile boomtown, seething with activity, deep in the interior of the Amazonian upland rainforests," stated one observer. "New urban centers have proliferated across the landscape in previously inaccessible [lowland] forest areas. Older towns and cities have become enveloped in a sea of peri-urban shantytowns. Unlike their remote counterparts on the 19th-century North American frontier, which were plagued by uncertain transportation and communications connections, the contemporary rainforest cities are permeated by global currents of information, trade, and politics. . . . Some virtually vaporize into ghost towns, after riding brief boom-bust waves of the extractive activity so typical of the region. Others grow to become permanent settlements of continuing economic importance. (ibid.)

Political Changes and Economic Development in Latin America

Latin America has undergone a dramatic shift away from military dictatorships toward more democratic forms of government in the past two decades, and several nations shaken by internal conflict during the 1980s enjoyed relatively peaceful conditions during the 1990s. In Central America, especially, the 1990s saw generally positive progress in the realms of political and social stability. Countries such as El Salvador and Nicaragua, where war and civil strife rendered the 1980s a veritable "lost decade" in terms of economic development, finally returned to levels of economic productivity that they enjoyed back in the 1970s and early 1980s. "The importance of ending the decades of authoritarianism and armed conflict cannot be overestimated in terms of the region's ability to restart the path toward economic growth," commented one analysis. "Today, no social or political group [in Central America] justifies social inequality in the name of political stability or national security" (UN Development Programme 2002).

Figure 1.1 GDP per capita (U.S.$1995/Year): Latin America and the Caribbean

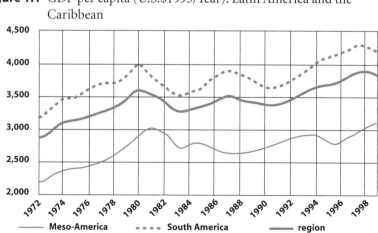

SOURCE: United Nations Environment Programme. 2002. *GEO: Global Environment Outlook 3*. Data estimated from World Bank 2001.

Severe Weather Events Contribute to Land Alteration in Latin America

People watch the overflowing waters of the Choluteca River on October 31, 1998, in Tegucigalpa, Honduras, a result of Hurricane Mitch. AFP/CORBIS

In addition to the hand of humankind, weather phenomena and natural disasters have played a significant role in shaping the current character of Latin America's jungles, deserts, marshlands, and coasts. Central America and the Caribbean, in particular, occupy a geographic zone in which severe weather events are a "constant threat" (UN Development Programme 2002), but all of the region is vulnerable. "The nature of the region's physical environment means that there is a particularly serious risk of the occurrence of phenomena capable of causing a disaster," added one UN agency. "The Sierra Madre, the chain of new volcanoes, the Central American isthmus and almost the whole length of the Andean range are very active tectonic elements responsible for the

occurrence of large-scale earthquakes and volcanic eruptions. In tropical latitudes, the region is prone to tropical storms and hurricanes which occur seasonally in both the Atlantic and the Pacific" (UN Economic Commission for Latin America and the Caribbean and UN Environment Programme 2001). Droughts (which heighten the risk of major forest fires) and flooding are also frequent phenomena in various parts of Latin America, in part because virtually all of the region is affected by the El Niño–Southern Oscillation, a recurrent global weather phenomenon.

The region's exposure to severe weather events and other natural phenomena is further exacerbated by human development and settlement patterns. In many countries, population centers are clustered along coastal

(continues)

areas that are particularly vulnerable to hurricanes. Moreover, infrastructure in these urban centers is often inadequate to withstand severe storms, and the prevalence of unsustainable consumption and development patterns further aggravates the impact of cyclones, wildfires, and floods. "[Unsustainable practices] include the inadequate disposal of wastes, the overuse of hydro resources, the poor treatment of sewage, the use of herbicides and insecticides in agriculture, deforestation, and hillside agriculture without plans for soil management and conservation. Some countries have begun actions dealing with disasters (early warning, evacuation, first aid), but few have done anything in terms of prevention and mitigation. The latter would include attacking the sources of vulnerability to reduce the impact of these events, given the impossibility of avoiding their occurrence" (UN Development Programme 2002).

Over the last thirty years, it has been estimated that natural disasters have cost Central America alone more than U.S.$50 billion (in 1998 dollars). Hurricane Mitch, which thundered across the region in October 1998, was perhaps the most powerful hurricane to hit Central America in more than a century. In Honduras, for instance, this storm brought winds and flooding that wiped out nearly a decade of development (losses were estimated to be equivalent to about 80 percent of the country's gross domestic product) (UN Economic Commission for Latin America and the Caribbean and UN Programme 2001).

Sources:
UN Development Programme. 2002. *Central America and Panama: The State of the Region 2002*. New York: UNDP. UN Economic Commission for Latin America and the Caribbean and UN Environment Programme. 2001. "The Sustainability of Development in Latin America and the Caribbean: Challenges and Opportunities." Report prepared for World Summit on Sustainable Development, Rio de Janeiro, October 23–24, Rio de Janeiro: ECLAC.

Welcome developments ushered in by the emergence of more open and democratic governmental institutions include major reforms of judiciary systems, increased civic participation in addressing societal woes, improved institutional responsiveness to community viewpoints, strengthened local governments and municipalities, economic reforms designed to encourage investment and entrepreneurship, and privatization of large state-owned enterprises (though many powerful extractive industries remain under state control, especially in the energy sector). Proliferating free trade agreements and customs unions, including the North American Free Trade Agreement (NAFTA), the Andean pact, the Southern Common Market of Latin America (MERCOSUR),

Table 1.1 Latin America and the Caribbean: Natural Disasters between 1972 and 2001

Country and Year	Type of Disaster	Number of Persons Affected		Millions of 1998 Dollars
		Deaths	Directly Affected	Total Damage
Nicaragua, 1972	Earthquake	6,000	300,000	2,968
Honduras, 1974	Hurricane Fifi	7,000	115,000	1,331
Grenada, 1975	Tropical storm			29
Antigua and Barbuda, 1975	Earthquake		4,200	61
Guatemala, 1976	Earthquake	23,000	2,550,000	2,147
Dominica, 1979	Hurricane David	42	60,060	118
Dominican Republic, 1979	Hurricanes David and Frederico	2,000	1,200,000	1,869
Nicaragua, 1982	Floods	80	70,000	599
El Salvador, 1982	Earthquake, droughts, and flooding	600	20,000	216
Guatemala, 1982	Heavy rains and drought	610	10,000	136
Nicaragua, 1982	Floods and drought			588
Bolivia, Ecuador, and Peru, 1982–1983	El Niño		3,840,000	5,651
Mexico, 1985	Earthquake	8,000	150,000	6,216
Colombia, 1985	Eruption of Nevado del Ruiz volcano	22,000	200,000	465
El Salvador, 1986	Earthquake	1,200	520,000	1,352
Ecuador, 1987	Earthquake	1,000	82,500	1,438
Nicaragua, 1988	Hurricane Joan	148	550,000	1,160
Nicaragua, 1992	Eruption of Cerro Negro volcano	2	12,000	22
Nicaragua, 1992	Pacific tsunami	116	40,500	30
Anguilla, 1995	Hurricane Luis			59
Netherlands Antilles, 1995	Hurricanes Luis and Marilyn			1,112
Costa Rica, 1996	Hurricane Cesar	39	40,260	157
Nicaragua, 1996	Hurricane Cesar	9	29,500	53
Costa Rica, 1997–1998	El Niño		119,279	93
Andean Community, 1997–1998	El Niño	600	125,000	7,694
Dominican Republic, 1998	Hurricane Georges	235	296,637	2,193
Central America, 1998	Hurricane Mitch	9,214	1,191,908	6,008
Colombia, 1999	Earthquake	1,185	559,401	1,580
Venezuela, 1999	Torrential rain	—	68,503	3,237
Belize, 2000	Hurricane Keith	10	57,400	265
El Salvador, 2001	Earthquakes	1,159	1,412,938	1,518
Total		84,249	13,625,086	50,365

SOURCE: The Sustainability of Development in Latin America and the Caribbean: Challenges and Opportunities (LC/G.2145 [CONF.90/3]), document presented at the Regional Preparatory Conference of Latin America and the Caribbean for the World Conference on Sustainable Development (Johannesburg, South Africa, 2002), Rio de Janeiro, Brazil, October 23–24, 2001 (http://www.rolac.unep.mx/foroalc/brasil2001/finales/CRPSusti.pdf), pp. 99.

the Caribbean Community and Common Market (CARICOM), and the Central American Common Market have also been touted as powerful tools for economic growth (UN Environment Programme 2002).

Proponents of these changes believe that they will move the Latin American/ Caribbean region out of the economic doldrums that have typified many— though not all—countries over the last two to three decades. For example, it has been noted that deregulation and privatization initiatives have spurred major spikes in foreign direct investment (FDI) in such areas as financial services, infrastructure development, and extraction activities. In absolute terms, net foreign direct investment inflows into Latin America and the Caribbean jumped from U.S.$16.5 billion a year in the five-year period from 1991 to 1995 to U.S.$58.2 billion a year in the period 1995 to 2000 (UN Economic Commission for Latin America and the Caribbean and UN Environment Programme 2001).

In some sectors, these infusions have produced much-needed progress in corporate environmental performance, as foreign firms (especially those operating in high-tech industries) introduce more environmentally sensitive practices to production systems (Jenkins 2000). In the realm of mining, for example, some international companies have introduced cleaner extraction technologies and models of environmental management that have reined in some of mining's notoriously negative impacts on the environment, including land degradation, atmospheric pollution, and poisoning of rivers and other freshwater resources (ibid.). But in countries that have yet to impose meaningful environmental regulations on mining activities—such as Peru—larger companies continue to spew huge volumes of tailings and other mining waste into rivers and coastal waters with impunity (Runge et al. 1997).

In addition, the cost of purchasing and installing new technologies is prohibitive for many small- and medium-size enterprises. As a result, activities such as small-scale mining remain enormously destructive to the environment. A notorious example of this phenomenon can be found in Brazil, where the country's army of *gariempeiros* (independent poor miners not officially employed by any corporation) continues to wreak terrible damage to forests, rivers, and wildlife in the feverish quest for gold. In the process, the gariempeiros undermine the livelihoods of indigenous Indian communities that rely on healthy forests and rivers for their survival; expose tribes to malaria, venereal infections, and other diseases; and expose themselves and Indian communities to deadly levels of mercury contamination. In Roraima's Yanomami indigenous area, for example, mercury poisoning stemming from illegal gold mining was reported to be responsible for the deaths of an estimated 15 percent of the Yanomami population in the late 1980s (MacMillan 1993; Browder and Godfrey 1997). The Brazilian government has responded by creating indigenous reserves in some parts of Amazonia. But the expansion of reserves for indigenous peoples has not stopped incursions by outsiders, and it has aroused strong opposition from mining companies concerned about losing access to reserves of oil, gold, and other valuable minerals (De Onis 1992; Place 2001).

Obstacles to Sustainable Economic Growth

The region's architects of economic change and reform acknowledge that significant obstacles to the establishment of healthy, vibrant economies exist. One such impediment is continued South and Central American over-reliance on exports of natural wealth such as oil and its various derivatives, minerals, timber and related products, and agricultural production for most economic activity. This lack of diversification leaves regional economies quite vulnerable to the vagaries of international markets, places heavy pressure on natural resources, and damages ecosystems and the biodiversity they support. In addition, the heavy concentration of economic activity in coastal urban centers leaves many rural dwellers in grim economic straits. "We have heaped this abuse upon ourselves," lamented one Peruvian official. "We have not managed to distribute our growing populations away from the coast. We have not been able to encourage industries to go elsewhere, and so there are fewer jobs in the interior. Our uplands are starving for development, while our coasts are drowning in it" (Hinrichsen 1998).

Among the small island states of the Caribbean, meanwhile, tourism rather than extractive industry is the main driver of economic activity. But future growth for these countries is difficult to forecast, as their tourism-based economic structures are vulnerable to mounting international concerns about terrorism, severe weather, coastal pollution and other forms of environmental degradation, and potential sea level rise associated with global climate change.

Another major obstacle to economic growth is Latin America's astonishing debt burden. For much of the 1970s and 1980s, the region borrowed money to shore up sagging financial fortunes and crumbling infrastructure and to repair the wounds of civil unrest and warfare. But rising interest rates in the United States and Western Europe in the 1980s increased debt service payments, and state schemes to reduce inflationary conditions during this same period reduced the income from which to service the debt. Moreover, these schemes failed to rein in spiraling inflation, and several countries experienced severe financial crises, including Mexico (in 1995), Brazil (in 1998), and Argentina (in 2001–2002) (UN Environment Programme 2002). All told, the region's collective external debt burden jumped twenty-one-fold from 1971 to 1999, from U.S.$46 billion to U.S.$982 billion.

By the close of the twentieth century, Latin America accounted for more than one-third (38 percent) of total global debt (World Bank 2001). Some countries, including Guyana and Bolivia, have qualified for debt relief under the Heavily Indebted Poor Countries (HIPC) initiative, but the future of others—like Argentina's government, which became a financial pariah around the world in December 2001, when it made the largest debt default in history—is uncertain.

In addition, major inequities in income and wealth distribution continue to exist throughout most of the Latin America/Caribbean region. Among the nations of South America's Andes region and Southern Cone, only Uruguay was reported to have made gains in this area during the 1990s, and most Central American countries reported little progress in this regard during the same time frame. "Traditional export activities, especially agriculture and assembly plants, and above all textiles, continue to be sources of wealth for the owners but not necessarily for the workers. The latter receive low salaries throughout the region, though there are notable differences between countries. New export activities, the expansion of services and especially those in finance, tourism, and other activities of the modern sector, seem equally concentrated in a few hands" (UN Development Programme 2002). Not surprisingly, these inequities give rise to social conflict and intensify struggles for control of forests, rivers, coastal fishing areas, and other natural resources that are already under considerable pressure (Homer-Dixon 1999).

Unemployment and underemployment (or "subemployment") rates also remain stubbornly high, especially in economically troubled countries in South America. In this environment, many people have been forced to toil in low-paying, nonpermanent "informal" jobs with no job security, no employment benefits, and no prospects for career advancement. With the exception of Chile and Panama, the number of people working in the informal sector rose in most countries during the 1990s. In fact, seven out of every ten jobs generated in the region's cities in this period were in the informal sector (UN Economic Commission for Latin America and the Caribbean and UN Environment Programme 2001).

Trends in Human Development across Latin America

Latin America's continued concentration of wealth in relatively few hands— despite economic reforms, new entrepreneurial ventures, low inflation, and greater levels of public social spending during the 1990s—is a major factor in the high levels of poverty that persist across the region. "The level of distributive inequality in the region, the highest in the world, condemns millions of people to extreme poverty and seriously limits the poverty-reducing effects

A family looks for sellable items in a garbage dump in Mexico City, Mexico. BETTMANN/CORBIS

of growth," charged the UN Economic Commission for Latin America and the Caribbean. "This means that if Latin America and the Caribbean are to be able to achieve the development objective of a 50 percent reduction in poverty by 2015 laid down in the Millennium Declaration [a series of policy goals adopted by all 189 member states of the UN General Assembly in 2000], they will need to reorient current growth patterns drastically so that growth can begin to have a significant and positive impact on the poor" (ibid.).

At the beginning of the twenty-first century, only six of the forty-six countries located in Latin America and the Caribbean—Argentina, Bahamas, Barbados, Chile, Costa Rica, and Uruguay—are ranked as having a high level of human development (UN Development Programme 2001). Thirty-nine of the remaining forty countries are ranked as having achieved "medium" human development, while Haiti, which is in the throes of almost complete economic and ecological collapse, is the region's lone entrant in the "low" category. Widespread poverty is the single greatest culprit for these mediocre rankings, as its influence filters into a host of other social areas, including education, health, and political rights. At the beginning of the twenty-first century, it was estimated that about 200 million people in Latin America—nearly 40 percent of the region's population—live in poverty (Inter-American Development Bank 2000; UN Economic Commission for Latin America and the Caribbean 2000).

Some countries have made significant inroads in addressing the poverty issue. In Chile, for example, poverty fell by more than 15 percent during the

1990s as low inflation, low unemployment, economic reforms, and economic expansion boosted household incomes across the country. In Brazil, meanwhile, the poverty rate fell from 42 percent to 30 percent from 1990 to 1999, despite economic troubles in the late 1990s. And to the north, Central American countries such as Costa Rica and Panama shaved their poverty rates by a quarter and a third, respectively, during the decade (UN Economic Commission for Latin America and the Caribbean and UN Environment Programme 2001). But other countries in South and Central America made little progress. In Colombia, Venezuela, Bolivia, and Ecuador, 45 percent or more of households are poor, and the poverty rate in Mexico—by far the most populous country in Central America—continued to hover between 35 and 40 percent throughout the 1990s (ibid.). In the Caribbean states, meanwhile, overall living standards have declined over the last two decades, despite improvements in performance by a number of individual countries, such as Costa Rica (World Bank 1996).

Poverty rates in rural areas are higher than in metropolitan centers, and in many Latin American countries, the most impoverished communities are concentrated in geographic regions that house rivers, forests, and wetlands that are vital for human health and biodiversity maintenance alike. In many instances, this situation has created a dynamic in which desperately poor communities feel as if they have no other choice but to plunder their rich but fragile natural surroundings for short-term economic gain.

In terms of education, it has been noted that "inequality in educational opportunities is one of the great social dividers in Latin America. Heads of household of the region's wealthiest 10 percent have on average [seven more years of schooling] than the poorest 30 percent" (Iglesias 1999). Nonetheless, education is one of the areas in which Latin American countries have made notable, tangible improvement in recent years. Overall adult literacy rates across the region improved by better than 10 percent from 1980 to 1999, when they reached about 88 percent (UN Development Programme 2001), and a number of nations have made major new investments in educational funding for schools, teachers, textbooks, and the like. But nations such as Guatemala, Nicaragua, and Haiti continue to be saddled with extremely high illiteracy rates, and certain demographic groups—most notably women, rural people, and indigenous populations—have lower rates of literacy and educational attainment in virtually every Latin American country (UN Development Programme 2002).

Access to health and other human services is on the upswing in many parts of Latin America, but it still falls short of desired goals. For example, chronic malnutrition continues to affect nearly one out of four children in Central America (ibid.), and basic sanitation services have yet to be provided to one-quarter of Central America's population (UN Economic Commission for

Figure 1.2 Latin America: Social Spending, by Sector

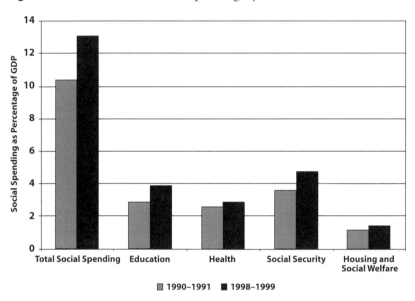

SOURCE: The Sustainability of Development in Latin America and the Caribbean: Challenges and Opportunities (LC/G.2145 [CONF.90/3]), document presented at the Regional Preparatory Conference of Latin America and the Caribbean for the World Conference on Sustainable Development (Johannesburg, South Africa, 2002), Rio de Janeiro, Brazil, October 23–24, 2001 (http://www.rolac.unep.mx/foroalc/brasil2001/finales/CRPSusti.pdf), pp. 26.

Latin America and the Caribbean and UN Environment Programme 2001). Pronounced differences in quality of care and access to care, depending on one's socioeconomic standing, also persist across Central America and the rest of the region.

Women in most Latin American countries enjoy greater quality of health care—including family planning—than they did even two decades ago. They also have greater employment opportunities than ever before and in a number of countries have made significant gains in the legal and political arenas (such as the right to hold elected office and equal legal status with men). Still, social, political, and economic gender inequities do persist across the region. In addition, Latin America has been troubled by an increase in incidents of domestic violence, especially toward women and children. In fact, it has been estimated that about half the women in Latin America face at least one episode of family violence in their life (UN Economic Commission for Latin America and the Caribbean 2000).

Finally, pronounced divisions in migration and employment patterns exist between genders, especially on the Amazon frontier and other geographic regions where resource extraction is a significant factor. Whereas women and children are entrenched in urban centers, large numbers of men—including husbands and fathers—spend weeks or months at a time in active resource extraction zones, where they jostle for employment in mining and timber extraction activities (Godfrey 1992). "Frequently men avoid urban households for extended periods, and sometimes they never return at all, leaving female-headed households without external means of support," observed one analysis. "For example, too often the income from male goldminers in remote camps does not filter back to urban households, which are by default headed by females" (Browder and Godfrey 1997).

Land Use and Degradation in Latin America

The natural landscape of Latin America and the Caribbean has been dramatically altered over millennia by its human inhabitants. Today, crop cultivation occupies nearly 160 million hectares of the region (approximately 8 percent of the total land area of the region), while pasturelands and other resources necessary for stock-raising activities account for another 600 million hectares (about 30 percent of the region's total land area). Forests and woodlands cover another 940 million hectares (46 percent of total land area) and nonforest plant cover accounts for about 290 million hectares (15 percent of total land area) (UN Economic Commission for Latin America and the Caribbean and UN Environment Programme 2001).

Alteration of land and extraction of resources for human use has accelerated in recent years, driven by growing populations, increased economic and industrial activity (in some places), and desperate poverty (in other locales). From 1989 to 1999, for instance, the total land area utilized for agricultural cultivation grew by 7.3 percent, from 149 million to 160 million hectares. Similarly, the region continues to add to its already enormous herds of livestock. From 1980 to 1999, the total number of head of cattle in the region increased by 8 percent, reaching the 350 million mark (ibid.).

All together, some countries have increased the amount of cultivated land and rangeland by 50 percent (Nicaragua, Cuba, and Brazil) or even 100 percent (Bolivia and Paraguay) over the past two decades—and virtually all Latin American countries have increased the size of their arable land holdings to some degree during this period (Pichón, Uquillas, and Frechione 1999). Overall, from 1972 to 1999, the area of permanent arable land and cropland expanded in South America by 35 percent, in Central America by 21 percent, and in the Caribbean by 32 percent (UN Food and Agriculture Organization 2001). "The main cause of deforestation in Latin America and the Caribbean has been the use of land for agricultural activities," confirmed one UN analysis. "The region is now devoting almost half of its natural ecosystems to agriculture and stock-raising. The risk run by natural ecosystems is that if they do not supply products that generate income and employment for the local inhabitants and they cease to be economically profitable, the use of the land in question is changed and . . . devoted to agricultural activities" (UN Economic Commission for Latin America and the Caribbean and UN Environment Programme 2001).

Wild forests have been the primary victim of the expanding appetite for land for livestock and crop cultivation. Indeed, Latin America currently loses more forest area on an annual basis than any other region of the world, including the continents of Asia and Africa, where unsustainable deforestation is a serious issue. Across Latin America, the annual average loss of forest cover between 1980 and 1990 was 7.4 million hectares, and from 1990 to 1995 it was 5.8 million hectares per year, with 95 percent of the forest loss in tropical regions (ibid.; UN Environment Programme 2001). Despite heavy rates of timbering and other forms of land clearance, Latin America and the Caribbean still contain the largest remaining tracts of closed forest in the world (32 percent of the whole), barely edging out North America (Canada and the United States, which have 30 percent) (UN Economic Commission for Latin America and the Caribbean and UN Environment Programme 2001). But based on current political, social, and economic pressures, further significant loss of intact, closed forests in Latin America seems inevitable.

Expansion of crop and livestock production is also often taking place at the expense of some of Latin America's most ecologically vital tropical forests, most notably the Brazilian Amazon (Nepstad 2001). Even Costa Rica, which is internationally renowned today for its proenvironment policies and its extensive protected-areas network, has experienced massive conversions of natural forests for agricultural use. "Despite regulations, management initiatives and international financial support, Costa Rica, formerly densely forested, has become an agricultural country. Virgin forests have become rare and are found nowadays only in remote or protected areas. Since the arrival of multinational companies, large areas have been transformed into monocultures, resulting in the pollution of both soil and water" (Sturm 2002).

In many places deforestation is not only reducing biodiversity and undercutting watershed functions but also exacerbating soil erosion, cited as the leading cause of land degradation in the region; it affects an estimated 14 percent of South America's land area and 26 percent of terrestrial Central America (UN Environment Programme 2002). Other soil degradation associated with the conversion of forests to farms is chemical contamination stemming from growing reliance on pesticides, fertilizers, and other agrochemicals, and salinization from inappropriate irrigation practices. By the close of the 1990s, the latter phenomenon affected more than 18 million hectares, with particularly large swaths of salinization-impacted land in high-population countries such as Argentina, Brazil, Chile, and Mexico (ibid.). Overuse of agricultural chemicals has also been blamed for an assortment of water pollution problems, including contamination of important potable water sources and damage to fisheries located downstream of pollution points.

Stemming the Tide of Unsustainable Land Use

The root causes of Latin America's unsustainable land use practices include poverty, population growth, and unplanned development. All of these factors contribute to incursions—both legal and illegal—into fragile natural areas that usually undergo significant, sometimes permanent, alteration or degradation. Effectively addressing these problems will require the involvement of all institutional sectors of government, with special attention paid to issues of population control, land reform, conservation education, adjustments in policies governing protected areas, and provision of economic incentives for improved land stewardship.

Implementation of sustainable forms of land stewardship will also require improved performance from agencies responsible for environmental protection and conservation. "The mandates of many [Latin American] government agencies and enterprises are muddled and at times even in conflict with those of other agencies," observed one expert. "When an agency has a mixed or contradictory mission, its accountability will be compromised: If it fails to achieve a particular objective, such as efficiency or conservation, it can dismiss this shortcoming as the cost of fulfilling its other responsibilities. For example, the Honduran forestry enterprise COHDEFOR was entrusted with four goals: exploiting timber, developing a forest-products industry, regulating forest uses for the sake of conservation, and promoting the economic development of low-income Hondurans living in and around the forests. It dismissed its very poor record in conservation and poverty alleviation as being part of the unavoidable tradeoff with pursuing its logging and industrial mission" (Ascher 2000).

The challenge to balance economic and ecological considerations is perhaps more striking in Brazil than any other Latin American country. Home to the planet's largest wetland complex (the Pantanal), the most species-rich savanna ecosystem (the Cerrado), and one-third of the earth's remnant tropical forests (the Amazon), Brazil is one of the world's great caches of biodiversity. But trends in population distribution and conflicting resource demands have transformed portions of this vast land into a checkerboard of (1) economically active but environmentally stressed regions and (2) environmentally sound but economically moribund regions.

Endangered Natural Areas in Guatemala

In many nations of Central America, unfettered exploitation of environmental resources has been the rule rather than the exception over the last half-century. Much of this unsustainable harvest of forest, mineral, land, and water resources has been undertaken under the banner of antipoverty initiatives, but with little appreciable improvement in standards of living for the vast majority of the populace (Place 2001). This dynamic can be seen in particularly stark relief in places like Guatemala, where feverish exploitation of natural resources has failed to relieve endemic poverty or absorb population growth rates that rank among the highest in the Western Hemisphere.

Many of Guatemala's unsustainable land management practices have been introduced in the past half-century, when the federal government first opened the nation's forests to loggers, cattle barons, and energy companies. In subsequent years, some forests and other species-rich areas were set aside as parks and other protected areas. But in many cases, protection of even the most highly valued parks and reserves has been inadequate. For instance, many parts of the world-famous Maya Biosphere Reserve, which encompasses several Guatemalan parks, have been heavily damaged by timber, oil, and ranching interests and impoverished communities of subsistence farmers and workers. "The laws of the biosphere reserve have hindered the destruction—but only slightly," contended one analyst. "Blatant violations of the rules continue, and the government often ignores them. But potentially most damaging, in the long run, are the illegal settlements. Fire is a normal part of the forest ecology, but the settlements have brought it to a level destructive to the ecosystem" (Meyerson 1998). In 1998 alone, for example, dry conditions and land clearance by burning combined to create wildfires that consumed or damaged one-quarter of northern Guatemala's tropical forests.

If Guatemala's government and people hope to salvage the Maya Biosphere Reserve and preserve its ecological integrity for the future, immediate implementation of higher levels of conservation protection and more sustainable land use schemes are essential. "One look at recent satellite photographs shows that the dream of a Maya Biosphere Reserve is slowly dying. The buffer zones have been developed indiscriminately. The park boundaries have been violated. In Laguna del Tigre [National Park, located within the reserve], settlements have sprung up both upriver and downriver. . . . Slash-and-burn *milpa* (corn) farmers and large-scale, well-funded cattle operations have turned the eastern part of the Sierra del Lacandón national park into swiss cheese" (ibid.).

Sources:
Meyerson, Fred. 1998. "Guatemala Burning." *Amicus Journal* 20, no. 3 (fall).
Place, Susan E. 2001. *Tropical Rainforests: Latin American Nature and Society in Transition*. Wilmington, DE: Scholarly Resources.
UN Development Programme. 2002. *Central America and Panama: The State of the Region 2002*. New York: UNDP.

In the state of São Paulo, for example, more than 4 million people in fifty-six municipalities now crowd into the Piracicaba-Capivari-Jundiai River Basin. Once carpeted in forest, the region is now almost completely deforested and suffers from high levels of air and water pollution, a paucity of green space, and growing freshwater scarcity. But the region also bristles with universities, research and medical centers, and high-tech businesses, all of which combine to provide residents with standards of living comparable to those of developed countries (Hogan 2000). The species-rich forests of the nearby Ribeira Valley, meanwhile, remain largely intact, thanks to formal protection measures and comparably low population pressure. But the income and education levels of its communities are the lowest in the state, and the mass exodus of young people from the region to more economically inviting urban centers has emerged as a major social problem (ibid.). One commonly touted solution to this problem is to provide rural communities with greater economic incentives to conserve habitat and protect biodiversity, whether through management of parks, ecotourism ventures, or other means. Supporters believe that such programs can help preserve wilderness treasures and also provide young people who stay in rural communities with a viable economic future (O'Riordan and Stoll-Kleeman 2002).

Brazil's ability to chart a new course of environmental and economic sustainability is uncertain, however. Over the last half-century, Brazilian administrations have time and again seen economic development as a higher priority than habitat conservation and environmental protection. Indeed, massive governmental initiatives of the 1960s, 1970s, and 1980s actively promoted development of the country's central and northern regions through mining, industrial logging, construction of roadways and other infrastructure, and various peasant settlement projects. These varied schemes spurred a massive migration of Brazilians into previously undeveloped areas (Egler 2002). More recently, Brazilian authorities have touted economic development plans that call for expansion of the length of paved highways in the Amazon from 12,000 to 18,000 kilometers (7,400 to 11,200 miles) (Nepstad 2001). If these plans come to fruition, the country's economic productivity will undoubtedly increase, as farming, logging, mining, and commercial interests gain access to resources and markets located deeper and deeper in the jungle.

But critics in the environmental, scientific, and development communities contend that this path to socioeconomic betterment is an illusory and ultimately ruinous one. They fear that the rate of destruction of the Amazon rain forest—already nearly 2 million hectares per year—will further accelerate under these development plans, with severe repercussions including significant biodiversity loss, reduced freshwater quality, devastated indigenous communities, and overall erosion of "quality of life" for the region's exploding human population (Laurence et al. 2001; Egler 2002). "This immense domain in the heartland of South America offers mankind the best chance it may have to develop a major tropical habitat in a life-sustaining way," claimed one observer. "If . . . the political and social forces at work in Amazonia produce an ecological debacle, the whole world will pay a price that will only be measured fully after the damage is done. There is an ethical imperative for cooperation between the countries that are sovereign in Amazonia and the industrial nations that, as consumers of raw materials and sources of capital, can influence policies on growth and environmental protection beyond their borders. The common objective must be the discovery of new and better patterns of economic development that combine efficient use of the region's abundant resources with the stability of its unique ecological systems" (De Onis 1992).

Land Reform in Latin America

In recent years, several Latin American nations have sought to address the link between poverty and environmental degradation by introducing land tenure reforms. Currently, land in many Latin American countries—most notably Chile, Mexico, and Paraguay—is concentrated in the hands of a small minority of people who utilize it for ranching, farming, and other economic purposes. This arrangement, which is rooted in colonial systems of land ownership and is exacerbated by a lack of land titles, leaves other rural families with little opportunity to improve their standard of living. Trapped on small plots with few prospects for expansion, these families often feel that they have no other recourse but to exhaust the resources of the tracts they do own or migrate to urban centers, where they add to the myriad social and environmental ills on display in those settings. "Without possibility of access to land, the [rural] worker cannot improve his living conditions," observed one study. "He cannot introduce new techniques, or change cropping patterns aimed at improving productivity. Without accessing land, he cannot have access to credit, technical assistance, improved marketing conditions. The experience of those countries which already passed through a successful agrarian reform process shows that a modification of land pattern, allied with an efficient agrarian policy, is favorable both for rural workers as well as for the State" (Groppo 1996).

Indeed, some Latin American countries have had tangible success in addressing the land tenure issue. In Costa Rica, for instance, it has been estimated that approximately one-third of the country's total land area—about 2 million hectares—has been redistributed through a variety of settlement programs and land title changes. To the north, the El Salvadoran government has earmarked significant sums for land-transfer programs and other agrarian reforms (UN Economic Commission for Latin America and the Caribbean and UN Environment Programme 2001). But despite land reform's clear benefits for alleviating rural poverty and reducing pressure on fragile environmental resources, indifferent government performance and opposition from politically powerful landowners have hampered redistribution and reform efforts in numerous countries. In fact, big agricultural enterprises are continuing to grow in size even as the number of smallholdings carved out of previously undeveloped forests rises.

Sources:

Ascher, William. 2000. "Understanding Why Governments in Developing Countries Waste Natural Resources." *Environment* 42 (March).

Bilsborrow, Richard, and David Carr. 2000. *Population, Agricultural Land Use and the Environment in Developing Countries.* Cambridge, MA: CABI.

Browder, John O., and Brian J. Godfrey. 1997. *Rainforest Cities: Urbanization, Development, and Globalization of the Brazilian Amazon.* New York: Columbia University Press.

De Onis, Juan. 1992. *The Green Cathedral: Sustainable Development of Amazonia.* New York: Oxford University Press.

Egler, Ione. 2002. "Brazil: Selling Biodiversity with Local Livelihoods." In *Biodiversity, Sustainability and Human Communities: Protecting beyond the Protected.* Edited by Tim O'Riordan and Susanne Stoll-Kleeman. New York: Cambridge University Press.

Godfrey, Brian. 1992. "Migration to the Gold-Mining Frontier in Brazilian Amazonia." *Geographical Review* 82 (October): 458–469.

Groppo, Paolo. 1996. "Agrarian Reform and Land Settlement Policy in Brazil: Historical Background." Sustainable Development Department, UN FAO. Available at http://www.fao.org/sd (accessed March 2003).

Hinrichsen, Don. 1998. *Coastal Waters of the World: Trends, Threats, and Strategies.* Washington, DC: Island.

Hogan, Dan. 2000. *Population Distribution, Conflicting Resource Demands and Quality of Life in Brazil.* Population Studies Center, NEPO, State University of Campinas, Brazil.

Homer-Dixon, Thomas F. 1999. *Environment, Scarcity and Violence.* Princeton: Princeton University Press.

Iglesias, Enrique. 1999. "The Challenges and the Opportunities." *Time International* 153 (May 24).

Inter-American Development Bank. 2000. *Annual Report 2000.* Washington, DC: IADB.

Jenkins, Rhys, ed. 2000. *Industry and Environment in Latin America.* London: Routledge.

Laurence, W. F., et al. 2001. "The Future of the Brazilian Amazon." *Science* 291, no. 5503 (January): 438–439.

MacMillan, Gordon. 1993. *Gold Mining and Land Use Change in the Brazilian Amazon.* Ph.D. diss., University of Edinburgh.

McGranahan, Gordon. 2001. *The Citizens at Risk: From Urban Sanitation to Sustainable Cities.* Sterling, VA: Earthscan.

Nepstad, Dan, et al. 2001. "Road Paving, Fire Regime Feedbacks, and the Future of Amazon Forests." *Forest Ecology and Management* 154.

O'Riordan, Tim, and Susanne Stoll-Kleeman, eds. 2002. *Biodiversity, Sustainability and Human Communities: Protecting beyond the Protected.* New York: Cambridge University Press.

Pan American Health Organization. 1998. *La Salud en las Américas.* Washington, DC: PAHO.

Pichón, Francisco J., Jorge E. Uquillas, and John Frechione, eds. 1999. *Traditional and Modern Natural Resource Management in Latin America.* Pittsburgh: University of Pittsburgh Press.

Place, Susan E. 2001. *Tropical Rainforests: Latin American Nature and Society in Transition.* Wilmington, DE: Scholarly Resources.

Population Action International. 2000. *People in the Balance: Population and Natural Resources at the Turn of the Millennium.* Washington, DC: PAI.

Population Reference Bureau. 2002. *2002 World Population Data Sheet.* Washington, DC: PRB.

Runge, C. F., et al. 1997. *Sustainable Trade Expansion in Latin America and the Caribbean: Analysis and Assessment.* Washington, DC: World Resource Institute.

Scherr, S., and S. Yadav. 1997. *Land Degradation in the Developing World: Issues and Policy Options for 2020.* Washington, DC: International Food Policy Research Institute.

Smith, Nigel J. H., et al. 1995. *Amazonia: Resiliency and Dynamism of the Land and Its People.* New York: UN University Press.

Sturm, Michael. 2002. "The Mixed Experience of Private Sector Involvement in Biodiversity Management in Costa Rica." In *Biodiversity, Sustainability and Human Communities: Protecting beyond the Protected.* Edited by Tim O'Riordan and Susanne Stoll-Kleeman. New York: Cambridge University Press.

UN Centre for Human Settlements. 2001. *The State of the World's Cities Report 2001.* Nairobi: UNCHS.

UN Development Programme. 2001. *Human Development Report 2001.* Oxford and New York: Oxford University Press.

———. 2002. *Central America and Panama: The State of the Region 2002.* New York: UNDP.

UN Economic Commission for Latin America and the Caribbean. 2000. *Social Panorama of Latin America 1999–2000.* Santiago: ECLAC.

UN Economic Commission for Latin America and the Caribbean and UN Environment Programme. 2001. "The Sustainability of Development in Latin

America and the Caribbean: Challenges and Opportunities." Report prepared for World Summit on Sustainable Development, Rio de Janeiro, October 23–24, Rio de Janeiro: ECLAC.

UN Environment Programme. 2000. *GEO Latin America and the Caribbean Environment Outlook.* Mexico City: UNEP.

————. 2001. *Global Forest Resources Assessment 2000.* Rome: FAO

————. 2002. *Global Environment Outlook 3 (GEO-3).* London: UNEP and Earthscan.

UN Food and Agriculture Organization. 2001. *FAOSTAT Statistical Database 2001.* Rome: FAO.

————. 2002. *The State of Food and Agriculture 2002.* Rome: FAO.

UN Population Division. 2001. *World Population Prospects 1950–2050.* New York: United Nations.

Vourvoulias, Alberto. 1999. "The Laboratory of Urbanism." *Time International* 153 (May 24).

World Bank. 1996. *Latin America and Caribbean Region—Poverty Reduction and Human Resource Development in the Caribbean.* Washington, DC: World Bank.

————. 2001. *World Development Indicators 2001.* Washington, DC: World Bank.

————. 2002. *World Development Indicators 2002.* Washington, DC: World Bank.

Biodiversity
—KIRSTEN SILVIUS

L atin America, which encompasses Central America, the Caribbean islands,
and the massive South American continent, houses the most species-rich
and the most intact terrestrial ecosystems on earth. Considering vascular
plants (all plants except mosses and ferns) and vertebrate animals combined,
Latin America supports more species than any other tropical region. Insect diversity is less well documented in the tropics, and we know nearly nothing
about fungal diversity. Nevertheless, the close coevolutionary relationship between these groups and their plant hosts suggests that they too may have high
diversity in Latin America.

Foundations of High
Biodiversity in Latin America
Three key factors are responsible for the region's high species numbers: first, a
large portion of Latin America lies in the geographic tropics, where biological
diversity tends to reach its highest levels. Second, it features extreme diversity
of landscapes and topographic features, including the Andes mountains and
extensive arid and temperate formations, as well as the better-known lowland
rain forests. And third, repeated extension and contraction of forests and savannas along the margins of the Amazon basin during past periods of glacia-
tion have helped drive an extremely dynamic evolutionary process.

   Biologists are still debating the causes of high species diversity in tropical regions. Suffice it to say that most, though not all, taxonomic groups have higher
species numbers in the tropics than in comparable arctic, temperate, or subtropical areas. In a surface area comparable to that of the continental United
States, for instance, the Amazon itself holds an estimated 10 to 17 percent of the
world's species (Gibson 1996). Five of the world's seventeen most biologically
diverse countries in the world are Amazonian countries: Brazil, Colombia,
Ecuador, Peru, and Venezuela. Only Indonesia, another geographically varied

tropical country, rivals them in overall species diversity (Mittermeier et al. 1997). The Amazon alone, however, does not tell the full story of Latin American biodiversity. Four of the five Amazonian countries mentioned above are also Andean countries, and three of them support extensive tropical savanna and shrubland systems, with their own unique flora and fauna. From the continent's "southern cone," Argentina, Chile, Paraguay, and Uruguay contribute species uniquely adapted to temperate grassland and montane (mountain) systems. To the north, the Caribbean islands, despite their relatively small collective surface area, contribute a high number of localized, endemic species.

Defining Biodiversity

The term *biodiversity* is utilized in several different ways, and an area's level of species diversity can vary with the person or institution doing the "accounting." Usually, both the absolute number of species (*species richness*) and the number of endemic species are considered in biodiversity assessments. *Endemic species* are those that occur in one geographic area and nowhere else. Although the scale of endemism is not fixed—one could say that the same species is endemic to just one river valley in Colombia, or to Colombia itself, or to South America as a whole—the term is usually reserved for species occurring in one geographically distinct region.

The term *diversity* itself is ambiguous, because different researchers use it in different ways. Originally, it denoted a mathematically calculated figure that included both the number of species and the abundance of individuals in that species relative to the abundance of all the other species. Thus, an area supporting 100 species, of which 10 are very abundant and 90 are rare, would be considered *less* diverse than an area of similar size also containing 100 species, all of which are equally abundant. However, it has become common practice in conservation and policy circles to use *biodiversity* as a synonym for species richness, and that is how the term will be used here.

Species Numbers

To understand species diversity in Latin America, it is useful to consider worldwide species diversity. The full range of species living on earth remains unknown, in large measure because developing countries have not carried out sampling and species inventories with the same frequency or the same level of care as industrialized countries. Even within the developing world, pronounced differences in species and habitat monitoring exist. For example, comprehensive species surveys have been carried out more frequently in the Amazon region than in Africa's Congo region in recent years. This should be taken into account when comparing species estimates between countries.

This qualifier notwithstanding, however, scientists estimate that there are about 300,000 species of vascular plants on earth, along with 9,881 species of birds, 4,809 species of mammals, 7,828 species of reptiles, and 4,780 species of amphibians (Mittermeier et al. 1999). The neotropics alone—all of Latin America except for the temperate southern cone—are home to more than 30,000 species of plants, three times more than either the African or Asian tropics. This includes over 8,000 species of orchids, again more than are found in Africa or Asia (Cody 1996). The sheer volume of the Amazon drainage (20 percent of the world's fresh water moves through the region) and the great variation in water quality, flooding regime, and size of the Amazon's many tributaries, make the neotropics the epicenter of freshwater fish diversity in the world (Groombridge and Jenkins 2000). Of more than 3,000 species of fish in the neotropics, 2,000 occur in the Amazon basin. Venezuela clocks in at 1,250 species, mostly in the Orinoco drainage, while Colombia and Peru support about 1,500 and 900 fish species, respectively (Mittermeier et al. 1997).

Three thousand species of birds are documented for the neotropics, 800 more than in Africa and 1,200 more than in Asia. Brazil, Colombia, Peru, and Ecuador each have more than 1,500 species of birds, and just the 15,000-square-kilometer (9,300-square-mile) Manu National Park in Ecuador has at least 1,000 species of birds (Cody 1996). Primates and many other mammal groups have similar diversity in all tropical regions. Species of amphibians are more numerous in the neotropics than in the Old World tropics, with the Andes as a center of frog diversity and endemism, but snakes and lizards have similar diversity in all tropical regions.

Butterflies are one of the best known insect groups. Latin America supports a greater diversity of butterflies than any other region in the world, and the seven top countries in the world for butterfly species richness are here. Peru leads the list with 3,532 species, closely followed by the much larger but less ecologically diverse Brazil, with 3,132 species. Ecuador comes in seventh with 2,200 species (Mittermeier et al. 1997). Up to 600 species of butterflies have been recorded at just one site in the central Amazon (Brown et al. 1997). One method currently being used to estimate insect diversity is canopy fogging, in which the canopy of an individual tree is sprayed with insecticides and all insects that fall to the ground are collected. When entomologist Terry Erwin sprayed nineteen individuals of one tree species in Panama, he obtained 1,200 different beetle species (Erwin 1982). Similar efforts in other areas have yielded up to 50 species of ant on individual trees, which can be extrapolated to about 300 species of ants in a few hectares of neotropical forest. However, ant diversity is probably similar in the New World and Old World tropics.

A yellow swallowtail butterfly COREL

Chief Threats to
Latin American Flora and Fauna

The World Conservation Union-IUCN maintains the *Red List of Threatened Species,* the most up-to-date and authoritative summary of information on the condition of species at the global level. This work tracks the status of mammals, birds, reptiles, amphibia, fishes, plants, mollusks, and other invertebrates. According to the IUCN's *2002 Red List,* the Mesoamerican (Central American) nation with the most threatened species is Mexico, which is also the largest country in terms of land area. It has 480 recognized threatened species, including 70 threatened mammal species, 39 threatened bird species, 88 threatened species of fish, and 221 distinct plants threatened with extinction. Other Central American nations with high numbers of threatened species include Panama (242, including 20 threatened mammal species and 192 threatened plant species), Costa Rica (155, including 14 threatened mammal species, 13 threatened bird species, and 110 threatened plant species), and Honduras (132, including 108 threatened plant species) (World Conservation Union-IUCN 2002).

According to the IUCN, there are many more threatened species in South America. The huge country of Brazil holds the highest number of threatened species, with 655. This total includes 381 plant species, 114 bird species, and 81 mammal species. Other South American nations with extremely high numbers of threatened species include Peru (404 species, including 269 plant species and 76 bird species), Ecuador (328 species, including 197 plant species and 62 bird species), Argentina (138 species, including 73 threatened species of mammals and birds), and Venezuela (138 species, including 67 threatened plant species and 50 threatened species of mammals and birds). Colombia, located at the juncture of Central and South America, is reported to have 354 threatened species as well, including 41 threatened mammal species, 78 threatened bird species, and 213 plants in danger of being extinguished (ibid.).

In the Caribbean Islands, meanwhile, Jamaica has more species on the *Red List* than any other country, with 241. Most of these threatened species (206) are plants, but Jamaica also is home to 12 threatened species of birds and 8 threatened reptile species. Other Caribbean nations and territories with high numbers on the *Red List* include Cuba (205 species, including 160 plant species), Puerto Rico (70 species), the Dominican Republic (62 species), and Haiti (58 species) (ibid.).

In virtually all of the above cases, species are being threatened by some combination of the factors listed here: population growth and unsustainable economic development; invasive species; gold mining and other types of mineral extraction; colonization politics; logging; subsistence hunting and the wildlife trade; and habitat fragmentation.

Population Growth and Unsustainable Economic Development

The greatest threat facing Latin American biodiversity is the inevitable impact of development on the natural landscape. The United States and other developed countries have already lost much of their natural capital to this threat—consider, for example, the clearcutting of the eastern forests of the United States and the conversion of the central and southwestern grasslands to agriculture and ranching, which led to the almost complete loss of the tall-grass prairie ecosystem, of bison, and of black-footed ferrets. All the threats that the United States has faced and still faces—mining, logging, agriculture, habitat conversion to cattle pasture, dams for hydroelectric power, inland waterways for more efficient product transport, and oil exploitation, among others—are currently at work in Latin America. However, the larger size and more extreme poverty of Latin American populations, and the avid market for natural resources provided by North America, Europe, and Japan make these threats potentially more destructive than they have been in the past.

Across Latin America, the number and extent of large roadless wilderness areas inhabited only by indigenous peoples continues to decline. The largest remaining areas are the forested highlands and surrounding savannas of southern Guyana, southern Venezuela, and the northern Brazilian Amazon, as

Table 2.1 Latin America Urban Sanitation Collection Rates

Country	Percentage Collected	Percentage Disposed of in Sanitary, Secure, or Other Landfills
Argentina	—	—
Bahamas	—	—
Bolivia	68	50
Brazil	71	28
Chile	99	83
Colombia	—	—
Costa Rica	66	68
Cuba	95	90
Dominican Republic	—	—
Ecuador	—	—
El Salvador	—	—
Guatemala	—	—
Haiti	30	20
Honduras	20	—
Mexico	70	17
Nicaragua	—	—
Panama	—	—
Paraguay	35	5
Peru	84	5
Suriname	—	—
Trinidad and Tobago	95	70
Uruguay	71	—
Venezuela	75	85

SOURCE: Pan American Health Organization. 2001. Adapted from the table "Coverage of Urban Sanitation" in *Health in the Americas.* 1998 ed. Scientific Publication No. 569, Washington, D.C.

well as the humid forests of the Japurá and Rio Negro basins, in the northern and western Amazon (Dinerstein et al. 1995). Smaller relatively intact areas occur in Central America, in the Talamancan montane forests of Costa Rica and Panama, the wetlands of Qintana Roo, and the Mosquitia region in Nicaragua and Honduras, but none of these approaches the magnitude of the Amazon and Orinoco basin forests. Colonization projects and logging and mining enterprises are degrading the edges—and in some cases the cores—of these wilderness areas.

Significant portions of the human population of Latin America, including both indigenous peoples and nonindigenous colonists, live off the land, practicing subsistence agriculture, hunting, and fishing. These people impact otherwise undeveloped lands, including legally protected areas not intended to support human activities. However, they also hold the greatest promise for conservation in Latin America, because they depend on the land and therefore have an incentive to protect it. Governments and nongovernmental organizations in Latin America are working to develop equitable systems of land protection and management, but these efforts are recent; resources are still being lost at a rapid pace both inside and outside of protected areas.

Invasive Species

Invasive species have their greatest effect on isolated areas—islands, lakes, rivers—and heavily disturbed areas, such as grazed pastures or cut forests. In fact, only habitat degradation ranks above invasive species as the greatest threat to freshwater biodiversity. In Colombia, for example, 58 fish species introduced from different regions or simply from different river basins are affecting—and in some cases decimating—native fish diversity. In particular, large species introduced into Andean rivers from the Amazon basin to improve local fishing industries prey on or compete with local fish species (Diaz-Sarmiento and Alvarez-Leon 1998).

In the Galápagos Islands of Ecuador, researchers have instituted a well-funded campaign to eradicate invasive species that have damaged native ecosystems. Targeted animals and plants include goats, rats, dogs, cats, pigs, fire ants, weedy plants, rock doves, and smooth billed anis. These species prey on sea turtle and tortoise eggs, kill reptiles and birds such as petrels that nest in burrows, compete for food and nesting sites with native species, carry diseases, and—in the case of goats and pigs—denude local vegetation and eliminate habitat critical for native species (Kaiser 2001).

Gold Mining

The Guyana Shield, including the country of Suriname, is under extreme pressure from mining. In Venezuela gold mining is increasingly mechanized, while in Brazil and the Guianas it is still largely artisanal in nature. Large concessions have already been granted throughout the Brazilian Amazon, paving the way for further development once compensation agreements are arrived at with local indigenous peoples.

This scenario is of great concern to environmentalists and other constituencies who cite appalling levels of environmental degradation associated with earlier exploitation operations. Indeed, Brazil's legions of independent poor miners, known as *gariempeiros,* have been notorious despoilers of area rivers and streams. Their operations make extensive use of mercury, which now laces numerous waterways and has accumulated to dangerous levels in predators such as carnivorous fish and raptors. In Brazil's Roraima state, for example, 40,000 gold miners invaded the Yanomami and Macuxi indigenous lands and adjoining national parks from 1987 to 1992. When they departed to exploit other areas of the forest, they left a legacy that included high mortality rates among indigenous peoples resulting from introduced diseases, collapse of traditional cultures, and extensive river degradation from mercury pollution and sedimentation, the latter churned up by construction of settlements and roads, as well as local deforestation of lands for cooking and heating purposes (MacMillan 1995).

Colonization Politics

State and federal governments have made extensive use of subsidized colonization projects into designated areas of the Amazon as a way to ease population pressure in Brazil, Ecuador, Peru, and Bolivia. This process reached its heyday in Brazil in the 1970s and 1980s, when projects supported by the World Bank led to the rapid deforestation of more than half the state of Rondonia and parts of the state of Acre in the southwestern Amazon. Colonization waves also occur spontaneously as urban poor move into forested areas, or abandon already degraded colonization areas to move into uncut forest. Colonists settle along recently opened roads or in areas several kilometers beyond the end of the roads. Bereft of income that could be used to buy fertilizers, these subsistence farmers resort to a pattern of shifting cultivation in which they till land to exhaustion, then move on to previously untouched land so that they can continue growing crops.

Logging

Unsustainable harvesting of tropical rain forests in Latin America is a problem that has attracted international attention in recent decades. In the Guayana region of Venezuela, for instance, gold mining and logging—and the squatter settlements that sprout up to support these activities—have taken a heavy toll on species-rich forests (Miranda et al. 1998). It is the diminishment of the vast Amazon rain forest, however, that has occupied much of the global spotlight. The best data on deforestation rates in the Amazon come from Brazil, where the National Institute for Amazonian Research (INPA) and its international collaborators use satellite imagery to closely monitor forest clearing and burning. The deforestation rate averaged 1.9 million hectares per year from 1995 to 1998 in the Brazilian Amazon (Laurance 2000). Colonization and oil exploration drive deforestation in Colombia and Ecuador, while in the Guianas and central Amazonia industrial logging is becoming an increasingly important factor. Forests are also weakened by selective logging and ground fires, both of which increase tree mortality and forest susceptibility to future fires. Such damaged areas are not detectable from satellite images, and

Figure 2.1 Annual Net Change in Forest Area by Region, 1990–2000

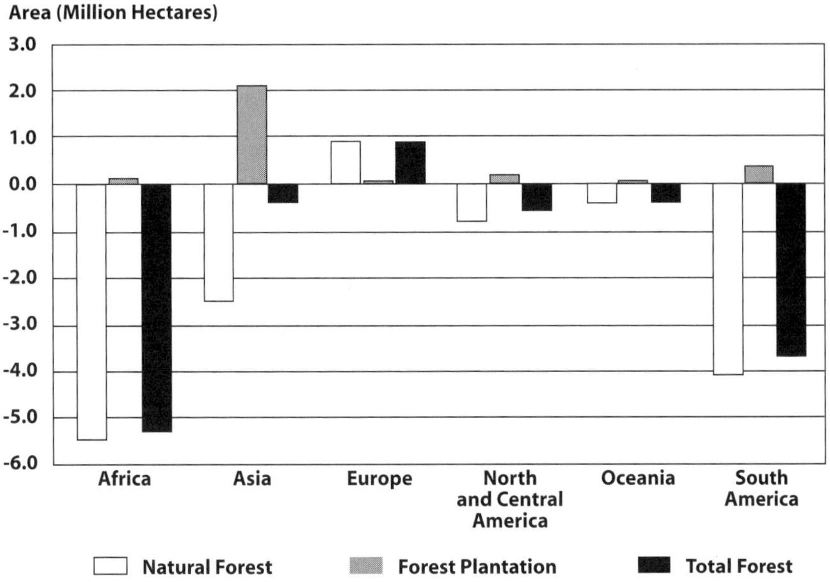

Area (Million Hectares)

Africa   Asia   Europe   North and Central America   Oceania   South America

☐ Natural Forest   ▨ Forest Plantation   ■ Total Forest

SOURCE: Food and Agriculture Organization of the United Nations. 2001. *Forest Resources Assessment 2000.* Rome: UNFAO.

they may be similar in extent to the more obvious clear-cut areas (Nepstad et al. 1999). The impact on animals caused by hunting and forest disturbance cannot be measured from satellites or by forest inventories; it is largely undocumented on account of the difficulty and labor intensity of sampling.

Past logging and colonization focused on the southwestern and easternmost portions of the Brazilian Amazon. Now, new highways and roads are being opened in the central Amazon by the Brazilian government, with the objective of opening up that area to colonization and development. These new roads may stimulate from 120,000 to 270,000 square kilometers (46 to 104 square miles) of additional deforestation, as well as collateral forest impoverishment from logging and understory fires (Nepstad et al. 2001). Conservation nongovernmental organizations (NGOs) are working with the government to design corridors of both existing and new protected areas, but the system is not yet in place. The final form that this plan takes will be shaped by discussion between Brazilian environmentalists, business interests, and politicians, but clearly development into the area will continue.

Galápagos turtles basking in the sun CRAIG LOVELL/CORBIS

Temperate forests in the region are also under threat from unsustainable logging and unrelenting demand for land for farming, ranching, industrial activity, settlements, and transportation. In Chile, for example, endemic forests that support a wide array of flora and fauna are being replaced by pine and eucalyptus plantations used to generate wood chip exports to Japan and other markets (Neira et al. 2002). And to the north, in Central America, nations such as El Salvador, Nicaragua, and Belize are losing significant tracts of their limited forests every year, mostly to wildfires, agricultural expansion (often subsidized by government policies and programs), and expansion of urban settlements in which fuelwood is usually the main energy source (UN Food and Agriculture Organization 2001).

Oil Exploration

Ecologically destructive forms of oil exploration and extraction are major despoilers of wildlife habitat in places such as Venezuela and Ecuador. In the latter country, for example, American and Ecuadorian companies have extracted oil continuously from lowland Amazonian Ecuador (the "Oriente") since 1972. Intentional discharge of toxins into the rivers (4.3 million gallons per day by 1991) as well as accidental oil spills have caused severe environmental contamination in the area (Jochnick 1995). Additionally, roads opened by oil companies become official and spontaneous targets of colonization. National parks and other reserves in the area are not off limits to oil exploration, either. In 1994, Maxus Oil Corporation began drilling within Yasuní National Park, an important protected area and part of a UN-designated biosphere reserve.

Signs of human activity—and corresponding pressure on species—seem likely to intensify in the future as well. One oil pipeline currently under construction will run from the Oriente across the mountains to the Pacific coast and has already stimulated an increase in investment into Oriente oil fields. Once completed, the pipeline will run through the Mindo Nambillo Cloud Forest Reserve, considered by BirdLife International as a center of bird endemism in the region. Given the poor track record of rain forest oil exploration in the areas of habitat and species conservation, critics of this project contend that environmental damage is likely to be significant. Access to the pipeline will affect several other protected areas as well, including Yasuní Park and Cuyabeno Wildlife Reserve. Because colonization along access roads is commonplace in South America, even with the best intentions the area will be opened to human incursion, with its concomitant forest fragmentation and hunting, in the classical pattern of Amazonian forest degradation (Amazon Watch 2002).

Subsistence and Market Hunting

During the last three centuries, South American wildlife has been subjected to extreme hunting pressure for the skin and meat trade. Turtles, turtle eggs, crocodilians, manatees, fur-bearing mammals, and large birds have been among the most affected. From 1946 to 1966, for example, more than 2 million collared peccary skins were sold in Iquitos, Peru, alone. In the 1950s and 1960s, an estimated 5 to 10 million crocodilian skins were traded annually in Amazonas state in Brazil. From 1976 to 1979, the port of Buenos Aires, Argentina, exported approximately 3.5 million gray fox skins, 9 million nutria (an aquatic rodent) skins, 5 million lizard skins (from large species such as the *Tegu* lizards), 400,000 skins from two species of small cats, and 3,500 puma skins. Chile exported 320,000 chinchilla pelts, 35,000 guanaco pelts, and 360,000 sea lion pelts from 1910 to 1984 (Redford and Robinson 1991). In some of these cases, strides have been made in reducing pressure on wild animals, but pressure on some prized species remains strong. Even with current controls and reductions in trade, many populations of large mammals, birds, and reptiles are still in peril from hunting. Fish populations in the Amazon, especially near large urban centers such as Manaus and Iquitos, have also been affected by overfishing, and many species show reduced abundance and body size.

The pet trade can have similar impacts, especially on parrots, lizards, and amphibians. For example, more than 90 percent of U.S. imports of live lizards in the late 1990s consisted of green iguanas bred in Central and South America. And heavy trade in Latin American mahogany and medicinal plants has drawn increased scrutiny in recent years. "There is evidence that trade volumes [in medicinal plants and derivatives] are considerable and that net sales exceed millions of dollars annually," declared TRAFFIC, a trade monitoring organization that works in concert with the secretariat of the Convention on International Trade in Endangered Species of Wild Fauna and Flora (CITES). "With many local communities depending on these plants for their healthcare, increasing harvest from the wild and current trade patterns of these resources can create a negative impact that threatens not only the sustainability of the species but also the health of the population" (TRAFFIC 2003).

In addition to large-scale market hunting, lower but widespread levels of subsistence hunting also affect populations of large animals. Especially affected are large mammals such as tapirs; white-lipped peccaries; deer; and spider, wooly, and howler monkeys; also large birds such as cracids, toucans, parrots, and waterfowl; and reptiles such as crocodiles, caimans, and river turtles. Human reliance on game animals for protein varies—some indigenous groups derive all their meat from game and fish, while colonists of European descent often bring cattle and pigs into the colonization frontier and may obtain less than 20 percent of their protein from wild animals. One study estimates that in the Brazilian state of Amazonas alone, a population of 600,000 people in the early 1980s killed approximately 3.5 million mammals, birds, and reptiles per year for subsistence purposes (Redford and Robinson 1991). Some of the most endangered bird species in Latin America are in the families *Cracidae* and *Tinamidae,* composed of large, chickenlike birds favored by hunters. Many studies have shown that species abundance is much lower in hunted than in comparable unhunted areas and that hunting alone or in combination with habitat disturbance such as fragmentation can lead to local species extinctions. Animals such as the chinchilla and Orinoco crocodile have been driven to the brink of extinction by hunting across their range; tapirs, white-lipped peccaries, spider monkeys, wooly monkeys, and giant river otters are locally extinct in many areas.

Although management plans have been put in place since the advent of the Convention on International Trade in Endangered Species in 1975, control is not always effective because of lack of biological data and enforcement capability; even legally harvested populations of capybara and caiman are overexploited. Subsistence hunting is officially forbidden in many Latin American countries, except in the case of indigenous peoples who hunt on their reserves. In fact, however, the practice is completely unregulated and largely undocumented.

Habitat Fragmentation

In recent years, three extensive studies (in Panama, in the central Brazilian Amazon, and at Guri Dam in the Guyana region of Venezuela) have helped ecologists gain a much greater understanding of the effects of fragmentation on neotropical forests. In some cases, species become locally extinct because the remaining habitat fragment is too small or does not have enough habitat diversity to support them. Plant and insect species that do well in hotter, drier edge areas eventually outcompete others that rely on the damp interior of continuous forest. Extinctions in fragmented areas are not immediate, however, which means that ongoing fragmentation of habitat may not show its toll in terms of species extinctions until many years later. For example, when the Gatun Lake impoundment was filled between 1911 and 1913 to supply water for the Panama Canal, one mountaintop isolated by the rising waters was protected as Barro Colorado Island Natural Monument and studied intensively by scientists from the Smithsonian Institution. Since its isolation, almost 100 species of birds have disappeared from the site, because of loss of specific habitats and greater vulnerability to chance events that affect small populations more than large populations (Sieving and Karr 1997). Several large mammals also disappeared: white-lipped peccaries, tapirs, spider monkeys, jaguars, and pumas. Although pumas are now recolonizing the area and tapirs and spider monkeys have been reintroduced, these populations remain vulnerable to regional extinction on account of low population size, and they may not provide the key ecological services—such as seed dispersal or control of populations of prey species—that they provide when they are present in normal abundances.

Vulnerable Regions of Exceptional Biodiversity

Over the last number of years, several international conservation organizations have undertaken exercises to highlight areas of particularly high biological diversity that are being threatened by anthropogenic activities such as logging, mining, and generation of air and water pollutants. Particularly notable studies along these lines have been compiled and maintained by the NGO groups Conservation International (which has identified 25 biodiversity "Hotspots" around the world) and the World Wide Fund for Nature (which has compiled a list of 238 distinct ecoregions that are endangered). The contents of these lists—developed with an emphasis on identifying areas of particular note in areas such as species richness, endemism, evolutionary phenomena, representativeness of distinctive ecosystems and ecological processes, and vulnerability to human activity—underline the importance of Latin America and the Caribbean as a center of global biodiversity. Indeed, 6 of Conservation International's 25 hotspots are located in Latin America (24 percent of the total), as are 53 of the WWF's 238 critical ecoregions (22 percent of the listed sites). Following is a brief rundown of some of the most notable ecoregions/habitat types identified in these and other conservation studies.

Tropical Andes

Encompassing nearly 1.26 million square kilometers (0.5 million square miles) in Venezuela, Colombia, Ecuador, Peru, Bolivia, and northern Argentina (the temperate Andes continue south into Chile and Argentina), this region is framed by the Pacific coastal forests to the west and the Amazonian lowlands to the east. The dominant habitat types are rain forests (forests receiving rain in every month of the year, for a total of at least 2,000 millimeters [79 inches] of rain per year), dry forests (forests that receive less than 2,000 millimeters of rain per year, undergo a marked dry season, and have a high proportion of deciduous species), puna (dry, high-altitude grasslands), and *páramo* (wet, high-altitude grasslands). More species of vascular plants (45,000, nearly half of them endemic) grow here than in any comparable area

A llama in the Peruvian mountains COREL

in the world. These include several plant species of economic importance to humans—potatoes, tobacco, quinoa, and the chinchona tree, the source of quinine used to prevent and treat malaria. The tropical Andes as a whole also houses 1,666 bird species (677 of them endemic), 830 amphibians (604 endemic), 479 reptiles (218 endemic), and 414 mammals (68 endemic) (Mittermeier et al. 1999).

The *yungas,* or cloud forests of Peru, Bolivia, and northern Argentina, are home to the spectacled bear, the only bear species in Latin America, and the mountain tapir, one of only four tapir species worldwide. The highest diversity of hummingbirds (a group of birds endemic to the New World) occurs here, as does a stunning array of "poison arrow" frogs. These highly poisonous amphibians are most diverse in the Andean and Chocó regions, although they also occur in the western Amazon and Central America. They acquire alkaloids from the ants, beetles, millipedes, and other insects they eat, and secrete them into their skin (Daly et al. 1994). Indigenous hunters rub their arrowheads on the backs of the animals to coat them with a long-lasting poison strong enough to kill large mammals. At least one pain-killing drug of potential benefit to humans has already been isolated from one of these frog species. As expressed by one conservation biologist, "[S]tudying these frogs . . .provides a shortcut to finding compounds that may be of importance to modern society" (Mittermeier et al. 1999). These and other mountain forests are under threat from colonization, and several of these frog species have gone extinct in recent years for reasons that are as yet not wholly understood—including some from relatively pristine mountain areas.

The páramo and puna grasslands grow above 3,000 meters (9,800 feet) and up to the snow line at about 4,500 meters (14,700 feet). The puna is home to the four native camelid species of South America—the llama, alpaca, guanaco, and vicuña. Although the llama and alpaca occur only as domesticated animals, the vicuña and guanaco live in the wild and are an important source of high-quality wool. The grassland and forest dwelling guanaco has been driven into a reduced range in Peru, northern Chile, and Argentina by hunting, habitat alteration, and perhaps by past climate change (Redford and Eisenberg 1992). The ecologically less flexible vicuña is completely restricted to the high-altitude puna. The Peruvian government has recently instituted a live-shearing program in which communities are given ownership and control over vicuña herds in their area. Each community builds a large corral for a once-a-year capture, in which animals are sheared and then released. Although potentially stressful to the animals, the system is a relatively successful example of sustainable use of a wildlife resource.

About 25 percent of the original extent of the Andean ecosystems is relatively intact, and 6.3 percent of its original surface area is included in a national park or other protected area (Mittermeier et al. 1999). Manu National Park and its surrounding Biosphere Reserve, one of the region's approximately eighty protected areas, is a particularly species-rich area of the Andes. The park's 1.5 million hectares extend from the Andean highlands down into the lowland Amazon flood plain of the Manu River. Despite its long history of protection and research, the park is currently threatened by invasion by colonists and must also deal with the changing aspirations of the indigenous peoples that live there, a situation common to many parks in Latin America. Other large current or planned protected areas in Peru (Tambopata Reserved Zone) and Bolivia (Madidi, Beni, and Pilón Lajas) provide some measure of protection to these montane forests and adjacent lowlands.

The Colombian Andes are especially threatened by large urban centers like Bogotá and Cali and by mechanized agriculture in the valleys. In Peru and Ecuador, similar pressure is exerted by the cities of Arequipa and Quito, respectively. Additionally, grazing, fire, and the establishment of exotic grasses are degrading the puna and páramo ecosystems. Rainbow trout introduced into high-altitude rivers and streams have impacted native fish populations, while the introduced American bullfrog preys on both native amphibians and the food sources upon which the amphibians rely. More recently, defoliants sprayed from the air to eliminate opium and other illegal plantations on the lower Andean slopes bring with them the danger of toxic soil and water pollution.

Mesoamerica

Tropical rain and dry forests are the dominant vegetation types in Central America, although extensive arid grasslands and shrublands occur in Mexico. In an area similar to that of the Andean hotspot (1,159,912 square kilometers), Mesoamerica supports 24,000 plant species (5,000 of them endemic), 1,193 bird species (251 endemic), 521 mammals (210 endemic), 685 reptiles (391 endemic), and 460 amphibians (307 endemic). After Australia, Mexico is the second richest country in the world in reptile diversity, and nearly half of its 510 reptile species can be found nowhere else on the globe. Similarly, Mexico's Chiapas region and neighboring areas in Guatemala are considered a center of origin for salamanders, and thirty-three out of the forty species in the area are endemic in nature (ibid.).

Human population densities are extremely high in Central America, with particularly strong growth registered in urban centers. In many cases, rapidly expanding human populations have exerted tremendous pressure for land clearing for subsistence agriculture and basic housing, while expansion of coffee, banana, and palm oil plantations has been driven by product demand from developed countries. Most of the old-growth forests on the Pacific side of the central mountain ranges have already been cleared, and logging and land clearance activities are now focused on the Atlantic slope forests, where much of the region's original forest cover has disappeared. One major factor in the demise of these forests is "the innocent-looking beef cow [which] is at the center of a destructive ecological cycle that is strangling Central America" (ibid.). Small-scale agriculturists sell their plots to large cattle ranch owners after a few years of slash and burn cultivation have robbed the soil of its nutrients. Approximately two-thirds of all agricultural land in Central America—land that was originally covered by dense forest—is now dedicated to cattle ranching.

Elsewhere, the pine and oak forests of southern Mexico and northern Central America (El Salvador, Guatemala, Honduras, and Nicaragua) constitute one of the richest subtropical conifer forests on the planet, with high levels of regional and local endemism. But populations of species ranging from the imperial woodpecker (likely already extinct) to the volcano rabbit to the dwarf jay have all been hammered by commercial logging, agricultural expansion, and overgrazing (World Wide Fund for Nature 2003).

Chocó-Darién Moist Forests

This 260,000-square-kilometer (100,400-square-mile) region on the Pacific coast of northern South America (Colombia, Ecuador, and Panama) is

Figure 2.2 Critical Ecoregions in Latin America and the Caribbean

Amazon River and Flooded Forests **147**
Antarctic Peninsula and Weddell Sea **196**
Atacama-Sechura Deserts **133**
Atlantic Dry Forests **59**
Atlantic Forests **48**
Brazilian Shield Amazonian Rivers
  and Streams **154**
Central Andean Dry Puna **109**
Central Andean Yungas **48**
Cerrado Woodlands and Savannas **93**

Chilean Matorral **122**
Chihuahuan Freshwater **194**
Chihuahuan-Tehuacan Deserts **131**
Chiquitano Dry Forests **58**
Chocó-Darién Moist Forests **39**
Coastal Venezuela Montane Forests **41**
Galápagos Islands Scrub **132**
Galápagos Marine **215**
Greater Antillean Freshwater **179**
Greater Antillean Marine **236**

(continues)

(continued)

Greater Antillean Moist Forests **37**
Greater Antillean Pine Forests **63**
Guayanan Highlands Moist Forests **45**
Guianan Freshwater **178**
Guianan Moist Forests **42**
Guianan-Amazon Mangroves **141**
Gulf of California **214**
High Andean Lakes **183**
Humboldt Current **210**
Llanos Savannas **92**
Mesoamerican Pine-Oak Forests **63**
Mesoamerican Reef **235**
Mexican Dry Forests **56**
Mexican Highland Lakes **192**
Napo Moist Forests **43**
Northeast Brazil Shelf Marine **238**
Northern Andean Montane Forests **40**
Northern Andean Paramo **108**
Orinoco River and Flooded Forests **148**

Panama Bight **213**
Panama Bight Mangroves **142**
Pantanal Flooded Savannas **101**
Patagonia Southwest Atlantic **205**
Patagonia Steppe **95**
Rapa Nui **228**
Rio Negro-J60urua6 Moist Forests **44**
Sonoran-Baja Deserts **130**
Southern Caribbean Sea **237**
Southwestern Amazonian Moist
    Forests **47**
Talamancan-Isthmian Pacific
    Forests **38**
Tumbesian-Andean Valleys Dry
    Forests **57**
Upper Amazon Rivers and
    Streams **152**
Upper Paraná Rivers and Streams **153**
Valdivian Temperate Rain Forests /
    Juan Fernández Islands **76**

characterized by high levels of rainfall and thick lowland forests. Isolated from the Amazon by the Andes range, the area is a globally significant repository of biological endemism (ibid.). It supports 9,000 plant species (2,250 endemic), an estimated 830 bird species (135 endemic), 235 mammals (60 endemic), 210 reptiles (63 endemic), and 350 amphibians (of which fully 60 percent are endemic to the region) (Mittermeier et al. 1999). Endangered species include the jaguar; the white-winged guan, a large bird rediscovered in 1977 in southern Peru; and Colombia's cotton top tamarin. Populations of the latter creature, a squirrel-size monkey, have been decimated by the pet trade, the medical research trade, and loss of habitat.

The Colombian Chocó and Panamanian Darién are in relatively good conservation condition because of their low human population densities. The Ecuadorian and Peruvian coastal forests, on the other hand, are in critical condition. Only 2 percent of the original forest cover remains in the Ecuadorian portion of this region, which has been heavily impacted by agriculture and sustains a large segment of Ecuador's population, which has one of the Western Hemisphere's higher fertility rates. Logging, overgrazing, and hunting have heavily impacted the Peruvian dry forests, while shrimp aquaculture and wood cutting for timber and fuelwood have greatly degraded mangrove forests in coastal Ecuador and Peru. Overall, 24.2 percent of the hotspot has relatively intact vegetation cover, and only 6.3 percent of this cover is located in formally protected areas (ibid.).

Caribbean

The entire surface area (263, 535 square kilometers) of the Caribbean bioregion is composed of islands. Numerous small islands in this corner of the world support one or more species that occur nowhere else, giving the area a high overall level of species richness and endemism. Less mobile organisms show particularly high endemism—of 497 reptile and 189 amphibian species in the Caribbean, 418 of the former species and 164 of the latter are classified as endemic. Among the better-known endemic reptiles are the legless lizards, rock iguanas, *Epicrates* boas, and a large diversity of *Anolis* lizards. The Caribbean also supports 12,000 plant species (7,000 endemic), 668 bird species (148 endemic), and 164 mammals (49 endemic). These figures, however, include the southernmost tip of the state of Florida, which is ecologically part of the Caribbean realm. Tropical rain forests, dry forests, and xeric shrublands are the primary vegetation types in the region (ibid.).

Exotic species pose a great threat to native Caribbean animals. Mongooses, feral cats, and Norway and black rats all prey on birds, mammals, and reptiles, including the unique Caribbean hutias and solenodons (endemic small mammals). Feral pigs and goats destroy native vegetation, affecting both endemic plant species and the animals that depend on the vegetation for cover and food. Introduced parrot species compete for nests and food with the endemic birds. One extreme example is the Puerto Rican parrot, considered critically endangered by the IUCN-World Conservation Union, whose population, like those of other parrot species in the Caribbean, has already been reduced by hunting and habitat loss. In fact, of twenty-six species of parrots originally occurring in the region, sixteen are extinct (including all the macaws); nine of the remaining ten are regarded as critically endangered by the IUCN (Snyder et al. 1997; World Conservation Union-IUCN 2002).

Approximately 11 percent of the original vegetation cover remains in this region, where many designated protected areas are highly degraded by human activities or too small to provide effective protection for many species (Mittermeier et al. 1999). For example, high human population pressure has led to extensive deforestation on Haiti—which has a population of 270 people per square kilometer—and elsewhere. Agricultural expansion is active in Cuba, and bauxite mining threatens several locations in Jamaica. On many islands, seasonal riverbeds and beaches are mined for sand for the concrete and construction industries. Additionally, large-scale tourist developments on small islands destroy entire patches of native habitat essential for the survival of endemic species.

For these reasons, and because local extinction equals global extinction for island endemics, extinction rates are usually higher on islands than on the mainland. The list of extinct species published by IUCN in its *Red List of Threatened Species* shows that at least fifty-nine species have gone extinct in the Caribbean in historical times, compared with only twenty-four and twenty-eight in Central America and South America, respectively. Of course, these numbers do not take into account the many insect, fungi, and small plant species that have become extinct before they were seen and described by scientists (World Conservation Union-IUCN 2002).

Gulf of California

Mexico's Gulf of California is one of the world's most biologically notable subtropical seas. Historically invigorated by the Colorado River's nutrient loads, this warmwater corner of the Eastern Pacific jutting between mainland Mexico and the Baja Peninsula is an important feeding and nursery ground for a wide array of marine species, including the blue whale, fin whale, the hawksbill turtle, the Pacific seahorse, the Mexican rockfish, and the totoaba fish. But exploitation of marine resources is rife throughout much of these waters, with overfishing looming as a potentially crippling threat to the ecoregion (World Wide Fund for Nature 2003).

Galápagos Islands

The Galápagos archipelago is a world-famous haven of rare and endangered terrestrial and marine species, including flightless cormorants and marine iguanas. Other species of note making their home in the forests or coastal waters of the Galápagos Islands, where wildlife has evolved separately from the rest of the world, include the waved albatross, Galápagos penguin, Galápagos giant tortoise, Galápagos hawk, banded ground-cuckoo, plumbeous forest-falcon, California sea lion, numerous species of whale (including the minke, fin, and humpback), killer whale, and the thirteen Darwin's finches.

But even on these remote Ecuadorian islands, human activities have had a deleterious effect on habitat integrity. Specific threats include overgrazing by domestic livestock and exotic species introduced to the islands over the years, poaching and other overharvesting of marine resources, environmentally destructive forms of tourism, unsustainable logging, and habitat loss and fragmentation resulting from expanding human settlements and continued reliance on shifting cultivation practices (ibid.). The most dramatic insult to the ecoregion in recent years, however, was a 2001 event in which

Marine iguanas on the Galápagos Islands COREL

an Ecuadorian oil tanker ran aground in the area, spilling 3 million liters of crude oil into the sea. Scientists believe that this accident caused the death of more than 60 percent of the Galápagos's marine iguanas—a species found nowhere else on earth.

Atlantic Forest

The coastal forests of Brazil and northern Paraguay and Argentina provide a cautionary illustration of how tropical habitats can be fragmented and degraded by development when adequate management and conservation plans are absent. Only 7.5 percent of the area can be considered intact, and this is made up of widely scattered forest fragments, most of them too small to represent fully functioning ecological systems. In the northern portion of the forests, as little as 1 percent of the area retains its original forest cover. Currently there are fourteen national parks, twenty biological reserves and ecological stations, a variety of Brazilian state and municipal parks, and nine additional protected areas in Argentina and Paraguay. But federal and state preserves encompass only 2.7 percent of the original area, and some of the largest remaining forest blocks are currently unprotected and in private hands (Mittermeier et al. 1999).

In southern and eastern Brazil, for example, a very small and wealthy segment of the population controls the vast majority of private land, a situation that has engendered social unrest that has further contributed to degradation of natural resources and biodiversity. Federal, state, and private lands are all currently threatened by invasion from Brazil's Landless Workers Movement (Movimento dos Trabalhadores Sem Terra, or "Sem Terras"), whose members settle on currently "unproductive" land in order to secure a living and force the government to institute desperately needed land reform. In the process, they clear forested land and hunt already endangered animal populations for food. At least one Brazilian NGO is working with the Sem Terra to educate them about ecologically sound ways of managing the land, but pressures to harvest resources in unsustainable ways for short-term gain remain significant.

The original extent of the Atlantic Forest region, a narrow strip of land that runs all along the eastern coast of Brazil, is estimated at 1,227,680 square kilometers (474,000 square miles). The first region to be colonized in Brazil, it currently supports two of the world's largest cities (São Paulo and Rio de Janeiro) and two-thirds of Brazil's population. The vegetation is primarily tropical and subtropical rain forest, with Araucaria pine forests in the south—many of which have been lost for the production of match sticks. Low mountains run throughout the region, being most concentrated in the southern states.

Although the Atlantic forest accounts for only 13 percent of the land surface of Brazil, it is the second most biologically diverse region in the country after the Amazon and has stunning levels of endemism. Of 20,000 plant species, 6,000 are endemic, and more than 50 percent of the region's tree species are endemic in nature. Of 620 bird species, 73 are endemic, as are 60 of the 200 reptiles and 253 of the 280 amphibians. More than half of the mammals (160 of 261 species) are endemic as well, including half of the rodent species and 80 percent of primate species and subspecies (Mittermeier et al. 1997).

The best known and most threatened of the primates of this region are the lion tamarins (four species—one endangered and three critically endangered). Approximately 600 individuals of the golden lion tamarin remain in the wild after thirty years of concerted conservation and education efforts, including the reintroduction of captive-bred populations from zoological institutions in the United States. Populations of the black-faced tamarin have dropped to fewer than 400 individuals, while an estimated 1,000 black lion tamarins still roam the region. The healthiest of the tamarin species may be the golden-headed lion tamarin, but habitat fragmentation has cut its estimated population to about 1,100 individuals. The majority of all of these individuals still existing in the wild are limited to two protected areas along the coast, the Poco das Antas Biological Reserve and Morro do Diablo State Park (Dietz 1996; National Zoological Park 2003).

Brazilian Cerrado

The Cerrado, an extensive open ecosystem composed of 1,783,169 square kilometers (688,500 square miles) of savanna, savanna woodland, and closed canopy dry forest represents 21 percent of Brazil's surface area (Mittermeier et al. 1999). Although annual rainfall is not necessarily low—up to 1,600 millimeters (63 inches) of rain fall per year in some portions of the region—the long six-month dry season precludes the occurrence of moist forest, and many plants are drought-adapted. Gallery forests growing along rivers and streams are important dry season refuges for many animals, and over evolutionary time scales they have served as refuges for forest species isolated in a sea of savanna. They also serve as corridors connecting the Cerrado to adjacent forested habitats such as the Atlantic forest to the east.

Plant diversity (10,000 species) and endemism (4,400 species) are very high, with a surprising 39 percent of genera endemic to the region. Herbaceous species, which do not disperse well and have strict adaptations to the open habitat, have an even higher proportion of endemics than shrubs, trees, and grasses. Bird diversity is also high, at 837 species, although only 29 of these are endemic to the region. In addition, the Cerrado supports 161 mammal species (including 5 deer species), 120 species of reptile, and 150 amphibian species (Mittermeier et al. 1999). In the open grasslands large animals such as the giant anteater, the rhea (a large, ostrichlike bird), and the maned wolf are easily sighted. The latter is a beautiful, red-furred, foxlike wolf that feeds largely on fruits and is therefore an important seed disperser for Cerrado shrubs and trees. Threatened bird species, meanwhile, include the Spix's macaw, the red-legged seriema, the cone-billed tanager, and the dwarf tinamou (World Wide Fund for Nature 2003).

The Cerrado ecosystem is adapted to fires started by lightning strikes and by indigenous peoples hunting with fire. In recent years, however, ranchers, farmers, and indigenous people have stopped restricting their burns to appropriate times of year. Indeed, observers worry that they are making more extensive use of burns as a land clearing tool than local ecosystems can support. Since the mid-1960s the Cerrado has been Brazil's most important agricultural frontier, especially for cattle, soybeans, and irrigated rice plantations. In 1963, Brazilian president Juscelino Kubitschek established the country's new capital—Brasília—in the middle of the Cerrado, with the express purpose of opening up this "hinterland" and exploiting its potential. Since then only a few protected areas have been declared, covering about 1 percent of the original extension of the habitat. Some parks, such as Emas and Serra da Canastra, are threatened by anthropogenic fires, road building, and illegal cattle pasturing. At least 80 percent of the Cerrado has been modified by human activities, primarily for ranching and agriculture. Fully one-quarter of Brazil's grain production comes from this area, and land clearing will continue as Brazil positions itself to compete with the United States as the world's primary exporter of soybeans.

Central Chile

"Mediterranean" climate areas are characterized by winter rainfall and aridity, and are dominated by drought- and fire-adapted plants. The central Chile hotspot includes both winter rainfall deserts and true Mediterranean scrub. Overall species diversity is low, because of the aridity and limited extent of the region, but endemism is relatively high: 1,605 of 3,429 plant species are endemic, as are 34 out of 55 reptiles and 14 out of 26 amphibians. Only 4 out of 198 birds and 9 of 56 mammals, however, are endemic to the region (Mittermeier et al. 1999). Araucaria pine and *Nothofagus* beech forests grow at the southern extreme of the region, and an alpine flora dominates in the mountains, with grasslands developing at the highest elevations.

Because Mediterranean habitats are excellent habitats for humans, and because Chile's national economy is growing at a rapid pace, central Chile has a high population pressure and has been impacted by logging, forest fires, overgrazing, development of coastal areas for tourism, and exotic species such as goats, European rabbits, Old-World Mediterranean plants, and *Acacia* shrubs. Eucalyptus and other exotic tree plantations divide the natural forest into isolated fragments. Because colonization and aggressive logging began early in this area, even currently forested areas in many cases support secondary regrowth rather than the original vegetation cover. Approximately 30 percent of the original vegetation cover remains intact, and a little over 3 percent is included in protected areas (about 1.8 percent of the desert region and 4.2 percent of the shrubland are protected). Native animals such as the chinchilla rodent and reptiles and lizards have been heavily impacted by the fur, skin, and pet trade, and native frogs are threatened by several introduced fish species and by introduced *Xenopus* frogs.

In addition, some of Chile's most species-rich—and critically threatened—forests are south of this region, in Administrative Region X. This area, which constitutes the second-largest patch of coastal temperate rain forest in the world after Alaska, is characterized by high levels of endemism in tree species, but many of these native trees are being cleared to make way for monocultural pine and eucalyptus plantations for wood production.

The Pantanal

The exact boundaries of the Pantanal are somewhat amorphous, given the diversity of wetland definitions and difficulty of delineating wetland borders. But it extends over an estimated 170,000 square kilometers (65,000 square miles) of central-western Brazil, eastern Bolivia, and northeastern Paraguay, making it the largest wetland complex in the world. It is an important wintering destination for swallow-tailed kites and other migratory birds that breed as far north as the southern United States (Dinerstein et al. 1995).

The Pantanal is also home to a spectacular array of animal wildlife, including several species that have experienced significant population declines as a result of rapacious rates of harvest. The Paraguayan caiman, for example, is only now recovering from the 1970s and 1980s, when hunters exported an estimated 1 million skins annually. Other animals affected by past and current hunting are the jaguar, the giant river otter, the marsh deer (the largest deer in Latin America), and the hyacinth macaw, which has been heavily exploited for the pet trade.

Most of the Pantanal is owned by cattle ranchers and other private landowners. Only about 0.3 percent of the Pantanal is in government-protected areas. The environmental impact of this land ownership situation varies. Vegetation has been disturbed by grazing, but wholesale habitat conversion is thus far limited and little competition occurs between cattle and native deer species for food. However, the environmental community has expressed concern about schemes to straighten and extend a river-based waterway through the Pantanal to facilitate soy grain transport from the Cerrado to a major port in Paraguay, citing the loss and disruption of habitat that would accompany such an effort. Other cited threats include agricultural expansion, charcoal production, mercury pollution from gold mining, overfishing, and habitat fragmentation and loss from road construction and attendant development (World Wide Fund for Nature 2003).

Venezuelan Llanos Savannas

The Venezuelan Llanos are smaller in extent than the Pantanal, but the World Wide Fund for Nature has described it as "the best example of tropical savannas in South America, with regionally high floristic and habitat diversity" (ibid.). Indeed, these savannas provide a haven for myriad species of wading birds and waterfowl (fourteen species of herons, three species of storks, a variety of shorebirds, and eight species of ducks, including the migratory blue-winged teal from North America), as well as exotic species such as the white-bellied spider monkey, the Orinoco crocodile, and the giant anaconda.

But this valuable habitat is threatened by all manner of anthropogenic activity, including overhunting, land conversion for grazing and cultivation, and diversions and other modifications of freshwater resources. A recent survey suggests that all duck species are declining in the Llanos, because of overhunting for food, shooting as pests, and contamination by pesticides sprayed on the expanding rice plantations. Caiman and capybara (a large, wetland-dependent rodent) are commercially harvested in this area for their skin and meat, and although government and private management plans are in place, both species have experienced population crashes in the recent past (Mittermeier et al. 1999; World Wide Fund for Nature 2003).

Pampas Grasslands

The humid and dry pampas grassland region has no formally protected areas, supports the highest human population densities in Argentina, and has been heavily degraded by grazing and agriculture. As a result, many of the 24 species of marine mammals and more than 300 species of marine and coastal birds that occur in the coastal section of the pampas are in some jeopardy (World Wildlife Fund). Inland, the pampas support key wetland areas for migratory birds. Freshwater and saline wetlands abound in the drier *espinal* and *monte* to the south and west of the pampas, including the nesting grounds of the Chilean flamingo. The Patagonian grasslands and marshes to the south are threatened by desertification caused by overgrazing; this habitat extends into the Falkland Islands, which support important bird nesting areas.

Valdivian Temperate Rain Forests and Juan Fernandez Islands

South America's only major temperate rain forest—and one of only five in the world—is tucked away on the West Coast of Argentina and Chile and the Juan Fernandez Islands that lie offshore. This ecoregion supports stands of enormous and unique trees. Particularly noteworthy are the southern beech forests, which are one of only three major forests of this type on the planet (the others are located in Australia and New Zealand). Species making their home in this region include the monkey puzzle tree and the Andean deer, but these and other flora and fauna are jeopardized by intensive logging and conversion of land to monocultural tree plantations (World Wide Fund for Nature 2003).

Sources:

Amazon Watch. 2002. "Ecuador: Environmentalists Continue Forest Occupation in Mindo to Block Pipeline Construction." Amazon Watch news release, January 9.

Amazon Watch. 2001. "OCP Pipeline Profile." Amazon Watch news release, August.

Brown, K. S., and R. W. Hutchings. 1997. "Disturbance, Fragmentation and the Dynamics of Diversity in Amazonian Forest Butterflies." In *Tropical Forest Remnants: Ecology, Management and Conservation of Fragmented Communities.* Edited by W. F. Laurence and R. O. Bierregard. Chicago: University of Chicago Press.

Cody, M. L. 1996. "Introduction to Neotropical Diversity." In *Neotropical Biodiversity and Conservation.* Edited by A. C. Gibson. Los Angeles: Mildred E. Mathias Botanical Garden.

Daly, J. W., et al. 1994. "Dietary Source for Skin Alkaloids of Poison Frogs." *Journal of Chemical Ecology* 20, no. 4 (April): 943–954.

Diaz-Sarmiento, J. A., and R. Alvarez-Leon. 1998. "Fish Biodiversity Conservation in Colombia." In *Proceedings of the International Conference on Conservation of Fish Genetic Diversity.* Edited by B. Harvey et al. Victoria, BC: World Fisheries Trust.

Dietz, L. 1996. "The Golden Lion Tamarin." In *WWF: Changing Worlds: 35 Years of Conservation Achievement.* Banson, UK: WWF International.

Dinerstein, E., et al. 1995. *A Conservation Assessment of the Terrestrial Ecoregions of Latin America and the Caribbean.* Washington, DC: World Bank.

Dobson, A. P. 1998. *Conservation and Biodiversity.* Basingstoke, UK: Palgrave.

Erwin, T. L. 1982. "Tropical Forests: Their Richness in Coleoptera and Other Arthropods." *Coleopterists Bulletin* 36: 74–75.

Gibson, A. C. 1996. *Neotropical Biodiversity and Conservation.* Los Angeles: Mildred E. Mathias Botanical Garden.

Groombridge, B., and M. D. Jenkins. 2000. *Global Biodiversity: Earth's Living Resources in the 21st Century.* Cambridge: UNEP-World Conservation Monitoring Centre, World Conservation Press.

Jochnick, C. 1995. "Amazon Oil Offensive." *Multinational Monitor* (January–February).

Kaiser, J. 2001. "Galápagos Takes Aim at Alien Invaders." *Science* 293 (July 27): 590–592.

Laurance, W. F. 2000. "Mega-Development Trends in the Amazon: Implications for Global Change." *Environmental Monitoring and Assessment* (March).

Laurance, W. F., and R. O. Bierregaard Jr. 1997. *Tropical Forest Remnants: Ecology, Management and Conservation of Fragmented Communities.* Chicago: University of Chicago Press.

MacMillan, G. 1995. *At the End of the Rainbow: Gold, Land and People in the Brazilian Amazon.* New York: Columbia University Press.

Miranda, M., et al. 1998. *All that Glitters Is Not Gold: Balancing Conservation and Development in Venezuela's Frontier Forests.* Washington, DC: World Resources Institute.

Mittermeier, Russell A., Norman Myers, and Cristina Goettsch Mittermeier. 1999. *Hotspots: Earth's Ecologically Richest and Most Endangered Ecoregions.* Monterrey, Mexico: CEMEX, Conservation International.

Mittermeier, Russell A., P. Robles-Gil, and Cristina Goettsch Mittermeier. 1997.

Megadiversity: Earth's Biologically Wealthiest Nations. Monterrey, Mexico: CEMEX, Conservation International.

National Zoological Park. 2003. *Golden Lion Tamarin Conservation Program.* Available at http://natzoo.si.edu (accessed April 2003).

Neira, E., H. Verscheure, and C. Revenga. 2002. *Chile's Frontier Forests: Conserving a Global Treasure.* Washington, DC: World Resources Institute.

Nepstad, Dan, et al. 1999. "Large-Scale Impoverishment of Amazonian Forests by Logging and Fire." *Nature* 14 (April): 505–508.

Nepstad, Dan, et al. 2001. "Road Paving, Fire Regions, and the Future of Amazon Forests." *Forest Ecology and Management* 154 (December).

Osborne, P. L. 2000. *Tropical Ecosystems and Ecological Concepts.* Cambridge: Cambridge University Press.

Redford, K. H., and J. Eisenberg. 1992. *Mammals of the Neotropics: The Southern Cone.* Chicago: University of Chicago Press.

Redford, K. H., and J. G. Robinson. 1991. "Subsistence and Commercial Uses of Wildlife in Latin America." In *Neotropical Wildlife Use and Conservation.* Edited by J. G. Robinson and K. H. Redford. Chicago: University of Chicago Press.

Rickleffs, R. E. 2001. *The Economy of Nature.* 5th ed. New York: W. H. Freeman.

Sieving, K. E., and J. R. Karr. 1997. "Avian Extinction and Persistence Mechanisms in Lowland Panama." In *Tropical Forest Remnants: Ecology, Management, and Conservation of Fragmented Communities.* Edited by W. F. Laurance and R. O. Bierregaard Jr. Chicago: University of Chicago Press.

Snyder, N. F. R., J. W. Wiley, and C. B. Kepler. 1997. *The Parrots of Luquillo: Natural History and Conservation of the Puerto Rican Parrot.* Camarillo, CA: Western Foundation of Vertebrate Zoology.

Stattersfield, A. J., et al. 1998. *Endemic Bird Areas of the World: Priorities for Biodiversity Conservation.* Cambridge, UK: BirdLife International.

Terborgh, J. 1999. *Requiem for Nature.* Washington, DC: Island.

TRAFFIC. 2003. "25 Years of TRAFFIC." Available at http://www.traffic.org (accessed April 2003).

UN Food and Agriculture Organization. 2001. *Global Forest Resources Assessment 2000.* Rome: FAO.

World Conservation Union-IUCN. 2002. *2002 IUCN Red List of Threatened Species.* Available at http://www.redlist.org (accessed March 2003).

World Wide Fund for Nature. 2003. "Global 200." Available at http://www.panda.org/resources/programmes/globa1200 (accessed April 2003).

World Wildlife Fund. *Ecoregions.* Available at http://www.worldwildlife.org/wild-world/profiles/2001 (accessed April 2003).

Parks,
Preserves, and
Protected Areas
—KIRSTEN SILVIUS

L atin America contains some of the planet's greatest treasure troves of un-
spoiled wilderness, biodiversity, and species endemism—animals and
plants found nowhere else in the world. This biological wealth is widespread,
from Mexico's Yucatan Peninsula and Sierra Madre mountains southward
through the Amazon rain forest of equatorial South America (home to more
species of flora and fauna than any other ecosystem in the world) and the
Andes Mountains to Argentina's rugged Patagonia region. But formal protection of these and other natural habitats is spotty through much of Central and
South America and the Caribbean. In places where establishment and maintenance of protected area systems has foundered, chief reasons include funding
shortfalls, resource consumption pressure from growing communities in surrounding areas (and sometimes from communities within the parks themselves), and inadequate legal provisions for habitat protection.

The Changing Face of Habitat
Conservation in Latin America
The relationship between parks and people in Latin America is very different
from that in North America, Europe, and many other parts of the world.
Whereas national parks in North America are regarded as nearly inviolate (at
least in principle), many protected areas in Central and South America are
managed for multiple purposes. For example, Henri Pittier National Park, the
oldest protected area in Venezuela, is renowned in international conservation
circles for its level of biodiversity, especially for avian fauna. Fully 43 percent
of Venezuela's bird species—and 7 percent of all the world's bird species—live

within the park's boundaries. But several towns also exist within Henri Pittier National Park. Some of these are farming communities that still maintain a variety of traditional cultural practices, such as the sustainable cultivation of cocoa. Others are resort towns that cater to tourists from around the world (Parks Watch 2002).

People living within the boundaries of protected areas are a reality that Latin American conservationists and managers must deal with. The situation stems in large part from high levels of poverty, inequality in land distribution, and social instability, all of which have driven people to seek "available" land—land that is not privately owned and protected. But cultural and historical factors play a role as well. The boundaries between humans and nature that are evident in the United States, for example, are much more porous in Latin America, because so many people there still depend on products harvested from the wild for their daily survival. Cultural and religious background also helps to establish a direct emotional and practical link between humans and nature in Latin America that is very different from the wilderness or recreation approach to nature that currently dominates in North America. When this attitude toward nature is combined with chronic underfunding of protected areas, the result is that many national parks and other protected areas in Latin America are currently in poor conservation shape, and their capacity to withstand future threats to their integrity as extensive functioning ecosystems is in question.

In the 1980s and 1990s, however, two new processes began to alter the face of protected areas in Latin America. First, sustainable use of resources rivaled biodiversity protection as a dominant paradigm for international conservation. Second, national level nongovernmental organizations (NGOs) have proliferated in Latin America, giving rise to what some have termed the age of "NGOism." These conservation organizations have launched multiple initiatives to establish new protected areas, improve protection of already established areas, and carve out a role for themselves in the management of parks, wilderness reserves, and other protected areas.

One result of these trends is that many countries have begun to emphasize protected area categories other than parks and forest reserves, including communal reserves and extractive reserves that are comanaged by local, subsistence-level dwellers. They have also given indigenous and local peoples a greater role in the management of more strictly protected areas, including national parks. Although national legislation is still catching up to these changes and the gap between legislation and reality sometimes causes conflicts, the trend toward participatory management and establishment of multiple-use areas is clear.

Discussion about protected areas in Latin America today is thus dominated by issues of synergism/conflict between indigenous areas and protected areas, by issues of sustainable use of resources, and by the participatory management paradigm. There is growing recognition that the intersection between human rights and biodiversity conservation may yet yield some innovative solutions for both people and biodiversity.

On the other hand, supporters of strictly protected areas justifiably argue that biodiversity and ecosystem function are inevitably degraded when humans and nature coexist in the modern world and that more attention needs to be paid to securing strictly protected areas that do not support people within their boundaries, both by adequately funding protections for existing areas and by establishing new areas that encompass as yet unprotected ecosystems. It is fascinating to trace the development of protected area policy in these times of rapid transition, given that protected areas mark the physical point at which nature as a scientific concept and nature as a cultural and political construct meet and jostle for priority.

Latin America's Protected-Area Networks

Latin America contains some of the largest and most biologically rich protected areas in the Western Hemisphere. Venezuela's Canaima National Park

Table 3.1 Protection of Natural Areas, 1997

	Square Kilometers Protected	As Percentage of Total Land Area
North America	2,147,140	11.7
Latin America and Caribbean	1,438,070	7.2
Europe	1,052,090	4.7
Africa	1,540,430	5.2
Asia	1,628,770	5.3
Oceania	603,820	7.1
World[1]	*8,410,410*	*6.4*

SOURCE: World Resources Institute

NOTE: [1] Includes areas not included in regional totals; excludes Greenland.

and Bolivia's Gran Chaco National Park and Management Area, for example, each cover more than 300,000 square kilometers (over 3 million hectares). The presence of these large blocks of protected habitat is one of the most positive aspects of Latin America's network of protected areas. Large protected areas are more effective for biodiversity conservation than small areas because flora and fauna contained therein are not as vulnerable to forces outside park boundaries and because the large populations of plants, animals, and other organisms they encompass are not subject to chance extinction events. Large areas also allow the operation of source sink dynamics, in which animals produced in an area of habitat suitable for reproduction are able to disperse into other areas (sometimes providing ecological services such as seed dispersal in the process), where they multiply to the point that they can be harvested sustainably. In addition, large populations tend to encompass larger genetic diversity, thus ensuring a more dynamic evolutionary process in the future.

Defining Protected Areas in Latin America

Protected areas around the world are managed for a wide range of purposes, including scientific research, wilderness protection, preservation of species and ecosystems, maintenance of environmental services, protection of specific natural and cultural features, tourism and recreation, education, sustainable exploitation of natural resources, and maintenance of cultural and traditional attributes. The specific design, objectives, implementation, and management of protected areas all vary in accordance with the home country's cultural, political, economic, and ecological orientations. Indeed, classification systems used by individual countries vary in accordance with objectives and levels of protection, and title designations are different from country to country as well. Therefore, comparing protected areas in different regions of the world, or in different countries within one region, can be a challenging task. To help countries decide what type of area to establish, select preservation objectives, and set management guidelines to achieve those objectives, the World Conservation Union (also known as IUCN from its former name—International Union for the Conservation of Nature) has over the years established and modified a classification system for protected areas that is used worldwide today. Fitting protected areas into this system based on their objectives, regardless of their local designations, also makes information comparable across national and regional boundaries, allowing an assessment of the effectiveness of different protected area categories. Data on all but the smallest of the world's parks and reserves are collected by the World Commission on Protected Areas (WCPA) and used to create the *United Nations List of Protected Areas,* the definitive listing of protected areas around the globe (World Commission on Protected Areas).

The World Conservation Union classifies each formally designated protected area in one of six management categories. Category I parks and reserves are protected areas managed primarily for science or wilderness protection. Strict nature reserves (Category Ia) includes ecological reserves, biological reserves, ecological stations, and other areas that are managed purely for biodiversity protection and scientific research and do not tolerate human visitation other than by scientists. In Latin America, Brazil, in particular, has made extensive use of this category. Wilderness areas (Category Ib) are protected areas managed primarily for wilderness ecosystem protection; they allow human visitation only at a primitive level—that is, without assistance from human-established infrastructure such as roads and housing. This category of protection, which is popular in the United States, is virtually nonexistent in Latin America. This state of affairs reflects the fact that the concept of wilderness as a spiritual—and limited—resource is less developed in Latin America than in North America, even though South America contains more extensive true wilderness areas than any other region of the world except for the boreal/Arctic, Antarctic, and Oceanic regions.

Category II protected areas are national parks managed for both ecosystem protection and human recreation. This is the most common category of protected area everywhere, including Latin America, because it is both the oldest of the categories and the one that is best suited to achieving the two objectives of greatest interest to the general public—conservation and recreation. Because of the emphasis on human recreation, however, clashes between humans and nature (such as conflicts between jaguars and human interest in Brazil's Iguaçu National Park) are frequently resolved in favor of humans rather than nature. In some countries and regions where humans occupy much of the landscape, human habitation is unavoidable in national parks. That is the case in densely populated Europe, but also in the more sparsely populated areas of Latin America still occupied by indigenous peoples.

Other management classifications are available for natural monuments and landmarks (Category III), species and habitat protection areas that are subject to tree felling and other active forms of management (Category IV), protected landscapes and seascapes with dual conservation and recreation management mandates (Category V), and "managed resource protection areas" (Category VI), which seek to balance biodiversity protection with extractive activities such as logging. Natural monument (Category III) designations are reserved for unique natural features (and sometimes anthropological features), such as mountains, canyons, or lakes that create a striking landscape feature. These areas, which receive stringent protection from development and are generally small in extent, receive relatively little funding and attention in Latin America.

Managed resource protected-area designations (Category VI), on the other hand, are widely used throughout most of Latin America, with the notable exception of the Caribbean. These protected areas are founded on the principle of sustainable use of natural ecosystems—that is, resource extraction is allowed on a sustainable basis. In Latin America, this often means that local communities that have a tradition of living within the area are partly responsible for managing the area. Whereas in North America this category would be dominated by forest reserves available for (presumably) sustainable logging and wildlife management areas open for hunting, in Latin America the category also includes extractive reserves such as those established for rubber tappers in the state of Acre, for açai palm fruit harvesters at the mouth of the Amazon, for fishermen in the flooded varzea forests of the central Amazon, and other communities practicing subsistence lifestyles.

Within Central America, Mexico protects the most total land area, at nearly 160,000 square kilometers (61,800 square miles) (8 percent of its total territory). Of this total, however, more than half is designated as Category VI in nature, meaning that logging and other manifestations of the multiple-use concept are a prominent feature. Elsewhere in Central America, Costa Rica and Guatemala have set aside large areas of land for habitat and species protection. Costa Rica has issued protection to nearly one-quarter of its total land area—about 12,000 square kilometers (4,630 square miles)—and about half of its protected area system is composed of Category I and II type parks and reserves. Guatemala, meanwhile, has set aside about one-fifth of its land— nearly 22,000 square kilometers (8,500 square miles)—with most of its parkland qualifying for Category I, II, or III status (Green and Paine 1997). Among Caribbean nations, data compiled to track the extent of protected areas is heavily skewed by the popularity of marine protected areas. Taking these reserves into consideration, the Dominican Republic, Cuba, and the Bahamas are the leaders in terms of land and water area protected (ibid.).

In South America, Brazil has officially designated more than 526,000 square kilometers (203,100 square miles) of rain forest and other wildlife habitat as one type of protected area or another. This land is distributed among all six recognized IUCN categories, but whereas the country has only a few national monuments (Category III), the size and number of its multiple-use parks and reserves (Category V and VI) is great. Other South American states that have set aside large expanses of land include Venezuela (560,000 square kilometers [216,200 square miles]), Bolivia (178,000 square kilometers [68,700 square miles]), Ecuador (156,000 square kilometers [60,200 square miles]), and Chile (141,000 square kilometers [54,400 square miles]). As in Brazil, however, protected area systems in most of these countries are heavily

Monteverde Cloud Forest Reserve in Costa Rica COREL

weighted toward designations that permit logging, mining, farming, and other extractive activities. In terms of percentage of total land area protected, Ecuador leads the way with more than one-third of its land in its system. Other countries with significant percentages of land under nominal protection include Chile (nearly 19 percent) and Bolivia (more than 16 percent) (ibid.).

Nonbinding Categories of Protected Areas— International Conventions

Internationally designated protected areas, especially Biosphere Reserves, are relatively common in Latin America. Biosphere Reserves, designated under UNESCO's Man and the Biosphere program, are usually extensive areas, centered around one or more strict protection zones such as national parks, and surrounded by inhabited areas zoned into different management categories. Agriculture, grazing, tree plantations, and even residential areas can occur within the buffer and transition zones of a biosphere reserve; for example, the Mata Atlântica Biosphere Reserve in São Paulo state, Brazil, includes the São Paulo city green belt and significant expanses of cultivated areas. Of nearly 29.6 million hectares in the reserve, only 4 million hectares are contained within a relatively intact core area (UN Educational, Scientific and Cultural Organization 2002).

Although no legal recourse can be brought to bear if Biosphere Reserves are degraded, such designations do draw public attention to sites of ecological significance, which in turn puts pressure on governments to protect the natural resources contained therein. These designations also help to publicize the potential for sustainable use and multiple-use management of natural areas, and in many cases they emphasize the linkage between human rights and environmental rights, as territories in designated Biosphere Reserves often encompass significant populations of indigenous and local peoples. For all of these reasons, designation of an area as a Biosphere Reserve is often a source of great pride in many Latin American regions, and recognition is highly sought after by NGOs working to enhance conservation of wilderness areas and other lands providing significant habitat for mammals, birds, plants, and other creatures.

In Venezuela, for example, the 860,000-square-kilometer (332,000-square-mile) Upper Orinoco Biosphere Reserve was declared in 1991 after feverish gold mining incursions into the traditional lands of the indigenous Yanomami tribe in neighboring Brazil wrought serious environmental and social damage on the Yanomami people and their way of life. National and international disapproval of this blatant disregard for indigenous rights provided fertile ground for the acceptance of the Upper Orinoco reserve. The Orinoco Biosphere Reserve has a core area composed of three national parks, which together make up just more than half the area of the reserve. The remaining territory is inhabited by Yanomami, Sanema, and Yekuana indigenous peoples and local nonindigenous peoples, who participate in biosphere management through their own organizations while continuing with their traditional subsistence lifestyles. Agro-ecosystems that produce crops of yucca, banana, palm fruits, and several root crops are among the activities permitted in the noncore area. Large-scale mining interests and timber concessions have thus far not been established within the reserve, in part because of the remoteness of the area. However, mining laws and agrarian reform are currently in flux in Venezuela—as is the government itself—and portions of the biosphere reserve that are not within the boundaries of the national parks may yet be opened for mining and other extractive activities at some point in the future. However, the very existence of the Upper Orinoco Biosphere Reserve guarantees that development proposals that endanger prime wildlife habitat or indigenous communities will not go unnoticed.

Cuba, despite its relatively small size, currently hosts six biosphere reserves, the last two declared in 2000. All are based on core areas of natural reserves, ecological reserves, and wildlife reserves. Cuba's biosphere reserves have been used extensively as a means of educating people in the sustainable

Environmental degradation has cast doubt on the future of Yanomami culture. HERVE COLLART/CORBIS
SYGMA

use of resources (all protected areas in Cuba are experiencing some degree of resource use or resource degradation). In Central America, and especially in Mexico, Belize, and Guatemala, many biosphere reserves are characterized by significant architectural sites and heavy levels of tourist visitation. As of 2001 there were a total of sixty-five UNESCO Biosphere Reserves in Latin America, with Argentina (twelve sites) and Mexico (ten sites) holding the largest number.

Many countries also have RAMSAR Wetlands, which have been designated by the Convention on Wetlands of International Importance, also known as the RAMSAR Convention. Since 1975, nearly 1,100 sites have been designated around the world, including more than 100 sites in South and Central America. Just as national protected areas form the core of biosphere reserves, RAMSAR sites often also fall within biosphere reserves. The convention essentially encourages international cooperation in wetland management, helps to disseminate expertise in wetland ecology, places media and other attention on critical wetland sites, and promotes a wise-use policy for the areas.

Overview of Threats to Protected Areas in Latin America

In general, South American countries have more coherent protected area systems than do Central American and Caribbean countries. That is, their legislation and central administration are stronger, and there is a longer tradition of incorporation of protected area systems into national level planning. Exceptions occur in the three smallest countries on the continent, two of which recently gained their independence from colonial powers (Guyana and Suriname) and one of which is still a French dependency (French Guiana). French Guiana is currently reviewing its wildlife management and protected-area system, which until two years ago was based on legislation more applicable to Europe than to a small tropical country. In Suriname, protected-area planning has recently been strengthened with the establishment in 1998 of the 1.6-million-hectare Central Suriname Nature Reserve, composed of three previously existing protected areas. Of the remaining protected areas in the country, only two are indirect use areas, all others being in Category IV or higher. Guyana has only one protected area, Kaiteur National Park. At about 60,000 hectares, it protects a minuscule proportion of the country's sparsely inhabited southern forests and savannas. Historically, the country's mining interests and indigenous peoples have opposed proposed expansions of the parks' area, though for different reasons. Mining companies wish to keep potentially valuable lands open for extraction, while indigenous peoples fear that their ability to use the area for subsistence purposes will be weakened, as will their overall ability to establish land claims in Guyana.

Figure 3.1 Regional Share of the World's Endemic Plants, 1990s

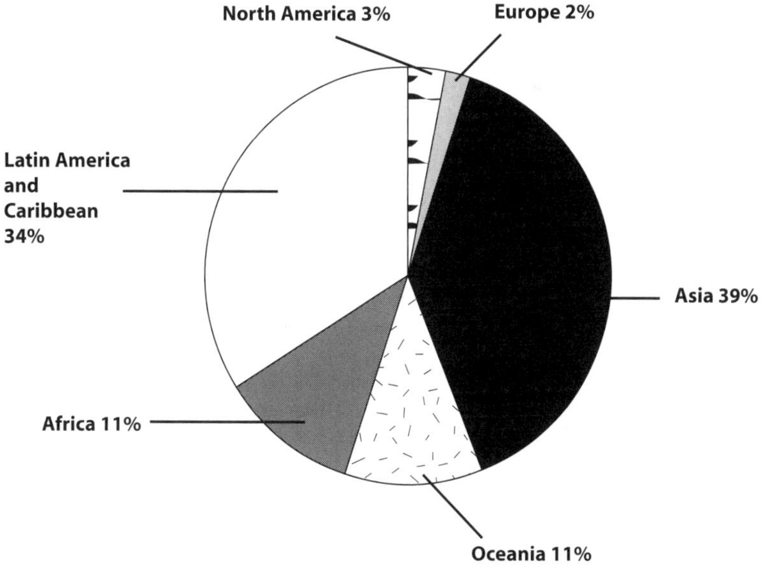

North America 3%   Europe 2%

Latin America
and
Caribbean
34%

Asia 39%

Africa 11%

Oceania 11%

SOURCE: World Resources Institute

In the Caribbean, inadequate funding for the creation and maintenance of protected areas trumps all other conservation challenges. For example, the World Conservation Monitoring Centre has estimated that the budgetary shortfall—the gap between what is actually spent on protected areas and what is required to make them fully functional—is U.S.$2,190 per square kilometer in the Caribbean (shortfalls were estimated at U.S.$142 per square kilometer in South America and U.S.$336 per square kilometer in Central America) (Green and Paine 1997). "The [protected areas] issues facing the region are basic and clear. What is needed in two-thirds of the cases is to build the capacity to manage at the local level. Without the essential building blocks of management in place, it is impossible to address the secondary issues such as community participation and awareness, involvement of the private sector, development of buffer zones, the application of science, amelioration of immediate threats, and transfrontier initiatives" (McNeely et al. 1994).

Among the nations of the Caribbean, Cuba probably has the best protected-area system. More than 16 percent of its land area enjoys protected status, and it boasts well-trained park staffs and a strong central administration. However, resource use and habitat modification occur within most of the parks, which are essentially managed as multiple-use areas. Among the other large islands in the Caribbean, Hispaniola (divided between Haiti and the Dominican Republic) has lost most of its native habitat. Protected areas in the Dominican Republic cover 23 percent of the country's surface area, but many of these protected areas have suffered extensive degradation. Haiti is in far worse conservation shape—its formally protected areas cover only 0.35 percent of its land, and original forest cover has been almost completely eliminated across the country. There is extreme pressure on natural resources by the desperately poor human population, and the country's political instability makes the enforcement of environmental legislation nearly impossible (Green and Paine 1997; McNeely et al. 1994). The smallest islands in the Caribbean have, for the most part, also fared badly in the realm of habitat conservation. The only fully functioning protected area in Saint Vincent and the Grenadines, for example, is a wildlife reserve established to protect the highly endangered St. Vincent parrot. Lobbying and funding from bird conservation groups have been largely responsible for the survival of this area.

Marine reserves are an important element of the protected-area systems that do exist in the Caribbean, and they are recognized as an important element in tourism, the region's only growth industry. Indeed, the size of some marine protected areas, such as those surrounding Bermuda, dwarfs the total land area of the governing nation. But the coral reefs and marine species contained within these protected areas are under pressure from the dense human populations that characterize most Caribbean islands. Overfishing, pollution, and sedimentation are among the specific threats to these protected areas, the administration of which remains separate from most other policy realms. "In general, Caribbean protected areas have not been effectively linked to other development sectors. In a few isolated cases, productive linkages have been made to fisheries, forestry, and tourism. However, few mechanisms for long-term linkages are in place even though in many islands there would appear to be great potential for productive partnerships with the tourism and education sectors, potable water authorities, and rural development programmes" (McNeely et al. 1994).

In Central America, political instability and population growth—with associated increases in demand for resources—has hurt protected-area management. In Guatemala, nearly half of the country's protected areas are located in the Petén, several of them within the 1.7-million-hectare Maya Biosphere Reserve. But illegal logging and planned road construction threaten these sites. Mexico, the largest country in the region, has a protected-areas system that covers more than 8 percent of its land area, but the system lacks coherence at the administrative and legislative level, and encroachment onto protected land by loggers, farmers, hunters, and others is a perennial problem. Perhaps one-quarter of Mexico's national parks are directly affected by encroachment, a major threat to the ecological integrity of the country's relatively small parks (ibid.). There is also extensive, unresolved overlap between that nation's protected-area system and the *ejidos,* the country's communal land ownership areas.

Nicaragua and Honduras, meanwhile, each have declared more than 10 percent of their land to be under official protection, but many of these parks and reserves have no staff, and in many cases their boundaries are undefined. The existence of these "paper parks"—protected areas formally declared by governments as reserves or sanctuaries, but given no financial, managerial, or other institutional resources to prevent them from being overrun by poachers, farmers, loggers, and other exploiters of the land—is a problem throughout the region. In the mid-1990s, the World Conservation Union-IUCN estimated that more than 30 percent of the region's formal protected areas (excluding Mexico) were parks in name only, including Panama's Darién National Park, Cerro Agalta National Park in Honduras, and Guatemala's Volcán Pacaya National Monument. "Many of the areas have no clear physical limits in the field, most of them do not have legal property titles, and, worst of all, many do not have a permanent institutional presence. . . . Experience also shows that mass declaration of protected areas, such as mangrove protection in Costa Rica or rain forests in Honduras, is not very effective" (ibid.).

Another shortcoming in Central America's protected-areas systems is that while mountain ecosystems have received a great deal of attention, many other ecosystems—including ones rich in endemic species—are poorly represented. Finally, states across Central America have been largely ineffective in addressing potential threats to parks and protected areas that shield still-viable ecosystems. These threats—concessions for tourist development and oil and natural gas extraction; illegal settlement by impoverished peasants; illegal deforestation; incursions by urban settlements and agricultural operations; poaching and illegal fishing; pollution of rivers, lakes, and aquifers that are cornerstones of healthy ecosystems; and increased isolation of protected areas in a sea of development—are eroding important habitats from Mexico to Panama. Indeed, conservation officials in countries like El Salvador and Nicaragua have warned that the integrity of all their protected area systems is in jeopardy (ibid.).

The same inadequacies that bedevil the protected-areas systems in Central America are also present in South America, home of the largest remaining blocks of intact rain forest on the planet. In 1999, for example, World Wildlife Fund-Brazil carried out a survey to determine the status of indirect use areas in that country, their ability to protect species and ecosystems, and the resources required to improve conditions within the parks. The results of the survey are applicable to national parks throughout Latin America, and especially those of South America. WWF-Brazil found that of eighty-six strict reserves (parks, ecological and biological reserves, and ecological stations) created before 1996, none had been fully implemented (five more were created between 1996 and 1999, and at least two more national parks and four ecological stations have been created since 1999). Full implementation would imply a fully operational management plan, settlement of all land claims, removal of all permanent human settlements, completion of physical demarcation of the protected area, establishment of headquarters and other facilities (where applicable), and provision of necessary personnel, funding, and equipment. The study concluded that 54.6 percent of the areas had almost no implementation, while 37 percent were minimally implemented and 8.4 percent were reasonably implemented and thus able to "guarantee the integrity of the ecosystems they should be protecting" (Ferreira et al. 1999). The most common problems cited in the study included absence of a management plan (which is required by law), incomplete establishment of boundaries, forms of use that are incompatible with the objectives for that category of protected area (e.g., tourists in an ecological station, hunting or gold mining in a national park), and insufficient funding. Other common problems included inadequate infrastructure, inadequate materials, and inadequate legislation of tenure.

As a result of these shortcomings, many protected areas in South America have been damaged by unsustainable mining and logging activities (both legal and illegal), incursions by subsistence farmers and other settlers, poaching of economically valuable animal species, and heavy levels of tourism. Some of the spectacular parks in Venezuela, for instance, have suffered extensive damage from tourism, in part because they attract high levels of domestic and international visitation, but also because few parks have adequate facilities to accommodate the tourists or educate them about appropriate behavior. For example, swarms of off-road vehicles (ORVs) drive across the savanna of Canaima National Park to reach its internationally renowned waterfalls, and ecologically destructive ORV rallies are a recurring problem in the park. In southern Brazil, the ecological balance within Iguaçu National Park has been derailed by a surge in the population of coatis, small raccoonlike animals that have thrived on the handouts of tourists.

Many South American parks suffer from poaching, which has disrupted delicate predator-prey balances and contributed to the endangerment of some species. For example, poachers in Iguaçu National Park have removed much of the natural prey base for jaguars living in the park. This has forced the cats to move into ranchlands outside of the park in search of prey, which has inevitably produced conflicts between jaguars and humans. Like all other parks in the Atlantic forest of Brazil, Iguaçu is a forest fragment, isolated by soybean and corn plantations and by cattle ranches. Although Iguaçu is probably large enough to sustain healthy populations of jaguars and other carnivores as long as the prey base is maintained, many other parks in highly fragmented areas throughout Latin America no longer provide adequate habitat for large animals such as jaguars, tapirs, white-lipped peccaries, and large eagles. Only large parks and protected areas will sustain these species in the future.

Even in remote areas, however, access by subsistence and commercial hunters can reduce animal populations to dangerously low levels, giving rise to what some have termed the "empty forest" syndrome—the intact green canopy of a forest hides the fact that the region may have already been defaunated. Even remote roadless areas of the Amazon are not immune to poaching, for hunters can access some areas by way of rivers (Peres and Terborgh 1995).

In addition to these internal problems, most Latin American protected-area systems are grappling with the impact of a host of destructive land use practices taking place just outside park boundaries. These activities—logging, drilling, mining, farming, residential and commercial development—can threaten the ecological integrity of parks, nature sanctuaries, and other protected areas in a variety of ways, from polluting rivers that pass through parks to degrading local air quality to destroying migration corridors. Increased recognition of the severity of this problem has prompted the introduction of a range of mitigation measures, including creation of "buffer zones"—landscapes around protected areas that are off limits to certain types of development. But in many countries, the fraying of the ecological integrity of park perimeters is accelerating rather than slowing.

Finally, while the level of legal, economic, and public support for protected areas varies significantly from country to country, few South American states have put together systems that emphasize protecting areas of particularly rich biodiversity. "The area under protection in some countries represents an important percentage of their national territories," acknowledged one analysis. "[But] in general the national systems do not well reflect the outstanding biological diversity which is characteristic of South America. This is due to deficiencies in the geographic distribution of protected areas, the lack of representation of many key ecosystems and a selection process which did not consider criteria such as diversity, endemism, and the degree to which species are threatened" (McNeely et al. 1994).

Indigenous Peoples
and Protected Areas

Many of the relatively intact areas left in Latin America are home to indigenous peoples, some of whom are distrustful of protected-area designations. Their concerns include erosion of their right to self-determination and restrictions of economic advancement by strict protection legislation. So, where conservationists sometimes claim a congruence of objectives between indigenous peoples and biodiversity conservation, indigenous peoples and human rights advocates sometimes see conflict.

The Ecuadorian Amazon alone is home to more than 100,000 indigenous people from six ethnic groups, which jointly claim about three-quarters of the region's surface area as indigenous land (Irvine 2000). Seven percent of Guyana's three-quarter million people are Amerindians from nine ethnic groups (Colchester 1996). In Brazil, as many as 300,000 indigenous peoples from 206 distinct ethnic groups live a traditional to near-traditional existence across nearly 12 percent of Brazil's total land area (urbanized populations, regardless of ethnic background, are not included in the count) (Ramos 1998).

The presence of these human communities in areas of high ecological value has proven to be a sensitive issue for many Latin American states. When these nations first began designating national parks and other protected areas in the 1940s and 1950s, they relied in large part on the protected-area concepts of the United States, which emphasized protecting wilderness areas from harm from human activities. Naturally, this orientation led to efforts to keep commercial, agricultural, and ranching activities out of most national parks. This philosophy has been largely retained by some countries, but other nations such as Venezuela, mindful of the presence of large numbers of indigenous peoples in areas targeted for ecological protection, have made modifications to allow for subsistence use of resources within national parks.

Today, Latin American governments wishing to establish a formal protected area on land occupied by indigenous peoples have two options: (1) declare a traditional protected area but allow comanagement with indigenous peoples, as Colombia and Bolivia have done; or (2) declare an indigenous reserve. Countries in the Amazon region have been particularly receptive to the latter arrangement. In Colombia, Brazil, Ecuador, Peru, and Bolivia, far more lands have been recognized as indigenous lands than as protected areas. Indeed, the Colombian government has publicly declared its belief that securing indigenous land ownership is the best means of ensuring conservation of important wildlife habitat, and it has set aside 60 percent of its Amazonian territory as indigenous lands, either as *resguardos,* where the people themselves hold title to the land, or as *reservas,* where the government retains land ownership (Colchester 1996).

Private Lands Conservation in Mexico

In developing countries like Mexico, where investment in protected area networks often falls victim to other budget priorities, private landowners are increasingly filling the void. Indeed, private, community-based conservation of biodiversity and associated habitat is on the rise in many Mexican states, a trend that has not escaped the notice of international conservation agencies, environmental nongovernmental organizations (NGOs), and the scientific community. "NGOs—many of which were founded by private citizens to support public reserves—[have evolved] to take full advantage of the conservation opportunity that exists in privately held lands. By extending conservation's reach into private lands and joining forces with their colleagues in the public sphere, Mexican conservation efforts have been greatly strengthened" (Jolly 2002).

Mexico's rural communities wield extensive legal rights concerning the governance of their territories and management of natural resources contained therein. In some places, these rights have been used to resist imposition of federally mandated protected area systems. In the state of Oaxaca, for example, "communities have resisted or distrusted the establishment of official protected areas on their lands, which they consider detrimental to community interests. In some cases this has been an additional reason for the adoption of local community strategies for biodiversity conservation" (Oveido 2002).

But the drive to conserve privately held lands intensified in 1992, when the Mexican government declared that communal *ejidos* (property parcels) that had been distributed to peasants following the Mexican Revolution of 1910 could now be sold either as collective parcels upon agreement of the entire *ejido* or as subdivided plots owned by individual peasants. Observers in the conservation community instantly recognized that this announcement held both peril and promise for the nation's extensive natural areas. On the one hand, the change was a boon to resort developers and other commercial interests keen on exploiting previously undeveloped lands. But conservationists also characterized it as an "extraordinary opportunity" to negotiate agreements that would keep private lands undeveloped in perpetuity while simultaneously improving the economic circumstances of *ejidos* and other private landowners (Jolly 2002).

Strategies and tools utilized by conservation organizations in this regard have ranged from outright land acquisition to conservation easements, wherein landowners agree to limit use of their property in order to conserve its natural resources, usually in exchange for economic benefit. To this end, conservation groups have emerged as an important resource for local people attempting to negotiate Mexico's complex land title system (ibid.).

Examples of private lands conservation are proliferating up and

(continues)

down the length of Mexico's sprawling lands. In the species-rich Gulf of California, which is home to sea lion colonies, nearly 900 fish species, and 65 percent of the world's species of whales, dolphins, and porpoises, conservation groups such as Niparajá are working to stave off unregulated tourism development and unsustainable commercial fishing through a blend of land purchases, conservation easements, and education programs. In the Chihuahua Desert in the state of Coahuila, private conservation efforts based on ecotourism are helping to preserve Cuatro Ciénegas, a rare desert wetland that includes freshwater springs, grasslands, alpine woodlands, and gypsum dunes. "Like a desert-bound Galápagos, the basin is, by reason of its geological remoteness, home to a notable diversity of animal and plant life—77 species found nowhere else on [earth]" (ibid.).

Private lands conservation is also growing in Oaxaca, one of Mexico's jewels of biodiversity. This region harbors 40 percent of the country's mammal species, including charismatic species such as cougars, jaguars, and river otters, as well as half of Mexico's plant species and more than 60 percent of its bird species. But Oaxaca's lands are also overwhelmingly (80 percent) in private ownership, which makes land-use practices on private lands a major factor in species and habitat conservation. Fortunately, ecotourism and other forms of nonextractive income generation have piqued the interest of many communities. "In the last few years, community experiences of biodiversity protection and conservation in Oaxaca have expanded in number, geographic coverage, and diversity of approaches. More than sixty cases have been registered [by 2002], providing protection or special conservation measures to nearly 200,000 hectares of land" (Oviedo 2002).

Sources:
Jolly, Mark. 2002. "Lands of Opportunity." *Nature Conservancy* 52 (winter).
Oviedo, G., ed. 2002. "The Community Protected Natural Areas in the State of Oaxaca, Mexico." Gland, Switzerland: WWF.

In Brazil, legislation that prohibits people from living within national parks has created serious conflicts. For example, Mount Roraima National Park, in the northernmost point of Brazil, was decreed in 1989. No effort at implementation was made, however, until 2001, when money became available from the United Nations to implement and manage parks throughout the country. At that time, the existence of the park, which had long been a mere paper entity, became a source of serious consternation among indigenous peoples within the park's crystallizing boundaries. When IBAMA, Brazil's national agency in charge of protected areas and the environment, began implementing its management plan for the park—which included es-

A boat full of tourists heads for a waterfall on a river in Canaima National Park, Venezuela. BUDDY MAYS/CORBIS

tablishing a headquarters building and exploring the possibility of removing people from the area—Ingariko and Macuxi communities that had long hunted, cultivated, and worshipped in the park's interior raised strong objections. Resolving this conflict will be difficult, for it would require major legislative change either to allow the park and the people to coexist or to de-gazette the park.

In Venezuela, Canaima National Park's vast interior (3 million hectares, including 2 million hectares of forested tabletop landscape and 1 million hectares of savanna) is home to about 10,000 people, primarily Pemón peoples living in the savanna region. They carry out subsistence agriculture and impact the environment through hunting and fires used to clear forest patches and encourage grassland regeneration. Indigenous peoples currently participate in the management of the extensive tourist facilities in the park, although their role appears to be marginal. Last year a high-tension power line was built across the park, running from the Guri impoundment to the north all the way to the Brazilian border in the south. The establishment of the power line will bring additional human visitation and impact (maintenance roads, vehicles, etc.) and has already caused conflict with the indigenous people in the area, who fear further development and the eventual incursion of mining interests.

The Mesoamerican Biological Corridor

The Mesoamerican Biological Corridor (MBC) is an ambitious proposal to conserve biological diversity in Central America on a scaffolding of formally designated protected areas and sustainable development initiatives. The MBC scheme reflects heightened concern about the continued erosion of regional plant and animal species and the wild habitats upon which they depend—as well as increasing recognition that wildlife preservation efforts cannot be addressed in isolation from socioeconomic realities that put pressure on fragile natural resources.

In recent decades, conservation biologists have taken increasing heed of the fragmentation of the world's natural landscape. This fragmentation—stemming from agricultural expansion, urbanization and industrialization, road development, and logging, mining, and oil drilling activities—has reduced many areas of wildlife habitat to "islands" floating in a sea of development. Many of these islands lack adequate food, water, shelter, and breeding resources for long-term sustenance of native species. As a result, these areas—many of them formally recognized protected areas armed with an explicit conservation mandate—gradually lose species, with large predators vanishing first, followed by creatures and plants further down the food chain. In addition, even if the habitat patch is large enough to support a small population of a particular species under normal conditions, such populations are vulnerable to "winking out"—local extinction (Soulé and Terborgh 1999). The Mesoamerican Biological Corridor was born out of the growing conviction that conservation of species and habitat exclusively through the creation and maintenance of protected areas was a losing battle and that protected wildlands would be far more likely to maintain their ecological integrity if they were linked to each other and to environmentally sustainable forms of land-use in the wider landscape (Miller et al. 2001).

The earliest incarnation of the MBC initiative arose in the 1980s. At that time, conservationists intent on re-establishing the historic migratory corridor of the endangered Florida panther broached the subject of creating a ribbon of wild land that would extend the length of Central America. This project, known as Paseo Pantera (Path of the Panther), eventually gave way to a scheme of even greater scope and complexity—the MBC. This initiative was formally endorsed by Central American nations in the 1992 XII Reunion de Presidentes Centroamericanos Convenio Para la Conservacion de la Biodiversidad y Proteccion de Areas Silvestres Prioritas en America Central and the 1994 Alliance for Sustainable Development in the Americas. The latter agreement, known as the *Alianza,* made the obvious but politically important acknowledgement that Central America is not composed of seven distinct tropical ecosystems contained within

(continues)

artificially constructed political boundaries. Rather, it is a single ecosystem that supports a startling array of mammals, birds, reptiles, and plants that are oblivious to colorful maps and flags of sovereignty.

As currently proposed, the Mesoamerican Biological Corridor will extend from the southeast states of Mexico (Chiapas, Tabasco, Campeche, Quintana Roo, and Yucatan) down through the Atlantic coast of Belize and Guatemala, then spread into the interiors of Honduras, Nicaragua, and El Salvador before culminating in the Choco region of Panama and Colombia. All told, the MBC will encompass an estimated 768,000 square kilometers (297,000 square miles). This land accounts for only 0.5 percent of the total global land mass, but it also harbors approximately 8 percent of the planet's biodiversity, including some 24,000 plant species and more than 500 mammal species.

The most important building blocks of the proposed Mesoamerican Biological Corridor are *core zones*—formally designated protected areas. Existing parks and reserves currently constitute about 11 percent of the region's land area, but supporters of the MBC hope that this percentage can be increased significantly in the next several years. *Buffer zones* located immediately adjacent to parks and reserves will complement the core zones, absorbing destructive activities and serving as a transitional zone between wilderness areas and lands that sustain logging, farming, and other

activities. *Corridor zones,* meanwhile, will link core areas to one another by emphasizing environmentally sensitive forms of land use within their boundaries. The final proposed category of land use in the MBC scheme is the *multiple-use zone,* which is devoted primarily to human use but managed to minimize ecological disruptions to the aforementioned land-use categories (ibid.).

The MBC enjoys strong support from many members of the conservation community, both in Central America and around the world. But even the scheme's most enthusiastic advocates acknowledge that executing the MBC blueprint is a formidable task that will require years of sustained work and funding. The single greatest impediment to successful creation of the MBC is the poverty that prevails across much of the region. Of the 45 million people who live in the Mesoamerica region, approximately 27 million (60 percent) are poor, according to the World Bank. "The region possesses one of the world's richest concentrations of biological resources, but the viability of these resources is threatened by economic underdevelopment, social inequality, and population pressure," stated one World Resources Institute study. "A [vicious circle] of environmental degradation and socioeconomic stagnation exists" (ibid.).

With this in mind, the MBC's conservation goals are blended with a heavy sustainable development component. Indeed, much of the MBC

(continues)

focus is on encouraging the pursuit of alternative economic strategies in the region that: (1) reduce environmental degradation and loss of natural resources; and (2) lift families and communities out of their present state of impoverishment. Specific economic strategies being pursued in these regards include ecotourism, organic farming, and forest conservation schemes that increase carbon sequestration capacity (the international Kyoto Protocol climate agreement provides financial incentives for countries to maintain carbon-storing forests). Finally, proponents of the MBC assert that a fully operational corridor network would provide a host of underappreciated financial and cultural benefits, from heightened protection of watersheds on which Mesoamerica's residents rely to preservation of vital cultural and archeological sites (ibid.).

Finally, anecdotal evidence suggests that the MBC program, though still in its infancy, is already acting as a catalyst in improving overall environmental performance in Mesoamerican states. For example, the proposed MBC network has been credited with spurring Guatemala to introduce its first meaningful legal mechanisms for the conservation and responsible use of natural resources. Reforestation efforts in Mesoamerica are also being aided by the MBC program. And increased attention is being paid to types of agriculture that are compatible with conservation goals. For example, the discovery that some shade-tolerant

coffee plantations in El Salvador contain more than 400 species of birds has heightened interest in these crops not only as potential threads in the fabric of the MBC but also as an ecologically sensitive, economically viable farming choice in other parts of Central America.

Keys to Success

Conservation biologists, environmentalists, human rights advocates, and economists cite several important challenges that must be effectively addressed if the Mesoamerican Biological Corridor is to be successful (ibid.; World Bank, n.d.), including the following:

Continued funding. Thus far, the proposed MBC has received significant amounts of financial and research assistance from donors, including international finance organizations, conservation organizations, and foreign governments. In December 2002 a meeting convened by the World Bank and attended by Central American government officials and representatives from other interested constituencies approved a $470 million budget for the program through 2007. This kind of support and interest will need to be sustained for years to come for the MBC vision to become a reality.

Reconciling stakeholder interests. At the present time, many Central American policy-makers and stakeholders (including businesspeople, farmers, and indigenous communities) remain wary of the MBC and its likely impact on their lives. According to one World Resources Institute analysis, "the

(continues)

initiative's success requires the development of a shared vision of its goals and functions—a vision that recognizes the divergent needs at stake and identifies the common interest all regional actors share in achieving ecological and socioeconomic sustainability. The ability to build trust and confidence among various stakeholders of the MBC will, in the end, determine its fate" (Miller et al. 2001).

Education and outreach. Supporters of the MBC contend that its chances of success are directly linked to the ability of program advocates to disseminate reliable and complete information to local residents and other stakeholders on the benefits and sacrifices associated with instituting environmentally sustainable practices and respecting national parks and other protected areas.

Respect for civil rights. "Long-term approaches to land use can only thrive if secure title is recognized, an issue of particular importance to the region's indigenous peoples," notes the World Resources Institute (ibid.). To accomplish this, democratic forms of governance and greater citizen participation in affairs of state need to be fostered and encouraged.

Spread the wealth. Economic benefits accrued from ecosystem goods and services are currently not reaching rural and indigenous peoples with any consistency or in meaningful amounts. Increased investment in ecologically sensitive activities, however—such as ecotourism or organic farming—can

not only improve the standard of living of participating families and communities but also generate funds that can be reinvested in habitat conservation and species protection programs. These investments can, in turn, ensure the continued viability of ecosystems and improve overall quality of life for local participants.

Given the epic scale of the MBC endeavor, there are widespread doubts about whether the vision of a continuous ribbon of green connecting Mexico to Colombia will ever become a reality. As one recent analysis acknowledged, the corridor "now stands at a critical threshold between concept and reality" (ibid.). But conservationists also note that every block of habitat that is safeguarded in the name of the Mesoamerican Biological Corridor constitutes a victory—however small—in the battle to save the region's wildlife from the twin threats of land conversion and environmental degradation.

Sources:

Miller, Kenton, Elsa Chang, and Nels Johnson. 2001. *Defining Common Ground for the Mesoamerican Biological Corridor*. Washington, DC: World Resources Institute.
Soulé, Michael, and John Terborgh. 1999. *Continental Conservation*. Washington, DC: Island.
World Bank. N.d. *Central American Environmental Projects Home Page*. Available at http://worldbank.org/ca-env (accessed February 2003).

Colombia, on the other hand, has developed one of the most innovative systems in Latin America for dealing with the overlap between national parks and lands claimed by indigenous peoples. The overlap zone between parks and indigenous reserves is recognized as a distinct legal designation with unique management requirements and legislation. NGOs, federal and state governments, and indigenous organizations are currently collaborating to find management plans for these overlap zones that will both sustain the livelihoods of indigenous tribes and satisfy the goals of biodiversity conservation.

Unlike Canaima, which was created at a time (1962) when indigenous peoples had few rights in South America—and almost none in Venezuela—Latin American parks of more recent vintage take into account the presence of indigenous peoples during the original design and implementation of the area. A case in point is Bolivia's Kaa-Iya del Chaco National Park and Integrated Management Area, established in 1995. This 3.4 million hectare area was designed to have a core protected national park area, and a surrounding management area. Additionally, an indigenous reserve is being established for the Izoceño-Guaraní people adjacent to the park. The local people are comanagers of the entire area, including the core protected park, and are working with researchers to collect data on deer, peccaries, parrots, and other wildlife populations that will allow them to sustainably use these resources.

The issue of sustainable use of resources—and especially animals—is a difficult one for many countries, however. In North America, the biology of the primary game species, such as deer, waterfowl, and turkeys, is well known. Surveys are taken frequently by well-trained staff of wildlife managers, and quotas are set and respected. In Latin America, data on the health of major game species such as white-lipped peccary, collared peccary, tapir, large terrestrial birds, and large rodents is usually incomplete. Populations are difficult to survey in forested habitats, and data on reproductive rates based on hunter-killed animals are just now beginning to accumulate for some sites. Therefore, management is experimental in nature, and the participation of local peoples in data collection is critical; they serve as parabiologists, providing information to trained conservation biologists, who then try to adapt accepted models of wildlife management (devised for sport hunting of deer and waterfowl in temperate areas) to subsistence hunting of a whole series of tropical species, including large reptiles and large rodents. Gauging sustainable levels of exploitation, then, is still an enterprise that is in its infancy in some regions. Noting the present experimental character of wildlife management in some areas, and the well-known impacts of overhunting on ungulates, large primates, and large birds, some conservationists have advocated a complete cessation of hunting in protected areas. But supporters of the multiple-use philosophy argue that some risks of overexploitation can not be avoided, since local subsistence peoples must be included in the management of protected areas.

The impact of indigenous peoples on natural ecosystems continues to be widely debated. Many indigenous peoples in Latin America have their own management rules, reserves, and systems for making decisions about resource use. Some indigenous groups that have retained a strong community-based system of organization and group identity are developing sophisticated management systems with the aid of conservation experts. Several projects are seeking to find the parallel between these traditional management systems and those recommended by conservation biologists, in order to develop site-specific, culturally appropriate, and effective resource management systems on indigenous reserves. But concerns have been raised that the natural resources held by these native groups are in jeopardy. Acculturated groups entering the national economy after acquiring formal rights to their lands have been accused of overexploiting natural resources, and some traditional management systems have been curtailed by sedentarization around health posts, missions, towns, and other sources of modern services and goods. Some indigenous groups will probably be unable to effectively conserve resources on their land for the long term under such pressures. "Destructive overexploitation of resources is generally not a part of [native peoples'] cultural heritage," acknowledged one study. "[But] the combination of political power with land rights may lead to vastly increased pressure on the natural resources of tribal homelands. . . . Native peoples are interested in pursuing economic development just as are people without tribal backgrounds. It would be unrealistic and unfair to expect otherwise" (Van Schaik et al. 1997). Indeed, native peoples ranging from the Kayopo of Brazil to the Lacandon Indians of Mexico granted major timber and mining concessions after acquiring title to their lands (ibid.).

Extractive and Communal Reserves

The "sustainable use" paradigm was initially considered to apply outside of protected areas, as a general way of maintaining an acceptable standard of living without harming the environment. It has since been incorporated into protected-area design, and protected areas have in turn been incorporated into overall strategies for sustainable use of resources at the national level. "National conservation strategies essentially aim to develop government policies towards the environment and, since they are founded on the same political assumptions as protected-area planning, tend to assume that the management of resources is something that is carried out through the development of national legislation to regulate natural resource use and government institutions to enforce such legislation. It thus tends to underemphasize the possibility of long-term management being achieved according to locally derived regulations and enforced by local peoples' own institutions" (Colchester 1996).

The establishment of communal reserves and extractive reserves by several South American countries in recent years denotes a significant shift in philosophy. Communal reserves are based on the premise that sustainable use of resources by community members will lead to long-term conservation of wildlife and trees and therefore also of habitat. Regulation is carried out by community members with the support of NGOs and the government. For example, Peru's Reserva Comunal Tamshiyacu Tahuayo was established in 1991 under the initiative of community members, who had been setting their own hunting and fishing limits for years while fighting to keep out commercial hunters and fishermen. Biologists are now helping them carry out the research necessary to establish hunting quotas, seasons, and complete bans if necessary.

Of course, such areas do not enjoy the same level of legal protection as strict reserves. Under these arrangements, mitigating the overexploitation of highly desired or economically valuable resources or species from outside sources still depends on external factors, such as enforcement of environmental protection laws. In addition, unsustainable levels of population growth remain an unresolved problem in all of these areas. Some observers believe that this trend, which has manifested itself dramatically in places like Peru's Manu National Park, constitutes an "insidious threat to biodiversity. . . . In the long run, population growth will overwhelm any park that contains human populations within its boundaries" (Van Schaik et al. 1997).

However, acknowledgement of the rights of indigenous peoples to make use of their traditional lands enables governments to avoid the serious social, economic, political, and environmental repercussions usually associated with relocation of traditional communities. Additionally, establishment of these types of reserves provides opportunities to educate local communities about ecologically sound management practices and to incorporate politically marginal populations into the country's political process.

The establishment of communally managed reserves has been particularly important in the flooded forest ecosystems that characterize the flood plain of the Amazon and its tributaries. Mamirauá Sustainable Development Reserve in Brazil, for example, is an 11,240-square-kilometer (4,340-square-mile) area established in 1993 to manage the freshwater fisheries in the area. Nearly 2,000 people in twenty-three communities inhabit the area, and another 40,000 people outside the reserve depend on its resources. Commercial fishermen from surrounding large towns have traditionally also entered the area and removed large numbers of fish using extensive net systems and freezer boats. In the early 1990s, residents and users caught about 300 and 320 tons of fish per year for subsistence and commercial uses, respectively. An additional 220 tons were caught by purely commercial fishermen. These levels seem to be biologically sustainable, as long as certain vulnerable species are protected and areas of intensive use are rotated. A management plan established in 1996 and currently being tested keeps out large commercial vessels, assigns community ownership of individual lakes, directs communities to rotate their use of lakes, and sets quotas on catches of fish species that studies have shown to be vulnerable. This program is such a model for conservation that it has become an independent program within Brazil's Ministry of Science and Technology (SCM 1996).

The Future of
Latin American Protected Areas

Latin America continues to support a rich bounty of biological diversity, but habitat and species loss on a major scale is inevitable without significant new investments in environmental protection, of which protected areas are a central component. Currently, protected-area systems in most areas of the Caribbean, Central America, and South America are hampered by enormous funding shortfalls for management, maintenance, research, and law enforcement of parks, reserves, and sanctuaries. The institutional weakness of organizations and agencies charged with managing and developing protected areas is further exacerbated by inadequate and poorly enforced resource protection policies and laws at the national and regional levels. In addition, current park systems provide inadequate protection to many areas with particularly high biodiversity and rates of endemism. A siege mentality also prevails among managers of some parks, which are being buffeted by a variety of internal threats (such as uncontrolled tourism, agricultural activity, and legal and illegal timber extraction) and external threats (such as destructive land use practices adjacent to park boundaries) that are worsened by high levels of population growth and impoverishment. And efforts to enlist more broad-based support via community outreach programs, cooperative projects with international organizations, and other mechanisms have been pursued only fitfully.

If the nations of Latin America hope to reverse these troubling trends in their protected-area systems, decisive steps are needed. These include increased funding for protected-area systems at the local, regional, and national levels; increased attention to programs that educate the public and provide communities with tangible reasons to support parks and their protection; and a new level of dedication to the principles of sustainable environmental stewardship in a wide range of policy areas. Many states also need to expand the size of their protected area systems, paying particular attention to large, biologically rich habitats that are currently under-represented, and investigate collaborative possibilities with neighbor countries with which they share transfrontier wilderness areas. Finally, the fortunes of protected areas and the wild habitats they shield will improve dramatically if Latin America can alleviate the high rates of impoverishment and swelling populations that are putting so much pressure on its diminishing natural wealth.

Sources:

Bodmer, R. 1994. "Managing Wildlife with Local Communities in the Peruvian Amazon: The Case of the Reserva Comunal Tamshiyacu-Tahuayo." In *Natural Connections: Perspectives in Community-Based Conservation.* Edited by E. Western and R. M. Wright. Washington, DC: Island.

Bodmer, R., et al. 1997. "Linking Conservation and Local People through Sustainable Use of Natural Resources: Community-Based Management in the Peruvian Amazon." In *Harvesting Wild Species.* Edited by C. H. Freese. Baltimore: John Hopkins University Press.

Brandon, K., K. H. Redford, and Steven E. Sanderson. 1998. *Parks in Peril: People, Politics and Protected Areas.* Washington, DC: Nature Conservancy, Island Press.

Colchester, M. 1996. "Salvaging Nature: Indigenous Peoples, Protected Areas and Biodiversity Conservation." UNRISD Discussion Paper No. 55. United Nations Research Institute for Social Development.

———. 1997. *Guyana, Fragile Frontier: Loggers, Miners and Forest Peoples.* London: Latin American Bureau (Research and Action Ltd.).

———. 2000. "Self-Determination or Environmental Determinism for Indigenous Peoples in Tropical Forest Conservation." *Conservation Biology* 14, no. 5 (October): 1365–1367.

Farrell, T. A., and J. L. Marion. 2001. "Identifying and Assessing Ecotourism Visitor Impacts at Eight Protected Areas in Costa Rica and Belize." *Environmental Conservation* 28 (September).

Ferreira, L. V., et al. 1999. *Protected Areas or Endangered Spaces.* Brasília: WWF-Brazil.

Green, M. J. B., and J. Paine. 1997. "State of the World's Protected Areas at the End of the Twentieth Century." Paper presented at IUCN World Commission on Protected Areas Symposium, Albany, Australia, November 24–29.

Huber, O. 2001. "Conservation and Environmental Concerns in the Venezuelan Amazon." *Biodiversity and Conservation* 10.

Irvine, D. 2000. "Indigenous Federations and the Market: The Runa of Napo, Ecuador." In *Indigenous Peoples and Conservation Organizations.* Edited by R. J. Butler and P. Larson. Washington, DC: World Wildlife Fund.

Kaiser, J. 2001. "Bold Corridor Project Confronts Political Reality." *Science* 293 (September 21).

McNeely, J. A., J. Harrison, and P. Dingwall, eds. 1994. *Protecting Nature: Regional Reviews of Protected Areas.* Gland, Switzerland: IUCN.

Meltzoff, S. K., Y. G. Lichtensztajn, and W. Stotz. 2002. "Competing Visions for Marine Tenure and Co-management: Genesis of a Marine Management Area System in Chile." *Coastal Management* 30 (January–March).

Miranda, M., et al. 1998. *All that Glitters Is not Gold: Balancing Conservation and Development in Venezuela's Frontier Forests.* Washington, DC: World Resources Institute.

Parks Watch. 2002. "Henri Pittier National Park." Available at http://www.parkswatch. org/parkprofiles/henrypittier.

Peres, C. A. 1994. "Indigenous Reserves and Nature Conservation in Amazonian Forests." *Conservation Biology* 8 (June).

Peres, C. A., and J. Terborgh. 1995. "Amazonian Nature Reserves: An Analysis of the Defensibility Status of Existing Conservation Units and Design Criteria for the Future." *Conservation Biology* 9 (February).

Ramos, A. R. 1998. *Indigenism: Ethnic Politics in Brazil.* Madison: University of Wisconsin Press.

RAMSAR Convention on Wetlands. 2002. "RAMSAR Wetlands Database." Available at http://www.ramsar.org.

Redford, K. H., and J. A. Mansour. 1996. *Traditional Peoples and Biodiversity Conservation in Large Tropical Landscapes.* Arlington, VA: America Verde Publications and the Nature Conservancy.

Sabatini, M. D., and R. M. Iglesia. 2001. "A Global Context for the Evolution and Current Status of Protected Areas in Argentina." *Natural Areas Journal* 21 (July).

SCM (Sociedade Civil Mamirauá). 1996. *Mamirauá Management Plan.* SCM, CNPq/ MCT.

Taber, A., G. Navarro, and M. A. Arribas. 1997. "A New Park in the Bolivian Gran Chaco." *Oryx* 31.

UN Educational, Scientific and Cultural Organization. 2002. *Man and the Biosphere Program.* Available at http://www.unesco.org/mab/.

Van Schaik, Carel P., John Terborgh, and Barbara Dugelby. 1997. "The Silent Crisis: The State of Rain Forest Nature Preserves." In *Last Stand: Protected Areas and the Defense of Tropical Biodiversity.* Edited by Randall Kramer, Carel van Schaik, and Julie Johnson. New York: Oxford University Press.

World Commission on Protected Areas website. http://iucn.org/themes/wepa/ (accessed April 2003).

World Conservation Monitoring Center. "WCMC Protected Areas Database." Available at http://unep-wcmc.org/protected_areas/data/index.html (last revision, October 29, 2001).

World Conservation Union-IUCN. 1998. *1997 United Nations List of Protected Areas.* Gland, Switzerland: IUCN.

———. 1993. *Parks and Progress: Protected Areas and Economic Development in Latin America and the Caribbean.* Washington, DC: IUCN and Inter-American Development Bank.

Forests

— KIRSTEN SILVIUS

Prior to the arrival of European peoples, much of the land surface area of South and Central America and the Caribbean was covered by forests. But as in North America, the colonization process took a heavy toll on forests, as trees were cut to make way for agriculture and to feed settlers' prodigious appetite for timber. Easily accessible dry forests, temperate forests, coastal forests, and forests growing along large rivers were the first to go. The colonization and land-clearing process then continued into the inland rain forests of Central America and South America's Amazon, where the largest expanses of tropical forest still occur. In many areas subject to alteration, extensive pine and eucalyptus plantations have been established, and countries such as Chile and Paraguay now export significant amounts of wood from these plantations. In many other areas, old-growth forests and other wildlands that have thus far escaped degradation or destruction are now under threat, a situation that has been exacerbated by continued population growth, corruption or apathy toward sustainability in the assignment of timber concessions, and a frequent absence of appropriate management, monitoring, valuing, and marketing systems.

The Value of Forests

The greatest impetus for current moist forest (rain forest) deforestation problems in Latin America comes from inequitable land tenure systems and government subsidies and socioeconomic pressures that encourage migration into forested and other relatively uninhabited areas, where land-clearing for ranching and other large-scale agriculture takes place on an epic scale. Historically, rates of deforestation also have been strongly affected by fluctuations in both national and international economies. For example, land clearing slowed in Brazil in the late 1980s and early 1990s as economic recession and reductions in government subsidies to the agricultural sector led to reduced investments in land development. Similarly, timber sales from French Guiana and Guyana to Asia decreased with the onset of the Asian financial crisis of the mid-1990s (Veening and Groenendijk 2000).

These fluctuations make it difficult to predict future trends in deforestation in South America with certainty. Additionally, the role of forests in national and international economies may change significantly during the next decade or two if new valuation systems stimulated by the ideal of sustainable use are put into place. At the present time, however, pressure on forest resources across the region is high, especially in countries still harboring large expanses of tropical rain forest.

In general, the dominant economic and social systems of today's world are able or willing to assign monetary value to forests only for the land on which they grow or the timber that is extracted from their trees. Value, however, could also be assigned to other functions and products of forested ecosystems, including carbon sequestration processes; moderation of climate and rainfall; maintenance of the animal populations that provide meat for subsistence and commercial purposes; nontimber forest products such as fruits, seeds, oils, resins, and chemicals with medicinal or insect-repellent properties; and biocontrol agents such as insects, bacteria, and nematodes. In some cases such products are valued when an appropriate market develops for them (as in the case of rubber and chicle), but on the whole, the economic value of ecosystem services are only beginning to be recognized and incorporated into institutional planning. Recognition of the importance of healthy and abundant forests in attracting tourists has also been underappreciated in some countries. Finally, the aesthetic and cultural properties of forested ecosystems remain an undervalued consideration in many forest management schemes.

Forest Types and Conservation Status

Tropical rain forests are not the only forest type in Latin America, nor, despite the heavy deforestation rates the Amazon basin has experienced in the last forty years, are they the most endangered. The dry forests of Central and South America are probably the most endangered major forest type in Latin America (Dinerstein et al. 1995), closely followed by the Atlantic forest of eastern Brazil and Argentina. Other forest types in the region include temperate rain forests in Chile and Argentina, coniferous and oak forests in Mexico and Guatemala, montane (mountain) or cloud forests on both slopes of the Andes, and drier forests in the inter-Andean valleys. Most of these ecosystems have experienced intense pressure from human development, colonization, and logging for several centuries—or for thousands of years, in the case of some Andean regions and the zones of Maya occupation in Central America. As a result, only the

Non-Timber Forest Products (NTFP)

In addition to wood, many species of New World trees produce commercially significant non-timber-forest products (NTFPs) or dietary staples. These products include edible fruits, nuts (Brazil nuts from the Amazon, cashew nuts from northeastern Brazil), oil (palm oil for soap), resins (pine resin for turpentine), latex from saps (rubber and chicle), dyes (the red and yellow dye annato), and spices (vanilla from a climbing orchid in Central America) (Smith et al. 1992).

In addition, many tropical forest plant species have been domesticated, and the genetic stock necessary to maintain and improve the domestic races resides in the wild trees. Commercially important forest-derived fruits from Latin America include: pineapple from the fringes of Amazonia, avocados from Central America, guavas from lowland Central America and tropical South America, papayas from the western Amazon and eastern Andes, passion fruit raised throughout South America, sapodilla from Central America and northern South America, cacao from the Amazon, and *cupuaçu* (a relative of cacao), which is very popular in Brazil and is beginning to enter the international market. Several of these economically valuable fruits are mainstays of local diets as well.

Historically, one of the most important NTFPs produced in Latin America has been rubber, which is made from the sap of the Amazonian *Hevea brasilensis* tree. Rubber made

from *Hevea brasiliensis* latex is of a better quality than that made from synthetic (hydrocarbon-derived) materials. Indigenous peoples in the Amazon have always used small amounts of the latex, and in the eighteenth and nineteenth centuries they showed it to European settlers, who took it back to Europe.

Rubber was initially used in Europe for erasers and other minor products, but it did not become an important commodity until Charles Goodyear invented the vulcanization process in 1839. This innovation sparked a "rubber boom" in Latin America in the mid-nineteenth century. Industrialists and investors grub-staked laborers who lived in the western Amazonian forest, where they collected rubber, hunted, grew crops on small plots, and relied on commercial products "bought" from the rubber barons in a debt peonage system. These were the original *seringueiros*, ancestors of the rubber tappers who still dominate the population in the westernmost Brazilian state of Acre.

Most of the rubber collected from the Brazilian, Bolivian, Peruvian, Ecuadorian, and Colombian Amazon was shipped through Manaus, which underwent a rapid transformation from sleepy village to bustling seaport as a direct result of soaring rubber demand. One thousand tons of rubber were shipped from Manaus in 1850, 20,000 tons by 1900, and 80,000 at the peak of the trade in 1908–1910, generating sufficient export duties to cover 40

(continues)

percent of Brazil's national debt at the time (Gheerbrant 1992). The boom ended when rubber plantations were established in Asia, where the absence of the fungal disease known as South American leaf blight allows trees to be grown at high densities.

Today, rubber plantations are still being established at the southern fringes of the Amazon, were the disease is less likely to reach the trees, and attempts are being made to breed trees resistant to the disease. Unfortunately, high deforestation rates in the western Amazon (in Rondonia, for example) have already led to a significant erosion of the genetic diversity in wild trees, which is required for breeding of resistant and more productive trees. Environmental consequences aside, this trend has troubling economic implications. Rubber may not be the cornerstone of the economy that it was

at the beginning of the twentieth century, but there is still a strong market for Amazonian rubber, and seringueiros have become an important political and social force in Brazil. Indeed, the state of Acre is strongly influenced by their philosophy of sustainable use of forest products, and its "government of the forest" is using this philosophy to establish statewide land use and economic development policies.

Sources:

Gheerbrant, A. 1992. *The Amazon: Past, Present and Future.* New York: Abrams.

Hall, A. 2000. *Amazonia at the Crossroads: The Challenge of Sustainable Development.* London: Institute of Latin American Studies, University of London.

Smith, N. J. H., et al. 1992. *Tropical Forests and Their Crops.* Ithaca, NY: Cornell University Press.

northern portions of the Amazon can be considered to be in excellent conservation condition. Incursions into these areas from Westernized peoples have been so insignificant that these forests are still occupied by indigenous tribes that have had little or no contact with the outside world.

Even within the area generally labeled "the Amazon" or "the rain forest," there are many different forest types, depending on total rainfall, seasonality in rainfall, proximity to large rivers, soil types, and elevation. Among the different Amazonian forest types, the flooded forests along the banks of the great river and its tributaries have been subjected to the most extensive exploitation. This pressure can be attributed both to the fertility of the soil, which attracts agricultural interests, and the accessibility of river transport (Barros and Uhl 1997). Rain forests proper occur only in areas with at least 2,000 millimeters (79 inches) of rainfall per year, and no prolonged dry season—that is, no month with less than 100 millimeters (4 inches) of rain (Kellman and Tackaberry 1997). As rainfall decreases or the length of the dry season increases, deciduous trees (those that lose their leaves simultaneously) gradually replace evergreen species, so that in the dry season the forest floor is littered with dry leaves and the forest canopy opens up, letting in sunlight that dries out the forest floor. These dry forests are more easily cut and burned and so have been the first to be cleared for agriculture and cattle ranching. Rainfall and seasonality usually decrease as one moves away from the equator, creating a dynamic in which the equatorial rain forests are framed by dry forests and then by grasslands. Near the oceans, however, moisture is high even away from the equator, and both temperate and tropical coastal forests occur. Notable examples can be found in the temperate coastal forests of Chile and the tropical-to-subtropical Atlantic forest of Brazil. As one moves up the mountain slopes, moisture is again high, at least on the windward side, and rain and cloud forest formations occur.

Another factor that can affect the vegetation is soil type and drainage. The very old soils of the Guyana shield area of Brazil, Venezuela, and Guyana, for example, have been leached of minerals for millions of years, so that even fewer nutrients are present than in the already nutrient-poor western Amazon. These forests tend to be low in productivity and in species richness. Flood plains, meanwhile, feature "flooded forest" ecosystems characterized by plant species equipped with roots and stems that can withstand seasonal submersion. *Varzea* forests are flooded by the whitewater rivers that drain the Andes mountain range; they carry high levels of sediments that turn the water pale brown and opaque, and the nutrients they carry replenish the soil in the area that is flooded. *Igapó* forests are flooded by "black water" rivers draining from the ancient Brazilian shield and Guianan shields; no sediment is carried, so the water is transparent, nutrient load is very low, and tannins and other chemicals leached from the leaves of trees make the water rather acidic and give the waterways their characteristic tea color.

Another class of periodically flooded forest common in lowland Amazonia is the palm swamps that grow on low-lying and poorly drained areas. The most common palm swamps are those dominated by the massively trunked *Mauritia flexuosa* palms, which grow in narrow strips along seasonal streams in a forest matrix or extend over thousands of hectares as in Amazonian Peru and Venezuela's Orinoco River delta. These swamp forests provide important resources for local human populations (fruits, fibers, insect larvae, thatch, starch) as well as for wildlife.

Altogether, forest types in South and Central America and the Caribbean can be classified into five major categories (Dinerstein et al. 1995):

Tropical Moist Broadleaf Forests
These cover about 38 percent of the surface area of Latin America and the Caribbean, extending from Southern Mexico through Central America and

into northern and northwestern South America, the middle and lower slopes of the northern and central Andes, and coastal Brazil. In the Caribbean, they are especially extensive on the larger islands of Hispaniola and Cuba. This category encompasses forests in which less than 50 percent of the trees lose their leaves seasonally, including true rain forests as well as more seasonal forests in areas where very little rain falls for up to three months of the year. It includes both flooded forests in the lowlands and montane forests in the highlands.

The most endangered of these forests can be found in the coastal Atlantic forest of Brazil, the seasonal moist forests of Costa Rica and Nicaragua, and the northern Andes of Colombia and Ecuador, where high human population densities and intense agricultural pressure have fragmented forests to the point that they are unable to sustain viable populations of many native plant and animal species. Relatively intact forests can still be found in Latin America in the Guiana Highlands, the forests of the Japura and Negro river basins, and the Juruá basin moist forests. These areas have only recently been reached by the colonization and agricultural frontier, so that the disturbed area is small relative to the extent of the ecoregion, and large, vulnerable animal species still occur.

Tropical Dry Broadleaf Forests

Tropical dry broadleaf forests are those in which more than 50 percent of the trees are deciduous. They cover about 4.8 percent of the region, occurring in southern Mexico, Pacific Central America, the Greater Antilles, central and eastern Brazil, eastern Bolivia, and northwestern South America. Many of these forests are critically threatened as well, and they have a low probability of survival in the decades ahead without intensive protection and management. These areas have been used by humans for centuries for agriculture, because they contain good soil and are easy to clear by burning in the dry season. Forests in particular peril include the dry forests of lowland Bolivia, where large-scale sugar cane, cotton, soybean, and sorghum plantations have cleared huge forest expanses in the past three decades (Pacheco 2002). Most of the remaining endangered dry forest areas are in Central America, especially along the Pacific coast, where cattle ranching has transformed large tracts of landscape, and in the northern Andes of Colombia (Kaimowitz 1996). Only one of thirty ecoregions recognized within this forest type—the dry forests of Baja California in Mexico—can be considered as stable, and none are intact.

Temperate Forests

These occur only in the southern cone of South America, covering about 1.5 percent of the region. Of the forest type's three ecoregions defined in the World Bank's *Conservation Assessment of the Terrestrial Ecoregions of Latin America,* one is endangered and the other two are vulnerable to human exploitation: that is, they are already impacted and various resources are being extracted, but fragmentation is not as severe as in critical and endangered habitats.

Tropical and Subtropical Coniferous Forests

These cover 3.6 percent of the region and are quite disjunct in distribution, occurring only in the central part of Central America (southern Mexico, Belize, and Honduras), in southern Brazil, and in the greater Antilles in the Caribbean. Pines native to Mexico, Belize, Guatemala, Honduras, and El Salvador are the source of most seed stock for extensive pine plantations throughout South and Central America. The single most planted species is Caribbean pine, which is native to the Caribbean Islands as well as to Central America. The genetic diversity of this species and others is threatened by extensive deforestation in their native habitat, and several organizations are carrying out extensive genetic research and experimental studies of growth and suitability to different habitats (Smith et al. 1992; CAMCORE Cooperative 2000). The most critically endangered forest stands in this category are located in Mexico and the Araucaria forests of southern Brazil.

Mangrove Forests

These are one of Latin America's most ecologically important natural resources. Mangrove forests provide essential nursery habitat for numerous species of fish, shellfish, and plants; serve as important spawning grounds for myriad fish species; and anchor vulnerable coastlines against erosion and seawater intrusion. Mangrove forests are common in the larger estuaries of South America's Atlantic Coast and also are found, albeit in smaller numbers, on the Pacific side of the continent. Brazil has the largest amount of mangrove forest of any South African country. Mangroves are also present on most Caribbean islands. All told, South America contains approximately 2.93 billion hectares of mangrove forest, while Central America and the Caribbean contribute another 1.51 billion hectares (World Resources Institute 1990–1999 data).

Regional Trends in Forest Cover and Health

The total forested area reported by the UN Food and Agriculture Organization for Latin America and the Caribbean in the year 2000 amounted to 956 million hectares, of which 11.7 million hectares are plantations (UN Food and Agriculture Organization 2000a). Of this total—which covers approximately 45 percent of the region's land area—more than 720 million hectares are classified as closed canopy forest (with 40 percent or more tree coverage).

Table 4.1 Central America, the Carribean, and South America

Country/Area	Land Area (thousands of hectares)	Forest Area, 2000			Forest Plantation (thousands of hectares)	Wood Volume in Forests (m^3/hectares)	Wood Biomass in Forests (t/hectares)
		Total Forest (thousands of hectares)	Percentage of Land Area (%)	Area per Capita (hectares)			
Central America							
Antigua and Barbuda	44	9	20.5	0.1	0	116	210
Bahamas	1,001	842	84.1	2.8	—	—	—
Barbados	43	2	4.7	n.s.	0	—	—
Belize	2,280	1,348	59.1	5.7	3	202	211
Bermuda	5	—	—	—	—	—	—
British Virgin Islands	15	3	20.0	0.1	—	—	—
Caribbean							
Cayman Islands	26	13	—	0.4	—	—	—
Costa Rica	5,106	1,968	38.5	0.5	178	211	220
Cuba	10,982	2,348	21.4	0.2	482	71	114
Dominica	75	46	61.3	0.6	0	91	166
Dominican Republic	4,838	1,376	28.4	0.2	30	29	53
El Salvador	2,072	121	5.8	n.s.	14	—	—
Greenland	34,170	—	—	—	—	—	—
Grenada	34	5	14.7	0.1	0	83	150
Guadeloupe	169	82	48.5	0.2	4	—	—
Guatemala	10,843	2,850	26.3	0.3	133	355	371
Haiti	2,756	88	3.2	n.s.	20	28	101
Honduras	11,189	5,383	48.1	0.9	48	58	105
Jamaica	1,083	325	30.0	0.1	9	82	105
Martinique	107	47	43.9	0.1	2	5	171

(continues)

Mexico	190,869	55,205	28.9	0.6	267	52	54
Montserrat	11	3	27.3	0.3	—	—	—
Netherlands Antilles	80	1	n.s.	n.s.	—	—	—
Nicaragua	12,140	3,278	27.0	0.7	46	154	161
Panama	7,443	2,876	38.6	1.0	40	308	322
Puerto Rico	887	229	25.8	0.1	4	—	—
Saint Kitts and Nevis	36	4	11.1	0.1	0	—	—
Saint Lucia	61	9	14.8	0.1	1	190	198
Saint Pierre and Miquelon	23	—	—	—	—	—	—
Saint Vincent and Grenadines	39	6	15.4	0.1	0	166	173
South America							
Argentina	273,669	34,648	12.7	0.9	926	25	68
Bolivia	108,438	53,068	48.9	6.5	46	114	183
Brazil	845,651	543,905	64.3	3.2	4,982	131	209
Chile	74,881	15,536	20.7	1.0	2,017	160	268
Colombia	103,871	49,601	47.8	1.2	141	108	196
Ecuador	27,684	10,557	38.1	0.9	167	121	151
Falkland Islands	1,217	—	—	—	—	—	—
French Guiana	8,815	7,926	89.9	45.6	1	145	253
Guyana	21,498	16,879	78.5	19.7	12	145	253
Paraguay	39,730	23,372	58.8	4.4	27	34	59
Peru	128,000	65,215	50.9	2.6	640	158	245
Suriname	15,600	14,113	90.5	34.0	13	145	253
Uruguay	17,481	1,292	7.4	0.4	622	—	—
Venezuela	88,206	49,506	56.1	2.1	863	134	233

SOURCE: UN Food and Agriculture Organization. 2001. *Global Forest Resources Assessment 2000*. Rome: UNFAO.

NOTE: n.s. = not significant, indicating a very small value

Latin America is losing more hectares of forest annually than any other region of the world, including the continents of Asia and Africa. Its annual average loss of forest cover between 1980 and 1990 was 7.4 million hectares, and from 1990 to 1995 it was 5.8 million hectares per year, with 95 percent of the forest loss in tropical regions (UN Economic Commission for Latin America and the Caribbean 2001; UN Food and Agriculture Organization 1999). But despite heavy rates of timbering and land clearance in Amazonia and other densely forested areas, Latin America and the Caribbean still have the largest extension of closed forest in the world (32 percent of the whole), barely edging out North America (Canada and the United States, which have 30 percent) (UN Economic Commission for Latin America and the Caribbean 2001).

International studies of forests in the region flatly declare that the main cause of deforestation in Latin America and the Caribbean has been the use of land for agricultural activities. "The region is now devoting almost half of its natural ecosystems to agriculture and stock-raising. The risk run by natural ecosystems is that if they do not supply products that generate income and employment for the local inhabitants and they cease to be economically profitable, the use of the land in question is changed and it is devoted to agricultural activities" (ibid.).

This perspective has been entrenched in the region for generations. The predominant approach has been to "mine" the forests—extracting all the species of commercial value from them and then abandoning them or changing the land use once its economic usefulness in its previous incarnation has been exhausted (ibid.). Moreover, this unsustainable, ecologically destructive approach has been actively sanctioned by state and federal governments in the region, as well as by private timber interests. "The promotion of private or governmental megaprojects has . . . played a very significant role in the deforestation of enormous areas of vegetation, especially in the tropics. The most significant examples of this are in Mexico (Chontalpa, Tenosique, Uxpanapa) and Brazil (Rondonia), with the conversion of tropical areas to stock-raising in the 1970s and 1980s" (ibid.).

Caribbean

The forests of the Caribbean—composed of island nations ranging from the southern tip of Florida (Bahamas, Cuba) to just off the South American mainland (Grenada, Trinidad, and Tobago, Saint Vincent and the Grenadines)—boast a rich abundance of flora and fauna and complex ecosystems. In addition, these forests and their attendant wildlife are cornerstones of the economic and social fabric of many Caribbean nations. "The nations in this region depend heavily on the health and beauty of the natural world to generate tourist income," observed the UN Food and Agriculture Organization. "However, with tourism comes the pressure for land and infrastructure development, which can impinge on the forest. A careful balance is required. The loss of the forest may well lead to the loss of tourism. This balance is one of the major problems facing the Caribbean forest sector and tourism industry today" (UN Food and Agriculture Organization 2001a; Fripp 2000).

Indeed, the forests of the Caribbean are freighted with economic and ecological importance, even though they account for only 0.1 percent of the planet's total forest area. Within this region, the Greater Antilles islands (Cuba, Jamaica, Hispaniola—composed of Haiti and the Dominican Republic—and Puerto Rico) have a total land area of 21 million hectares, of which more than 4 million (22 percent of the land) are forested. The Lesser Antilles islands and isolated island groups in the Caribbean add another 2 million hectares of land, approximately 59 percent of which is forested. Among Caribbean nations, the highest levels of deforestation are found in Saint Lucia and Haiti, where poverty and growing populations are catalysts in expansion of agriculture activities that require forest clearing. Cuba, meanwhile, has reported a significant increase in forest cover, but this increase stems primarily from its ambitious plantation program (nearly 500,000 hectares in size by the close of the 1990s), which is seen as essential in fulfilling the country's ambitious timber production goals (UN Food and Agriculture Organization 2001a).

Central America

Within Central America, Mexico's forest resources dwarf those of any other nation. Approximately 29 percent of Mexico's 190 million hectares of land area are under forest cover. By comparison, the other countries of Central America—Belize, Guatemala, El Salvador, Honduras, Nicaragua, Costa Rica, and Panama—have a combined land area of 51 million hectares, about one-third of which is covered by forest. Altogether, these countries account for less than 2 percent of the world's total forest cover (ibid.).

These forests serve a host of important ecological functions, from watershed protection to habitat for a rich array of flora and fauna. Indeed, this relatively small corner of the world harbors about 7 percent of the world's biological diversity, with much of this biological wealth concentrated in its tropical hardwood and pine forests and coastal mangroves (Calvo 2000). In addition, the presence of forests in Central America has made the region a vital biological corridor between North and South America. But many of these wildlands are in jeopardy, for Central America is posting some of the highest negative rates of forest area change in the world. Mexico and

An aerial view of logged-over land in Rondônia, Brazil HERVE COLLART/CORBIS SYGMA

Nicaragua have struggled the most in terms of total forest lost; in the latter country, for instance, deforestation rates increased dramatically in the early 1990s when a cessation of military conflict made remote areas safer for colonization and development (Kaimowitz 1996). The highest rates of negative change in terms of percentage of forest lost are in El Salvador, Nicaragua, and Belize. The main factors cited in this alarming decline in forest area include wildfires, which are fueled by the region's dry climate; extraction for fuelwood, which is pursued by 80 percent of the population in countries like Guatemala and El Salvador; expansion of urban settlements; and expansion of agricultural activity, especially in places like Nicaragua where government programs continue to provide economic incentives to clear forests (ibid.).

South America

South America is home to about 23 percent of the world's forests, with about 885 million hectares of forestland scattered from Colombia to the Argentine island of Tierra Del Fuego at the continent's southern tip. Most of the continent's forests, however, are located in its tropical midsection, home of the Amazon rain forest. Indeed, the presence of the Amazon rain forest, regarded as the world's richest ecosystem in terms of biodiversity, gives South America about 54 percent of the globe's total tropical rain forest area. The Amazon ecozone alone accounts for 85 percent of tropical South America's total forest

Figure 4.1   Countries with the Largest Percentage of the World's Forests

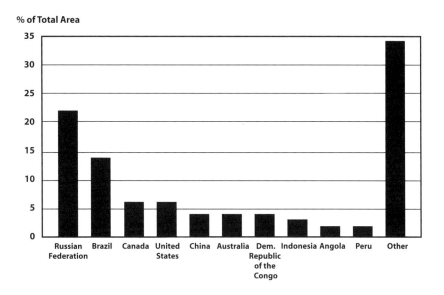

SOURCE: UN Food and Agriculture Organization. 2001. *Forest Resources Assessment 2000.* Rome: UNFAO.

cover and accounts for about 60 percent of the region's total land cover (ibid.).

Brazil, which is nearly eight times larger than any other country in tropical South America, is also the nation with the greatest amount of forest cover. Armed with an enormous swath of the Amazon rain forest, Brazil holds an estimated 65 percent of the subregion's total forest area. Obviously, then, Brazil's forest management practices and policies are major factors in overall forest health on the continent. To date, Brazil has failed to implement sustainable forestry practices, and it has been ineffective in halting illegal logging and slash-and-burn practices that clear forest areas for farming and livestock.

All in all, tropical South America has treated its forest resources poorly in the past half-century, with deforestation riddling many areas of the Amazon basin. This forest loss accelerated with the mid-1970s construction of the Trans-Amazon Highway and a lateral road system that penetrated previously untouched areas, providing landless people and loggers alike with access to the forested interior. Government subsidies are another factor that have encouraged land clearing for cattle ranching and other purposes (Wood and Porro 2002).

Today, it is estimated that annual net loss of forest in South America is 3.7 million hectares annually. Recognition of the importance of forest preservation is on the increase throughout much of tropical South America, as evidenced by the growing utilization of formal management plans and expansion of protected area networks. But decisive changes in forest stewardship and other policy areas that influence environmental conservation still need to be made. "More stable and consistent policies and administration of natural resources can contribute to a positive trend, but lack of alternative income sources and extreme poverty will continue to provide the incentive to clear forests for agricultural purposes" (UN Food and Agriculture Organization 2001a).

In the temperate "southern cone" of South America, forest resources are modest compared with those to the north. The natural forest cover contained within the countries of Argentina, Chile, Uruguay, and the Falkland Islands amounts to only 5 percent of South America's forest resource and 0.85 percent of the global forest total. This region does contain 10 percent of the world's temperate forests, but the volume of frontier (old-growth) forest in Chile, Argentina, and Uruguay has diminished greatly over the years. In Chile, for instance, only about one-third of the country's forests now quality as frontier forest—mature forests or dense timberline forests of 5,000 hectares or more that are still intact. In addition, only 27 percent of Chile's frontier forests are formally protected, and smaller remnants of native forests—including those in protected areas—have had their ecosystems rent asunder by destruction of migratory corridors, nursery areas, and hunting grounds (Neira et al. 2002).

Plantations in Latin America

In Chile and many other nations in Latin America, native forests are being converted to plantations, some of which focus on raising exotic species that mature quickly. Indeed, plantations are a more profitable source of timber than managed natural forests in Latin America. Most plantations in Latin America are of Caribbean pine or eucalyptus, although several countries have also established teak, "white teak," and native hardwood plantations. Both teak and white teak are exotics from Asia and represent relatively recent plantation species in the New World, established for an emerging market. Their resistant wood is used to make furniture and, in the case of white teak, high-quality pulp. In many instances, policy makers are actively encouraging plantation development through some combination of incentives that serve to subsidize part of the cost of reforestation, pruning, and thinning. In Argentina, Chile, and Uruguay, for example, 22,000 hectares of forest were planted between 1992 and 1998, providing 35,000 new jobs and representing a U.S.$1.2 billion investment in the region's industrial forestry sector (UN Food and Agriculture Organization 2001a).

Brazil has the greatest area of land under forest plantation in Latin America, at 5 million hectares. Chile (2 million hectares) and Venezuela (1 million hectares) also have extensive holdings set aside for forest farming. Brazil has the most extensive hardwood plantations, but these are mostly of eucalyptus rather than of native species. With the exception of those in Venezuela, Latin American plantations are primarily in private hands rather than state-owned. Uruguay, meanwhile, is experiencing the greatest rate of plantation growth, increasing its total area under cultivation from 50,000 hectares to 360,000 hectares (all in eucalyptus and pine) during the 1990s. Much of this expansion has been financed by the World Bank and by European and North American investors. In some places, such as Uruguay and Brazil, the rapid growth in plantation activity has masked—or at least obscured—continued loss of natural and old-growth forests.

Among the northern Andean countries, only Colombia has significant areas in plantation, including pine, eucalyptus, and several native hardwood species. Ecuador and Peru both have extensive eucalyptus plantations in Andean habitats. Bolivia has only about 40,000 hectares converted to plantation use, and it produces wood primarily from its native forests.

In the Caribbean, Cuba is the only country with significant forest plantations (pine, eucalyptus, casuarinas, and white teak), in part because of policies that strongly encourage both reforestation and investment in plantations and in part because of international sanctions that spurred policies of self-reliance. In Central America, Mexico has set aside more land area for plantations than any other country in the region, but investment remains only moderate. Elsewhere, Costa Rica supports significant plantations of teak and white teak, while Belize, El Salvador, Honduras, and Panama all have small pine and eucalyptus plantations. Combined, the nations of Central America contribute less than 1 percent of the world's total plantation area.

Leading Causes of Deforestation

The main cause of deforestation in Latin America since the 1970s has been the expansion of the agricultural frontier into the rain forests of both Central and South America. A combination of government colonization projects (which stimulated the migration of poor peoples into previously undeveloped, lightly populated areas), government subsidies for the establishment of livestock operations (which allowed large landowners to aggregate large land holdings on speculation of their future value), and the opening of roads into previously uncolonized areas have all speeded this conversion process. In addition, commercial logging operations have exerted significant pressure on natural forests in Brazil and some other countries in recent years.

Central America—The Cattle Connection

The international market for beef has been a strong driver of forest clearance in Central America. In the 1960s and early 1970s, escalating levels of meat consumption in the United States created a demand for beef imports. Several Central American countries, most notably Costa Rica, Nicaragua, Honduras, and Guatemala, responded to this demand. Existing cattle operations expanded their holdings into the rain forest regions, and new meat processing plants were established. Pasture land in the Guatemalan Petén increased by more than 200,000 hectares between 1979 and 1996, largely at the expense of previously undisturbed rain forest, and by approximately 275,000 hectares in Honduras during the same period.

The number of cattle raised in Central America doubled from 1958 to 1978, then stabilized and began to fall. As meat demand dropped in the United States in the late 1970s, growth of the beef industry slowed and the large ranchers stopped expanding and clearing forest. Some of these areas have reverted to secondary forest and brush vegetation, contributing to the expansion of forest cover that has been reported by some countries in recent years. Secondary forest, however, does not have the same characteristics and species diversity as primary (old-growth) forest.

In the meantime, small landholders that clear a few hectares of forest every year for crops and pasture continue to clear land at more or less constant rates. Collectively, these small operations can be a significant contributor to deforestation. For example, in 1996 small farmers accounted for 43 percent of all cattle in Honduras and 33 percent of the cattle in Costa Rica and Panama. But while livestock held by subsistence farmers can have a pronounced negative impact on local environments, they seldom affect the same large areas of land as medium- to large-scale landholders.

The Amazon Region:
The Forest-to-Crop-to-Pasture System

The best estimates of deforestation rates in Latin America come from the Brazilian Amazon, where organizations such as the Instituto Nacional de Pesquisas Espaciais (INPE) have used satellite imagery to track trends since the early 1990s. The Amazon of Brazil covers approximately 5 million square kilometers (1.9 million square miles), of which 80 percent were forested at the time of European conquest. By 1997, 13 percent of this area, about 530,000 square kilometers (205,000 square miles)—an area the size of France—had been cleared. Eighty-two percent of the clearing took place after the construction of the Trans-Amazon Highway in 1970. In the following year, another 17,000 square kilometers (6,560 square miles) were cleared, the same as the average rate of clearing in 1988–1997 (Fearnside 2000). This transformation of wildlands to human use includes all forms of land clearing, from small slash and burn plots to continuous areas of pasture. Additional areas of forest have been damaged by fires following selective logging or simply because they are at the edge of the clearing front. These areas are not considered in deforestation estimates, even though they are very susceptible to future fires and likely to burn completely given current fire regimes in the area.

Current studies show that areas that are close to population centers, can be accessed by road, and are easily cleared by burning in the dry season are at the highest risk. Much of the deforestation is illegal—as soon as a road is opened, squatters and land speculators move in. Moreover, conversion to cropland and pasture is often undertaken regardless of soil quality and drainage characteristics—all available land is cleared, regardless of its suitability for agriculture.

Traditional small-scale agriculturalists in the region, including indigenous peoples, detribalized indigenous peoples, and other local peoples who have lived in the region for multiple generations, allow the land to go fallow for significant periods (ten to twenty years) after two to three years of cultivation. Once secondary forest has come in, the land can be cleared again and put back into crop production. At this point clearing is easier than in old-growth forest landscapes, and the area still contains valuable fruiting trees and other useful plant species left over from the initial cultivation, when native fruiting trees were protected or planted in the agricultural plots. In this way, relatively small areas of old growth are cleared every year. However, some new immigrants into the region are not familiar with this traditional system—or consciously reject the system—choosing instead to convert large tracts of land to pasture for cattle, the traditional mark of land ownership in the Amazon.

Although small landholders can have a significant impact on forest clearing, it has been estimated that at least 70 percent of deforestation in the Brazilian Amazon in the 1990s was attributable to medium- and large-scale landholders (those who hold more than 100 hectares) (ibid.). Tax breaks and cheap credit in the 1970s and 1980s in Brazil made it easy for people with access to money to purchase land, which was much less expensive in the Amazon than in the more heavily populated south. Land was bought on speculation of future value. In addition, the government's policy of levying taxes on "unproductive" (i.e., forested) land encouraged new owners to clear land and put it to active use (Wood and Porro 2002). Most of the subsequent forest loss has come in the southern Amazonian state of Mato Grosso, a traditional stronghold for large landowners involved in the cattle industry.

Timber workers sitting on logs in Pará, Brazil COREL

Logging and
Timber Production

The leading timber species exported from Latin America during the 1990s included Spanish cedar (1.767 million cubic meters of timber from 1994 to 1996), mahogany (1.22 million cubic meters), Brazilian cherry or "jatoba" (926,000 cubic meters), several species of *Tabebuia,* which includes the ornamental "tree of gold" (503,000 cubic meters), and Araucaria pine (240,000 cubic meters). Another twenty-two species were exported, but only four of them contributed more than 100,000 cubic meters (Jansen and Zuidema 2001).

When compared with Asia and Africa, Latin America as a whole is not an important source of export timber from logging of native forests. For example, Asia exported nearly 49 million cubic meters of timber from 1994 to 1996, while Latin American nations contributed approximately 9.9 million cubic meters during the same period. However, several countries do produce large volumes of wood and wood products for internal consumption, and Brazil's presence on the international timber scene has grown steadily greater in recent years. Indeed, Brazil ranks not only as by far the biggest wood producer in Latin America but also as the world's leading source of tropical wood (ibid.; UN Food and Agriculture Organization 2001b). Other Latin American nations with commercially significant timber production include Chile, Colombia, Guatemala, Ecuador, Paraguay, and Peru. Not coincidentally, these countries are also among the Latin American nations with the greatest amount of land area devoted to forest plantations.

The current logging frontier in the region—that is, the area of greatest expansion of the timber industry—is in the Amazon. Elsewhere, with some notable exceptions, logging is not an important *direct* cause of deforestation in Latin America. Amazonian forests are very species rich, supporting many more tree species than one would typically find in the same land areas in tropical Asia or Africa. Only a few Amazon species have significant market value, however, and logging enterprises have traditionally relied on "high-grading" the forests—extracting only the valuable species—rather than on clear-cutting. As a result, extraction rates can be as low as 0.12 tree per hectare in the western Amazon (in the eastern Amazon, where more tree species are harvested, extraction rates can be as high as 6 trees per hectare) (Putz et al. 2001).

Within the environmental community, selective harvesting is regarded as a much less invasive and destructive practice than clear-cutting, in which all trees are cut and removed from a targeted area. However, poorly conceived and executed selective logging can also result in rapid forest degradation. One problem is that colonists often settle along the roads opened by the logging companies and proceed to open small farm plots, which eventually enter into the cycle of farm-to-pasture conversion and land consolidation by large landholders. Selectively logged forests also have a more open canopy and so are drier and more susceptible to fire than the original forests; fire can cause significant damage in these areas because trees and other plants are not adapted to fire. The removal of large canopy trees also provides a window of opportunity for vines, trees, and other species that may crowd out valuable timber species, thus altering forest composition and reducing the future value of the forest for timber extraction. Finally, regeneration of target and nontarget tree species can be delayed or prevented by soil compaction, incidental destruction of nearby seedlings and saplings, or failure to leave adequate numbers of trees standing to ensure their continued existence. For example, it has been reported that bulldozers damage up to fifty-one trees per hectare in Paragominas, eastern Brazil, for each tree extracted. Recent research shows, however, that with appropriate planning, such collateral damage can be dramatically reduced and postlogging regeneration improved. Improved mapping of targeted trees to minimize road building, removal of lianas (heavy vines that link trees together) prior to felling, increased use of small machinery or animals to pull logs, and sparing of seed-producing trees are among the measures that can help reduce the impact of logging (ibid.).

Unsustainable logging in the Amazon has been further exacerbated by illegal timber harvesting, a persistent problem on state, indigenous, and private lands (Wood and Porro 2002; Veening and Groenendijk 2000). Management plans are required by law in most countries, but they are often ignored or applied to areas for which they were not intended. In addition, logging companies are given short-term concession agreements that give them no financial incentive to pursue long-term sustainable management goals.

Not surprisingly, deforestation and degradation have hurt biodiversity in Latin America in a host of ways. An important indirect effect of logging is that the removal of trees reduces the number of fruits and seeds available to animals. Gaps also reduce connectivity between canopy trees, making it difficult for arboreal animals to move through the forest as they search for food or try to avoid predators. Disturbance and especially hunting also reduce populations of animals. Many of the affected animals play key roles in forest regeneration as seed dispersers or as seed predators that prevent any one species from becoming dominant in the area. With the decline or loss of these animals, the forest's capacity to regenerate is reduced, and forest ecosystems are disrupted and altered in myriad ways.

Fuel Wood and Charcoal

Wood is an important energy source in many Latin American countries, both as fuelwood and for charcoal production. Brazil and Colombia are the largest consumers of fuelwood in South America, followed by Peru and Paraguay. In Central America, Honduras, Nicaragua, and El Salvador rely heavily on fuelwood for energy, with 70 percent of total energy consumption in Honduras produced by fuelwood. In Haiti, wood also provides the main source of household energy, and 80 percent of wood extracted in Jamaica is ultimately consumed as fuelwood (UN Food and Agriculture Organization 2001a).

Protecting Forests through Improved Management and Protected-Area Networks

The future of Latin American forests, including the Amazon, will hinge on improved forest management and control of forest resources; increased monitoring and research of forest ecosystems and associated flora and fauna; and increased investment in protected-area networks.

In South America, several countries have passed new forestry laws or significantly strengthened existing laws and forest services since the early 1990s, in part because some foreign markets are placing pressure on timber exporters to operate in sustainable fashion. Indeed, Argentina, Bolivia, Chile, Paraguay, and Brazil have all launched major initiatives to manage their timber resources more carefully. Bolivia, for example, passed the Forestry Law of 1996, which requires more detailed management plans for all logging operations and seeks to enforce sustainable logging (Rumiz and Aguilar 2001). As a result of these changes, indigenous groups are developing management plans for their communal lands. In Argentina and Chile, major forest inventories have been undertaken. In Brazil, meanwhile, the government has announced its intention to increase the size of its national forest system to 50 million hectares by the year 2010; in 2001 the system contained sixty *Flonas* (national forests) covering 16.5 million hectares, with 99 percent of this surface area in the Amazon (Barreto and Arima 2002). These forests are managed with a multiple-use mandate that seeks to provide for the extraction of timber and nontimber plant products; protect watersheds and other important ecosystem elements; preserve sites of aesthetic, cultural, and historic interest; pursue scientific research; and provide environmental education and recreational opportunities. In order for the *Flona* system to achieve its objectives of sustainable resource use, however, the government will have to crack down on illegal and predatory logging and place greater emphasis on environmental stewardship in all policy areas.

Brazil's efforts in this regard are being aided by its forest monitoring programs, which are the most complete and reliable in South America. Unfortunately, few other countries have adequate monitoring and research systems in place, which makes it extraordinarily difficult to make informed decisions about forest and habitat care (UN Food and Agriculture Organization 2001a).

Protected-area networks are another tool that can be used to preserve old-growth forests and fragile forest ecosystems, and they are being increasingly utilized across the continent, though serious problems with funding persist. In 1990, less than 10 percent of the forest cover in tropical Latin America was estimated to be protected, but in a decade that percentage increased to 14 percent. Bolivia has made particularly extensive use of parks and other protected areas as a conservation tool, designating nearly one-third (31 percent) of its forest area as a park, reserve, or other protected area. Other countries that have given formal protection to large areas of forest include Guyana (25 percent of total forest), Colombia (24 percent), Ecuador (20 percent), and Brazil (17 percent) (UN Food and Agriculture Organization 2000b).

The nations of Central America have haltingly moved toward sustainable forest management philosophies, but funding shortfalls have kept many conservation initiatives from being implemented. Indeed, development and approval of sustainable management plans have been largely contingent on the support of international nongovernmental organizations (NGOs). Still, recognition of the need for greater care in stewardship of diminishing forest resources is on the rise, and the timber industry, national forestry institutions, and campesinos—local people who work the land and forests—have shown an increased willingness to work together to improve management of forests (UN Food and Agriculture Organization 2001a).

In the Caribbean, forestry and environmental agencies have embarked on a range of programs designed to improve forest health and preserve relatively pristine wilderness areas. These range from soil and water conservation initiatives to habitat and biodiversity conservation programs, all of which support the tourism industry that is the economic lifeblood of numerous communities (ibid.).

Halting Deforestation through Carbon Credits

Many NGOs, research institutions, and national governments are working to develop economic incentives for countries to refrain from deforestation.

The Mahogany Forests of Latin America

The story of mahogany extraction throughout Central America, the Caribbean, and the Amazon basin exemplifies the pattern and consequences of high-grading without reinvestment in the forest. Mahogany is a canopy emergent of tropical forests that can grow to 70 meters (230 feet) in height, although 30 to 40 meters (100 to 130 feet) is the average. It is most abundant in dry forests (those that receive between 1,000 and 2,000 millimeters [40 and 80 inches] of rain per year), but it also occurs in true rain forests and on a diversity of soil types. It is not a rare species—its range extends from Mexico, throughout the Atlantic Coast of Central America, southward through Colombia, Venezuela, Ecuador, and Peru, and then in a broad band along the southern Amazon in Bolivia and Brazil. It usually grows in low densities of about one tree per hectare, interspersed by areas with no mahogany at all, but it can grow at much higher densities along rivers and in other areas subject to some degree of natural disturbance (which opens up the canopy and provides adequate light for regeneration).

Despite mahogany's range, however, its extremely high value on the international market has driven many mahogany populations to local commercial extinction throughout large swaths of Latin America. Most mature trees of harvestable size have been removed, and in many instances attention to providing an environment conducive to natural regeneration has been lacking. Since the 1970s, most mahogany extraction has been accomplished via high-grading, with logging companies removing all marketable mahogany, ignoring other timber species, and then moving on without making any meaningful investment in the management or recovery of the logged area. Much of the logging has taken place illegally on state land and indigenous reserves, without appropriate government permits. Today, the only remaining mahogany stocks in Brazil are in the

(continues)

These advocates of forest preservation argue that forests provide such important global ecological services that they warrant conservation investment at the international level. For example, forests are enormously effective storehouses of carbon, a notorious contributor to global warming. Both existing and newly established forests store carbon by incorporating it into woody tissue through photosynthesis. In recognition of this capacity, forests are known as "carbon sinks." Conversely, deforestation both diminishes this carbon storage capacity and increases the volume of carbon in the atmosphere (through burning or decomposing vegetation).

Estimates of the volume of carbon that is released or taken up by forests are variable, because clearing of forests releases carbon in several ways—the initial

western state of Acre and in the southwestern portion of Pará, the state most heavily impacted by the timber industry in Brazil. The situation is similar in Bolivia, where most lowland forests have had all their commercial mahogany extracted, leaving only young trees behind.

Greenpeace led an international campaign in the 1980s and 1990s to prevent the continued overexploitation of mahogany, arguing that the species could be driven to extinction. Partly in response to this campaign, Brazil took several steps to address the illegal exploitation of mahogany in the 1990s, and in 2001 authorities cancelled all of the country's existing forest management plans because of concerns that many of them were fraudulent. In addition, the state imposed a halt on the export of mahogany that had already been harvested and was awaiting shipment. Finally, in 2002—a decade after the measure was first proposed—the Convention on International Trade in Endangered Species of Wild Fauna and Flora (CITES) added mahogany to its list

of flora and fauna considered to be endangered by uncontrolled trade. This means that all traded mahogany must be accompanied by export and import permits detailing its origin, greatly facilitating the control of mahogany exploitation. Mahogany-producing countries had fought this measure for years, arguing that there was not real evidence that the stocks were in trouble. Such evidence did not exist, of course, because the appropriate studies had not been carried out.

Sources:

Grogan, J., P. Barreto, and A. Veríssimo. 2002. *Mogno na Amazônia Brasileira: Ecologia e Perespectivas de Manejo* [*Mahogany in the Brazilian Amazon: Ecology and Perspectives on Management*]. Belém, Pará, Brazil: Imazon.

UN Food and Agriculture Organization. 2001. *Global Forest Resources Assessment 2000*. Rome: FAO.

Wood, C. H., and R. Porro, eds. 2002. *Deforestation and Land Use in the Amazon*. Gainesville: University of Florida Press.

burning of the wood, the continued decomposition of partly burned wood as it lies in the fields, and the release of underground biomass and soil carbon (Fearnside 2000). However, the contribution of carbon release from forests is ecologically significant. In some countries, carbon dioxide releases from deforestation do not approach the level of emissions generated by the consumption of fossil fuels, but in Brazil, for instance, deforestation is believed to release almost twice as much carbon dioxide into the atmosphere as the country's energy sector (Chandler et al. 2002).

Because of the contribution of deforestation to carbon emissions, many European nations have independently placed taxes on carbon emissions, while at the international level the Kyoto Protocol would place similar taxes on emissions. An additional proposal is that "avoided deforestation" be included in the protocol's Clean Development Mechanism (CDM). Under this proposal, countries that implement measures to reduce forest clearing would gain carbon credits and could sell these credits to countries that need to offset their own emissions in order to comply with the Kyoto Protocol. There has been strong resistance by the European countries to the inclusion of avoided deforestation in the protocol. These nations argue that within the context of the protocol, the only effective way to reduce carbon emissions is to reduce the consumption of fossil fuels. They contend that signatories to the protocol should not be given a mechanism for avoiding these reductions by buying carbon credits from tropical countries that establish protected areas or plantations.

However, within the context of national policies, countries in Europe and elsewhere are very supportive of avoided deforestation as a way of reducing emissions and protecting biodiversity and ecosystem function worldwide (Fearnside 2001). Indeed, the World Bank has recently established a BioCarbon Fund, which will effectively "allow companies and public-sector organizations in the developed world to offset carbon emissions by investing in projects in the developing world, such as tree-planting schemes, which absorb carbon from the atmosphere. Investors will earn credits that can be used to meet regulatory requirements or voluntary pledges to cut greenhouse gas emissions" (McDowell 2002). In addition to cutting greenhouse gas emissions, projects must also contribute to biodiversity conservation and incorporate sustainable livelihood considerations and other poverty reduction goals.

There exists inherent uncertainty in the calculations of carbon content per hectare, in the value estimates, and in the degree of damage that global warming will do to both ecosystems and human systems. But as one expert on global deforestation observed: "[T]he basic outline of the problem, namely that widespread deforestation would bring tremendous impacts that must be avoided, is not likely to change as research progresses. The rest is mere detail" (Fearnside 2000).

Sources:

Acopa, D., and E. Boege. 1998. "The Maya Forest in Campeche, Mexico: Experiences in Forest Management at Calakmul." In *Timber, Tourists and Temples: Conservation and Development in the Maya Forest of Belize, Guatemala, and Mexico.* Edited by R. B. Primack, D. Bray, H. A. Galletti, and I. Ponciano. Washington, DC: Island.

Adalardo de Oliveira, Alexandre, and D. C. Daly. 2001. *Florestas do Rio Negro.* São Paulo, Brazil: Compañia das Letras/Universidade Paulista/New York Botanical Garden.

Allen, William. 2003. *Green Phoenix: Restoring the Tropical Forests of Guanacaste, Costa Rica.* New York: Columbia University Press.

Barreto, P., and E. Arima. 2002. *Florestas Nacionais na Amazônia: Consulta a empresários madereiros e atores afins a política florestal.* Brazil: Ministerio do Meio Ambiente (MMA).

Barros, C., and C. Uhl. 1997. *Padrões, problemas e potencial de extração de madeira ao longo do Rio Amazonas e do seu estuario* [*Patterns, Problems and Extraction Potential of Wood along the Amazon and Its Estuary*]. Serie Amazônia No. 4. Belém, Pará, Brazil: Imazon.

Barton, D. 1994. *Indigenous Agroforestry in Latin America: A Blueprint for Sustainable Agriculture?* Chatham, UK: National Resources Institute.

Bellefontaine, R., A. Gaston, and Y. Petruci. 2000. *Management of Natural Forests of Dry Tropical Zones.* Rome: UN Food and Agriculture Organization.

Calvert, P. 2001. "Deforestation, Environment and Sustainable Development in Latin America." In *Deforestation, Environment, and Sustainable Development.* Edited by D. K. Vajpeyi. Westport, CT: Praeger.

Calvo, J. 2000. *El estado de la caoba en Mesoamerica: memorias del taller.* Costa Rica: PROARCAS-CAPAS, Centro Cientifico Tropical.

CAMCORE Cooperative. 2000. *Conservation and Testing of Tropical and Subtropical Forest Tree Species.* Raleigh, NC: CAMCORE.

Chandler, William, et al. 2002. *Climate Change Mitigation in Developing Countries: Brazil, China, India, Mexico, South Africa and Turkey.* Arlington, VA: Pew Center on Global Climate Change.

Dinerstein, E., et al. 1995. *A Conservation Assessment of the Terrestrial Ecoregions of Latin America and the Caribbean.* Washington, DC: World Bank.

Dugelby, B. L. 1998. "Governmental and Customary Arrangements Guiding Chicle Latex Extraction in the Petén, Guatemala." In *Timber, Tourists and Temples: Conservation and Development in the Maya Forest of Belize, Guatemala, and Mexico.* Edited by R. B. Primack, D. Bray, H. A. Galletti, and I. Ponciano. Washington, DC: Island.

Fearnside, P. M. 2000. "Deforestation Impacts, Environmental Services and the International Community." In *Amazonia at the Crossroads: The Challenge of Sustainable Development.* Edited by A. Hall. London: Institute of Latin American Studies, University of London.

———. 2001. "Saving Tropical Forests as a Global Warming Counter-Measure: An Issue that Divides the Environmental Movement." *Ecological Economics* 39, no. 2 (November): 167–184.

Fripp, E. 2000. *Socio-economic Trends and Outlook: Implications for the Caribbean Forestry Sector to 2020.* London: Data Collection and Outlook Effort for Forestry in the Caribbean.

Gheerbrant, A. 1992. *The Amazon: Past, Present and Future.* New York: Abrams.

Grogan, J., P. Barreto, and A. Veríssimo. 2002. *Mogno na Amazônia Brasileira: Ecologia e Perspectivas de Manejo* [*Mahogany in the Brazilian Amazon: Ecology and Perspectives on Management*]. Belém, Pará, Brazil: Imazon.

Groombridge, B., and M. D. Jenkins. 2000. *Global Biodiversity: Earth's Living Resources in the 21st Century.* Cambridge: UN Environment Programme, World Conservation Monitoring Centre, World Conservation Press.

Hall, A. 2000. *Amazonia at the Crossroads: The Challenge of Sustainable Development.* London: Institute of Latin American Studies, University of London.

Jansen, P. A., and P. A. Zuidema. 2001. "Logging, Seed Dispersal by Vertebrates, and Natural Regeneration of Tropical Timber Trees." In *The Cutting Edge: Conserving Wildlife in Logged Tropical Forests.* Edited by R. A. Fimbel, A. Grajal, and J. G. Robinson. New York: Columbia University Press.

Kaimowitz, D. 1996. *Livestock and Deforestation in Central America in the 1980s and 1990s: A Policy Perspective.* Jakarta, Indonesia: CIFOR (Center for International Forestry Research).

Kellman, M., and R. Tackaberry. 1997. *Tropical Environments: The Functioning and Management of Tropical Ecosystems.* New York: Routledge.

McDowell, N. 2002. "Developing Countries to Gain from Carbon-Trading Fund." *Nature* (November 7).

Miranda, M., et al. 1998. *All that Glitters Is Not Gold: Balancing Conservation and Development in Venezuela's Frontier Forests.* Washington, DC: World Resources Institute.

Monbiot, G. 1991. *Amazon Watershed: The New Environmental Investigation.* London: Sphere.

Neira, E., H. Verscheure, and C. Revenga. 2002. *Chile's Frontier Forests: Conserving a Global Treasure.* Washington, DC: World Resources Institute.

Pacheco, P. 2002. "Deforestation and Forest Degradation in Lowland Bolivia." In *Deforestation and Land Use in the Amazon.* Edited by C. H. Wood and R. Porro. Gainesville: University of Florida Press.

Place, Susan E. 2001. *Tropical Rainforests: Latin American Nature and Society in Transition.* Wilmington, DE: Scholarly Resources.

Primack, R. B., et al. 1998. *Timber, Tourists and Temples: Conservation and Development in the Maya Forest of Belize, Guatemala, and Mexico.* Washington, DC: Island.

Primack, R. B., et al. 2001. *Fundamentos de Conservación Biológica: Perspectivas Latinoamericanas.* Mexico City: Fondo de Cultura Económica.

Putz, F. E., L. K. Sirot, and M. A. Pinard. 2001. "Tropical Forest Management and Wildlife: Silvicultural Effects on Arboreal Animals." In *The Cutting Edge:*

Conserving Wildlife in Logged Tropical Forests. Edited by R. A. Fimbel, A. Grajal, and J. G. Robinson. New York: Columbia University Press.

Rumiz, D. I., and F. Aguilar. 2001. "Rain Forest Logging and Wildlife Use in Bolivia: Management and Conservation in Transition." In *The Cutting Edge: Conserving Wildlife in Logged Tropical Forests.* Edited by R. A. Fimbel, A. Grajal, and J. G. Robinson. New York: Columbia University Press.

Smith, N. J. H., et al. 1992. *Tropical Forests and Their Crops.* Ithaca, NY: Cornell University Press.

Snook, L. K. 1998. "Sustaining Harvests of Mahogany (*Swietenia macrophylla King*) from Mexico's Yucatán Forests: Past, Present and Future." In *Timber, Tourists and Temples: Conservation and Development in the Maya Forest of Belize, Guatemala, and Mexico.* Edited by R. B. Primack et al. Washington, DC: Island.

Southgate, D. 1998. *Tropical Forest Conservation: An Economic Assessment of the Alternatives in Latin America.* New York: Oxford University Press.

Terborgh, John. 1992. *Diversity and the Tropical Rainforest.* New York: W. H. Freeman.

UN Economic Commission for Latin America and the Caribbean and UN Environment Programme. 2001. "The Sustainability of Development in Latin America and the Caribbean: Challenges and Opportunities." Report prepared for World Summit on Sustainable Development, Rio de Janeiro, October 23–24.

UN Food and Agriculture Organization. 1999. *State of the World's Forests 1999.* Rome: FAO.

———. 2000a. *Caribbean Workshop Data Collection and Analysis for Sustainable Forestry Management.* Rome: FAO.

———. 2000b. *Informes nacionales de los países.* Bogotá: FAO, Latin American and Caribbean Forestry Commission (LACFC).

———. 2001a. *Global Forest Resources Assessment 2000.* Rome: FAO.

———. 2001b. *State of the World's Forests 2001.* Rome: FAO.

Veening, W., and J. Groenendijk. 2000. "Extractive Logging in the Guianas: The Need for a Regional Ecosystemic Approach." In *Amazonia at the Crossroads: The Challenge of Sustainable Development.* Edited by A. Hall. London: Institute of Latin American Studies, University of London.

"Wildlife Protectors Switch Targets to Mean Business." 2002. *Nature* (November 21).

Wood, C. H., and R. Porro, eds. 2002. *Deforestation and Land Use in the Amazon.* Gainesville: University of Florida Press.

World Resources Institute. *Earthtrends Data Base.* Available at http://www.earthtrends.wri.org (accessed January 2003).

Agriculture
—Rafis Abazov

Agriculture is one of the most important sectors of the national economy throughout Latin America. It is the dominant economic activity in virtually every rural community, and crop cultivation and ranching activities together claim nearly 40 percent of the region's total land area (UN Economic Commission for Latin America and the Caribbean 2001). Latin Americans utilize a variety of methods in producing agricultural products and foodstuff, from subsistence hunting and fishing in the great rain forest of the Amazon basin to highly sophisticated and modern agricultural techniques in the large latifundias of Argentina or Mexico. But various elements of the region's agricultural and livestock raising practices—high reliance on water diversions from freshwater sources, heavy applications of agrochemicals, and rampant conversion of forests and other wild habitat to agricultural use—are damaging or destroying many Latin American rivers, wetlands, forests, and other habitats and jeopardizing the future of the flora and fauna contained therein.

Agriculture's Impact on
Latin America's Environment

Latin America's future economic and environmental prosperity is heavily dependent on introducing and maintaining sustainable development models in its agriculture sector. At the close of the 1990s, agricultural production alone was worth more than $90 billion in Latin America, more than 10 percent of the region's total gross domestic product. Moreover, healthy farming and ranching sectors generate a host of welcome economic ripple effects in transportation, retail, and processing areas. As it is, food and agriculture systems account for more than 20 percent of total economic activity in many Latin American countries, and they continue to account for better than 10 percent of total economic activity even in industrialized countries such as Mexico and Argentina.

But this productivity has come at a heavy ecological price. According to UN Environment Programme (UNEP) calculations, about 300 million hectares of land across Latin America—about 15 percent of its total land area—experienced ecological degradation between 1972 and 2002, "mainly due to the erosion caused by non-sustainable land use, nutrient depletion, chemical pollution, overgrazing, and deforestation" (UN Environment Programme 2000). The agriculture sector has played a major role in driving all of these negative environmental trends, for few of its principal cash crops and products—cocoa, coffee, sugar, tobacco, beef, cotton—are being produced in an environmentally sustainable manner.

Today, nearly 160 million hectares of land across Latin America (about 8 percent of the region's total land area) are devoted to crop cultivation, while rangelands and other stock-raising infrastructure account for another 600 million hectares (about 30 percent of the region's total land area). Yet in Amazonia and elsewhere, large tracts of species-rich rain forest continue to be cleared at a dizzying pace for livestock rangeland or crop cultivation. During the 1990s, for instance, the total land area utilized for agricultural cultivation in Latin America jumped by 7.3 percent (UN Economic Commission for Latin America and the Caribbean 2001). Overexploitation of arable land and consequent erosion of productive soil have also been reported across the region, causing siltation of rivers, reservoirs, and estuaries. In some places, excessive use of agrochemicals—fertilizers, herbicides, and pesticides—have degraded rivers, lakes, aquifers, and reservoirs that are vital habitat as well as important sources of drinking water for human communities. And diversions of water for irrigation have compromised water quality and altered aquatic ecosystems. In fact, agriculture is the single greatest consumer of water in Latin America, accounting for 56 percent of total water withdrawals in the Caribbean and 78 percent of all withdrawals in Central America (Nishizawa and Uitto 1995; UN Environment Programme 2000).

Social and economic inequities in the agriculture sector have also been cited as a major factor in Latin America's overall anemic socioeconomic performance of the past three decades. Some ranchers and farmers operating in Central and South America are fabulously wealthy. But most of the region's 16 million small farmers grind out an existence on small plots of marginal land, and their impoverishment has been linked to all sorts of environmental degradation in the countryside, from clearance of woodlands that provide a host of valuable ecological functions to increased siltation of rivers from erosion-prone hillsides that are stripped of native vegetation for planting (Groot and Ruben 1997; Schioler 2002).

Historically, rural farming communities in Central and South America have received only modest investments in hospitals, schools, roads and transportation services, electrical service, and other infrastructure (UN Children's Fund 2001). Moreover, these communities may become even more of an afterthought in the coming decades, since the regional population is growing increasingly urbanized with each passing year (Huber and Safford 1995). But rural-to-urban migration trends might be slowed, or even reversed, if governments made greater investments in sustainable forms of rural development and basic health and education programs. Such initiatives would also have the beneficial effect of reducing pressure on natural ecosystems that provide a host of benefits for society as a whole, from sustainment of commercially valuable fisheries and wildlife to carbon absorption to filtering pollutants. "Although their natural instinct is to conserve the land, small, poor farmers exhaust the land as they struggle to survive," confirmed one study. "Lack of appropriate technologies and economic opportunity will push the rural poor to work harder to extract a living from their fragile lands, and, when they fail, to move on to new forests or hillsides or to the cities. Of course, eliminating poverty will not automatically eliminate environmental degradation. Governments and wealthier producers contribute to degradation as well, as in the 1980s when inappropriate macroeconomic and sectoral policies encouraged ranchers to expand into the Brazilian Amazon" (Garrett 1998).

Some Latin American countries are seeking to address this problem through various land reform initiatives and other changes in agricultural policies. In addition, agencies at the local, national, and regional levels are all placing greater emphasis on sustainable development models and on integrating agriculture and land management goals with other economic and social development goals, such as poverty reduction. Decentralization of government responsibilities to the local and state level and increased emphasis on community and nongovernmental organization (NGO) participation have also created an environment in which antipoverty and sustainable agriculture programs are increasingly tailored to individual community needs and desires. But "for these bold experiments to succeed, citizen participation must be strengthened. Municipalities may need technical assistance from the central government or development organizations to design and manage their programs and to benefit from links to other municipalities and government agencies. Mexico has provided such support through its Decentralization and Rural Development Project. If service provision is privatized, governments must ensure that policies continue to encourage market competition and that a minimum level of services is provided to all" (ibid.).

Agriculture in Central America

Central America is a diverse region both in terms of climatic and geographic settings. The region is situated in the subtropical zone between Mexico and South America. Composed of seven countries—Belize, Costa Rica, Guatemala, El Salvador, Honduras, Nicaragua, and Panama (the latter is sometimes treated as part of South America)—the region has a combined area of 523,870 square kilometers (202,300 square miles). Comparatively, the region is slightly larger than California, the third-largest state in the United States, and is about one quarter the size of Mexico, which is also sometimes considered part of Central America.

Central America is predominantly mountainous, with a significant portion of the region situated at elevations between 900 meters (3,000 feet) and 2,400 meters (8,000 feet). There are also more than forty volcanoes dotting the region, and some of them are still active. Only about 13 percent of its land is arable and suitable for raising cattle or other livestock. Relatively cool temperatures and frequent rainfall in the elevated areas provide an environment suitable for the cultivation of some crops, and communities have capitalized on the presence of numerous small rivers originating in the mountains to erect a number of intensive large-scale agricultural operations. Thick rain forest and extensive swamps cover lowlands, especially along the east coast. Historically, they have been less populated and less altered by development than the Pacific Coast because of heightened vulnerability to various diseases, including malaria, as well as distance from population centers.

During the last two centuries the landscape of Central America has undergone significant change, as farmers and ranchers cleared valleys and forests of native vegetation to make way for crops and cattle and other livestock (Groot and Ruben 1997; Pelupessy and Ruben 2000). From 1972 to 1999 alone, the area of permanent arable land and cropland in Central America (including Mexico) jumped by an estimated 21 percent. As in earlier eras, agricultural activities remain the single leading cause of deforestation in the region (and throughout all of Latin America) (UN Economic Commission for Latin America and the Caribbean 2001).

Central America's proximity to the lucrative markets of the United States contributed to agriculture's development into an important sector of regional economies throughout the nineteenth and twentieth centuries. In the 1990s, agricultural production contributed between 15 and 30 percent of the regional gross domestic product (GDP) and provided employment for about 30 to 35 percent of the population. Today's Central American agriculture output is concentrated in five major export commodities: bananas, coffee, cotton,

Fields of coffee beans in Costa Rica's verdant Central Valley COREL

sugar, and beef, with almost half of its agricultural output destined for export to the United States (World Bank 2001).

Bananas are produced in the lowland of the Caribbean coast and are exported mainly to the United States. The production of bananas requires intensive low-skill labor throughout the year and large capital investments into infrastructure. Therefore, large local and overseas companies own most of the banana plantations. Sugarcane production is concentrated in Guatemala, El Salvador, and Nicaragua, all of which have long-established traditions of producing this crop. By the 1990s most sugar produced in the region, which is cultivated on small private plots as well as large plantations, was being raised for local consumption. The coffee plantations of Central America produce more coffee than any other region of the world, but most of the profits generated by this industry sector go to multinational companies and large plantation owners. Cotton and beef have been major income sources since the middle of the twentieth century, when worldwide demand for these commodities surged.

Production of these goods has had a number of negative impacts on the environment. In the case of cotton, for example, intensive use of various fertilizes, pesticides, and insecticides has polluted rivers and lakes and produced harmful concentrations of some chemical elements in the soil (Murray 1994; UN Environment Programme 2000). In places like Nicaragua and Honduras, meanwhile, large tracts of forest have been cleared for cattle operations, and overgrazing has degraded highland valleys and damaged river corridors.

Agriculture in Mexico

Mexico is one of the largest countries in Latin America. With a total land area of more than 1.97 million square kilometers (758,000 square miles), the country is slightly larger than Alaska, the largest state in the United States. Mexico is an extremely diverse country in terms of climate and geography. Much of the country is of a mountainous character, and its climatic patterns are heavily influenced by elevation changes. Northern Mexico is a dry desert region covered by cacti, desert shrubs, and some grasses. The higher-altitude regions of central Mexico are forested with oak, pine, and fir. Expansive grasslands also cover large parts of these plateaus. Low-lying southern Mexico once contained significant areas of tropical rain forest, but extensive logging has dramatically reduced its stores of natural forest.

Because of dry climate, only 14 percent of the land in Mexico is actively cultivated. Agriculture contributes about 5 percent of the country's total GDP annually, but it provides employment for about 25 percent of the working population. Traditionally Mexican agriculture yielded enough foodstuffs to cover domestic consumption, although extended droughts have necessitated importation of some food crops.

A significant proportion of Mexican farmers are engaged in subsistence agriculture on their small plots of land, which were distributed by the government between the 1920s and the 1970s. Many small farmers are extremely poor and thus unable to improve their outdated machinery and equipment, expand their holdings, or purchase high-quality seeds and fertilizer. These farmers produce corn, beans, wheat, barley, rice, soybeans, vegetables, citrus fruits, and some other crops, primarily for personal consumption and for local market. Big capital-intensive, export-oriented agricultural enterprises, on the other hand, utilize modern machinery and production technologies and advanced marketing techniques. These large farms, located primarily in the southern states of Chiapas and Oaxaca, focus on commercial crops such as coffee, citrus fruits, sugar, and tomatoes for export. Mexico is also a large producer of cotton, which is cultivated on irrigated land in northwest Mexico.

Together, subsistence and commercial forms of farming and ranching have radically transformed the character of large swaths of the Mexican countryside. Environmental problems originating within the agriculture sector include deforestation, desertification, freshwater shortages, and soil salinity and soil erosion stemming from cattle grazing and irrigation (Simon 1997; UN Environment Programme 2000). At this time, environmentally sustainable farming and livestock raising practices remain the exception rather than the rule. However, acceptance of these schemes is growing in farming communities, in part because international donor agencies, nongovernmental organizations, and regional governments alike are allocating more funds and expertise to land-use improvement schemes.

Agriculture in South America

The world's fourth-largest continent, South America extends from the subtropical zone of the Northern Hemisphere through the equator to the polar zone in the Southern Hemisphere. Because of the enormous size of the region, climate and landscape conditions differ considerably from region to region, providing each area's farmers and ranchers with different resources and challenges. For example, the tropical midsection of the continent contains fertile soils and abundant precipitation that make it possible for farmers to raise a wide assortment of crops. In Patagonia and other areas, however, arid or semiarid conditions prevail, making the land unsuited for many crops (barring irrigation measures) and types of livestock.

Historical Development of Agriculture

The indigenous population of South America had well-established traditions of crop cultivation prior to the arrival of European colonizers. Utilizing subsistence-based forms of cultivation and pastoralism, communities cultivated the crops for personal use and in some cases for barter between tribes; there was no indication of private ownership of the land or pasture.

The arrival of large groups of settlers from the Old World, however, radically changed the continent's agricultural character. Most of the rich settlers seized sizable areas of land and established large ranches or farms. This phenomenon accelerated in the eighteenth and nineteenth centuries as improved modes of transportation made it possible to ship large-scale exports of South American agricultural products to other parts of the world, especially Europe and the United States. In the meantime, South America's large population of subsistence farmers expanded their cultivation and livestock raising activities into previously undisturbed areas of Patagonia and Amazonia.

South America's agricultural sector has experienced turbulent changes since World War II. One of the most important changes was a pronounced downturn in the price of agricultural commodities in the international market. This development battered the economies of numerous South American countries, many of which traditionally exported between 50 and 60 percent of their agricultural products to the international market. In addition, galloping population growth put further strain on the agriculture sector, despite technological gains and innovations that boosted per-acre and per-head productivity. At the same time, agriculture's status as a major employer and economic driver was eclipsed somewhat by growing industrialization. Nonetheless, agriculture accounted for 10 percent or more of the GDP of several South American nations at the end of the twentieth century, and it continues to account for more than 30 percent of the labor force in Bolivia, Ecuador, Paraguay, and Peru.

Today, most of the countries of South America are self-sufficient in terms of food production, with basic foodstuffs such as corn, beans, sweet potato, potato, wheat, and various types of nuts all produced primarily for domestic markets. Still, nearly half of the continent's total agricultural output is produced for export to the world market. The major export commodities in the South American economies include grain and beef (Argentina, Brazil, Chile), coffee and cotton (Bolivia, Brazil, Colombia, Peru), sugar (Brazil), tobacco (Brasília and Colombia), and grape wines (Chile, Argentina).

Pillars of South America's Agriculture Sector

Coffee has been an important commercial crop in Brazil, Colombia, Ecuador, Peru, and Venezuela since the 1800s. Farmers in the highlands of these countries produce the world's highest quality coffee, and Brazil continues to maintain its rank as the largest producer of coffee on the planet. However, the importance of coffee for national economies has declined significantly since the 1970s. For example, Colombia's export earnings from coffee declined from 80 percent in the 1970s to 25 percent in the 1990s. This decline has been attributed to several factors, including low international prices, serious problems with pests that damage coffee beans, and increased competition from low-cost newcomers such as Vietnam and Indonesia.

Cattle breeding operations have been integral to the economies and cultures of South America since the colonial era, and grazing remains the primary form of land use in Argentina, Uruguay, Brazil, Paraguay, and Bolivia today. In Argentina, for example, ranchers owned some 55 million heads of cattle, 14 million sheep, 3.2 million pigs, and 3.3 million horses in 2000. Annual export earnings from meat, live animals, and other related products generated by these resources reached about U.S.$1.4 billion, or about 14 percent of the nation's total export earnings. Brazil is another country where cattle and animal breeding are an important sector of the national economy. In 2000 an estimated 167 million head of cattle ranged across the country, with many herds ensconced on pasturelands that once held species-rich rain forests. Many farmers in eastern and southern Brazil raise their animals for personal consumption, although meat, wool, and related products are sold in the local and international markets. Farmers in the Andes, meanwhile, raise

A herd of cattle in Santa Fe, Argentina FULVIO ROITER/CORBIS

llamas, alpacas, sheep, and goats. In Chile, where only about 3 percent of the land area is suited for cultivating cash crops, ranchers held about 4.1 million head of sheep and 590,000 horses in 2000.

Wheat and corn are the most important crops raised on the continent. In the 1990s Argentina was among the major producers of wheat in the world, while Brazil ranked among world leaders in the production of soybeans and maize. Cotton is produced in many countries on the continent, although large commercial crops are concentrated mainly in the Chaco province of Argentina, northeastern Brazil, and coastal Peru. During the 1980s and 1990s, Argentina and Chile emerged as international leaders in the production and export of grape wines.

Impoverishment and limited economic opportunity have also driven many farmers to turn to crops that are used to produce illegal drugs for distribution in the United States and other economically advanced nations. In the late twentieth century Colombia and Peru became the world's largest producers of coca, which is used to produce cocaine. By the turn of the twenty-first century coca production was a multibillion-dollar business, despite the interdiction efforts of national governments and international assistance to eradicate or reduce coca cultivation through various initiatives. But the economic incentives to grow these and other drug crops remain very high for poor farmers. In addition, some farmers have been forced to produce drugs by various paramilitary groups or by guerrillas, who also recruit their members among the local unemployed population.

The continued appeal of illicit drug production clearly indicates the need for serious agricultural reforms in South America. Indeed, the region's agricultural sector contains shocking contrasts in income distribution and disturbing pictures of social polarization. On the one hand, there are large, well-equipped, and comparatively modern farms—the latifundias. These large commercial operations, often owned by the same powerful families for generations, are the source of much of the region's agricultural exports. Across Latin America as a whole, these large commercial producers account for 5 percent of total landholders but possess more than 90 percent of the available land (Garrett 1998). The vast majority of farmers, though, are engaged in small-scale and labor-intensive crop cultivation and ranching operations. In fact, 75 percent of South America's farmers own less than 10 hectares (25 acres) of land. Many of these small farms (*minifundias*) are not productive enough to lift their tenders out of poverty—a situation that has been cited as a factor in social instability and unrest in Colombia, Peru, Bolivia, and poor regions of larger countries.

Brazil provides a classic example of the problems that stem from these entrenched inequities in land and income distribution. The country has a large number of landless rural dwellers that have no sources of income other than seasonal work at large farms. More than half of the country's landholdings consist of parcels that are 25 hectares or smaller; combined, these farmers account for only 2.5 percent of the farmed area. Conversely, less than 1 percent of the country's farmers and ranchers control 45 percent of the land; the average size of these establishments is about 1,000 hectares (2,500 acres) (UN Food and Agriculture Organization 2002).

Increasingly cognizant of the unwelcome environmental, economic, and social ramifications of their existing land distribution models, several South American governments have sought to introduce land tenure reforms in recent years. For example, Brazil has implemented some reforms in taxation, reclamation, and settlement, and in providing tenancy and credit protection. At the same time, most of the countries have abandoned or reduced agricultural subsidies, protective tariffs against imports of agricultural products, and other protective measures for their farmers. Advocates of these steps claim that over the long term the free market and international competition will motivate farmers to increase productivity and the efficiency of their farms, make food and other staples more affordable for South America's citizenry, and boost overall economic productivity. Critics contend, however, that these market reforms have harmed the most vulnerable groups of society—rural communities in general and small farmers in particular.

Bananas ripening in the sun in Port Antonio, Jamaica COREL

Agriculture in the Caribbean

The island nations and territories of the Caribbean Sea, a 4.15-million-square-kilometer (1.6-million-square-mile) area of the western Atlantic Ocean, curve in a great 4,000-kilometer-long (2,500-mile-long) archipelago between North and South America. The archipelago, sometimes called the Antilles or West Indies, is divided into three groups: the Bahamas; the Greater Antilles (consisting of Cuba, Jamaica, Haiti, the Dominican Republic, and Puerto Rico); and the Lesser Antilles (consisting of Barbados, the Leeward Islands, the Windward Islands, and Trinidad and Tobago). A variety of territories affiliated with the British, Dutch, French, Venezuelan, and U.S. governments round out the picture.

The Caribbean countries differ significantly in terms of their sizes. For example, the total area occupied by Cuba is 110,860 square kilometers (42,803 square miles), and it contains a population of more than 11.1 million people. The total area of Grenada, by contrast, is only 378 square kilometers (146 square miles) with a total population of about 93,000 people. The defining geographic and climatic features of the Caribbean countries are numerous small islands, warm tropical climate, and warm seawater. The mild climate found in the Caribbean creates excellent opportunities for cultivating various tropical fruits and vegetables. However, the region's agricultural sector is severely circumscribed by limited land area and low soil fertility. In fact, only about 10 percent of the region's territory is arable.

Since Caribbean nations have very limited land resources, virtually all of it is already utilized for agriculture or to support other industries (even parks and other protected areas are important elements of the all-important tourism industry). At the close of the 1990s, agricultural production contributed 11 to 29 percent of the Caribbean countries' GDP. These countries specialize in a handful of major commodities: bananas, coconuts, coffee, citrus fruits, sugar, tobacco, and some others. At the same time, the Caribbean countries import a large quantity of foodstuffs, particularly rice, maize, and wheat flour. The agricultural sector also provided employment for about 20 to 25 percent of the working population (World Bank 2001). But as in other parts of Latin America, high unemployment is a chronic problem in rural communities where farming and ranching are the main economic drivers.

The nations of the Caribbean practice widely divergent philosophies of agricultural management and land tenure. One of the most radical approaches was adopted by the government of Cuba after the 1958 revolution, and it is still in place today. After Fidel Castro's rise to power, his Communist government eliminated large plantations and expropriated the land owned by foreign companies. Public land on which economically vital rice and cattle were raised was converted into state farms, and sugar plantations were converted into cooperatives. Private ownership of land and private farming were permitted only on a very limited scale. The government also heavily subsidized the state-controlled cooperatives and farmers' associations and made significant investments into the building of rural infrastructure; it provided machinery, fertilizers, and equipment, as well as expertise for irrigation and reclaiming previously unused land. Although the cooperatives were successful in retaining a certain degree of productivity, they focused primarily on labor-intensive crops and made only fitful efforts to diversify. This was partly due to an embargo imposed by the United States (which remains in place) that placed the largest food market in the Western Hemisphere off limits to Cuban farmers, and partly to the inflexibility of the state-controlled farmers' association and cooperatives.

Other countries, such as Puerto Rico, have adopted quite a different approach. Most Puerto Rican farmers work on very small farms of less than 4 hectares (10 acres), producing subsistence commodities for personal consumption and for small-scale retail trade. About 1,600 larger farms (of 40 hectares [100 acres] or more in size) produce goods mainly for export, including vegetables, sugarcane, bananas, pineapples, tobacco, and rice. Both small and large farms produce dairy products, poultry, and beef, although at a very different scale. In Haiti, one of the most desperately impoverished nations in the world, about two-thirds of the population lives in rural settings, and most are engaged in subsistence agriculture. But endemic corruption, entrenched systems of inequitable land distribution, and unsustainable exploitation of forests, farmland, and other natural resources make it impossible for most families to produce anything beyond the most meager agricultural output.

During the second half of the twentieth century, several Caribbean countries actively worked to modernize their subsistence-based economies and to attract foreign investments in order to cope with rapidly growing population. Subsequent growth in the tourism and manufacturing industries has enabled a number of countries to elevate their standards of living. Indeed, by the end of the 1990s, most of the countries in the region were classified by the World Bank as lower-middle-income or upper-middle-income economies (ibid.). But these "quality-of-life" gains are concentrated mostly in the region's urban populations. Small-scale subsistence farming—still the primary source of income and employment for a significant proportion of the region's rural population—remains a labor-intensive way of life, with limited socioeconomic benefits.

The Future of Agriculture in Latin America

Rural poverty is at the root of many of Latin America's problems with environmental degradation, habitat and biodiversity loss, education and health shortfalls, and unrestrained urbanization. Impoverished families and communities are often engaged in such an everyday struggle for survival that they have little recourse but to work the limited resources at their disposal (crop fields, forests, fisheries) to ruination, then move on to another plot of land, where the vicious circle begins again (Schioler 2002). Or they simply migrate to urban centers, where the basic elements of infrastructure development—schools, health care facilities, roads, provision of basic water and sanitation services, electricity—have been overwhelmed by demand.

One key to improving the fortunes of rural farmers—and the ecological vitality of the lands in which they work—will be to improve the productivity and efficiency of land that has already been converted for cultivation or grazing. One potential avenue that may be pursued is the use of genetically modified (GM) strains of crops and livestock. Proponents of this new technology assert that the introduction of GM crops could dramatically boost the size of harvests, in part because of their resistance to pests and drought. Similarly, they argue that the introduction of genetically modified breeds, feeds, and vaccines will make livestock herds healthier and more productive. Advocates of transgenic farming believe that productivity gains from GM technology would economically invigorate rural communities throughout Latin America, improve the region's food security despite continued population growth, and reduce pressure to convert rain forest and other important wildlife habitat into new fields and pastures (Pinstrup-Anderson and Schioler 2001).

But the use of genetically modified seeds, feeds, and vaccines is strongly opposed by many constituencies, including contingents from the environmental and scientific communities. Concerns have been raised that introduction of genetically modified crops and livestock could have unanticipated repercussions on human health and natural ecosystems. Opponents also fear that if farmers in the developing world become reliant on GM seeds and feeds, they will be at the economic mercy of international agribusinesses and biotech firms that hold the reins to this new technology (McHughen 2000; Pinstrup-Anderson and Schioler 2001).

Another priority in addressing poverty and its impact on the environmental resources of Latin America and the Caribbean is greater investment in rural services and infrastructure. This constitutes a formidable challenge, given the clamor for upgrading infrastructure and services in Latin America's rapidly growing cities and towns, and the heavy foreign debt burdens that loom over most of the region's economies. But proponents of increased rural investment argue that spending in this area would carry a host of valuable benefits. Improved quality of life in rural communities would reduce country-to-city migration pressures and stimulate economic activity, which would in turn provide farmers with greater capacity to implement more environmentally sustainable cultivation and livestock raising practices.

Various environmental protection initiatives also have been launched to address the strong linkages between poverty and environmental degradation. To date, for example, several Central American states have introduced land tenure reforms designed to ease the strong development pressures on the region's remaining untouched lands. However, introduction of these reforms has been halting and inconsistent because of political and social pressures and conflicting demands from different groups of the population. "Access to and use of land constitutes a serious problem throughout the [Latin America] region," declared the UN International Fund for Agricultural Development (IFAD). "The majority of agricultural producers [continue to] work small plots, usually located in marginal, low-productivity areas, and this contributes to the deterioration of natural resources. As a result, off-farm activities, as well as remittances from workers who have migrated to other areas of their home countries or abroad, have become important sources of income for the rural poor" (International Fund for Agricultural Development 2002). In addition, IFAD points out that indigenous groups in Latin America have repeatedly been cheated out of productive land that is legally theirs by unscrupulous speculators and government officials.

Despite missteps and setbacks, however, many of the peoples of Latin America recognize that addressing land access and property rights issues remain an essential part of the equation in solving the vexing—and intertwined—issues of unsustainable environmental exploitation and rural impoverishment. "If the production base of the rural poor in Latin America and the Caribbean is to be improved, problems concerning access to land will need to be solved. Although agrarian reform based on the expropriation of land is no longer viable, the establishment of markets for land leasing, new types of sharecropping arrangements and contractual agreements for the use of communal forests or indigenous territories provide new opportunities for gaining access to land" (ibid.).

Finally, enhanced regional cooperation in addressing environmental issues in agriculture and other sectors is a high priority. Treaties and alliances already established toward this end include the Central American Alliance for Sustainable Development (*Alianza Centroamericana de Desarrollo Sostenible*), the Central American Commission of Environment and Development (*Comisión Centroamericana de Ambiente y Desarrollo, CCAD*), and the Central American Council of Forests and Protected Areas (*Consejo Centroamericano de Bosques y Areas Protegidas*).

"The greatest challenge for the [Latin America] region in the next 25 years will be to harness the winds of economic and political change to benefit all the region's people," concluded one study. "With a significant proportion of the population dependent on agriculture-based enterprises for their livelihoods, the crucial role of agriculture and the food system must be acknowledged. With many women, indigenous groups, and poor people participating directly in agricultural production, processing, and distribution, a vibrant food and agricultural system can also promote social and economic equity. Agricultural policies should work to increase the use of knowledge-intensive and environmentally friendly technologies; improve productive infrastructure; and invest in agricultural research, with an overall stable and transparent macroeconomic environment" (Garrett 1998).

Sources:

Bell, Stephen. 1999. *Campanha Gaucha: A Brazilian Ranching System, 1850–1920.* Palo Alto, CA: Stanford University Press.

Birdsall, Nancy, Carol Graham, and Richard H. Sabot, eds. 1998. *Beyond Tradeoffs: Market Reforms and Equitable Growth in Latin America.* Washington, DC: Inter-American Development Bank: Brookings Institution Press.

Garrett, James L. 1998. "Challenges to the 2020 Vision for Latin America: Food and Agriculture since 1970." 2020 Vision Brief 48, February 1998. Washington, DC: International Food Policy Research Institute.

Gleick, Peter H. 2000. *The World's Water, 2000–2001*. Washington, DC: Island.

Gonzalez, Roberto. 2001. *Zapotec Science: Farming and Food in the Northern Sierra of Oaxaca*. Austin: University of Texas Press.

Groot, J. P., and R. Ruben, eds. 1997. *Sustainable Agriculture in Central America*. New York: Macmillan.

Huber, Evelyne, and Frank Safford, eds. 1995. *Agrarian Structure and Political Power: Landlord and Peasant in the Making of Latin America*. Pittsburgh: University of Pittsburgh Press, 1995.

International Food Policy Research Institute. 1997. *The World Food Situation: Recent Developments, Emerging Trends, and Long-Term Prospects*. Washington, DC: IFPRI.

International Fund for Agricultural Development. 2002. *IFAD Strategy for Rural Poverty Reduction in Latin America and the Caribbean*. Available at http://www.ifad.org/operations/regional/2002/pl/pl.htm (accessed March 2003).

Kay, Cristobal, and Patricio Silva, eds. 1992. *Development and Social Change in the Chilean Countryside: From the Pre-land Reform Period to the Democratic Transition*. Amsterdam, Netherlands: Centre for Latin American Research and Documentation.

Larson, Brook. 1998. *Cochabamba, 1550–1900: Colonialism and Agrarian Transformation in Bolivia*. Durham, NC: Duke University Press.

McHughen, Alan. 2000. *Pandora's Picnic Basket: The Potential and Hazards of Genetically Modified Foods*. New York: Oxford University Press.

Murray, Douglas L. 1994. *Cultivating Crisis: the Human Cost of Pesticides in Latin America*. Austin: University of Texas Press.

Nishizawa, Toshie, and Juhi I. Uitto, eds. 1995. *The Fragile Tropics of Latin America: Sustainable Management of Changing Environments*. Tokyo: United Nations University Press.

Pelupessy, W., and R. Ruben, eds. 2000. *Agrarian Policies in Central America*. New York: Macmillan.

Pinstrup-Anderson, Per, and Ebbe Schioler. 2001. *Seeds of Contention: World Hunger and the Global Controversy over GM (Genetically Modified) Crops*. Washington, DC: Johns Hopkins University Press.

Population Reference Bureau. 2002. *2002 World Population Data Sheet*. Washington, DC: PRB.

Postel, Sandra. 1997. *Last Oasis: Facing Water Scarcity*. New York: Norton.

Roseberry, William, Lowell Gudmundson, and Mario Samper Kutschbach, eds. 1995. *Coffee, Society, and Power in Latin America*. Baltimore: Johns Hopkins University Press.

Schioler, Ebbe. 2002. *From the Rural Heart of Latin America: Farmers, Agricultural Research and Livelihoods*. Washington, DC: Future Harvest and International Food Policy Research Institute.

Schumann, Debra A., and William L. Partridge, eds. 1989. *The Human Ecology of Tropical Land Settlement in Latin America.* Boulder: Westview.

Simon, Joel. 1997. *Endangered Mexico: An Environment on the Edge.* San Francisco: Sierra Club.

Twomey, Michael J., and Ann Helwege. 1991. *Modernization and Stagnation: Latin American Agriculture into the 1990s (Contributions in Latin American Studies).* Westport, CT: Greenwood.

UN Children's Fund-UNICEF. 2001. *State of the World's Children 2001.* New York: UNICEF.

UN Development Programme. 2001. *Human Development Report 2001.* New York: UNDP.

UN Economic Commission for Latin America and the Caribbean. 2001. "The Sustainability of Development in Latin America and the Caribbean: Challenges and Opportunities." Report prepared for World Summit on Sustainable Development, Rio de Janeiro, October 23–24.

UN Environment Programme. 2000. *GEO Latin America and the Caribbean Environment Outlook.* Mexico City: UNEP.

———. 2002. *Global Environment Outlook 3 (GEO–3).* London: UNEP.

UN Food and Agriculture Organization. 2002. *The State of Food and Agriculture 2002.* Rome: FAO.

World Bank. 2001. *World Development Indicators 2001.* Washington, DC: World Bank.

6

Freshwater

The countries of Latin America and the Caribbean enjoy plentiful supplies of freshwater compared with other continents. But this overall abundance masks significant shortfalls in some locales, especially fast-growing urban centers, arid and semiarid sections of Central and South America, and Caribbean island states with limited annual rainfall. Stewardship of the region's freshwater resources is also increasingly problematic. Many poor people in both urban and rural communities do not have reliable access to safe drinking water and sanitation services, unsustainable levels of consumption have been reported across the region, and water distribution systems are often inefficient and wasteful. To date, institutional and governmental efforts to provide remedies for these trends have been inadequate.

In addition, some of the planet's largest, wildest, and most biologically significant rivers and wetlands wind through South America, but many of these waterways have suffered extensive damage from pollutants emitted by the industrial, agricultural, and household sectors, as well as by deforestation, mining, and other activities within their watersheds. Hydroelectric development of rivers is also expanding in some parts of the region at a time when international debate over the environmental and economic consequences of such projects has intensified.

Freshwater Supply and Use
The freshwater riches contained within Latin America and the Caribbean are the envy of most other regions of the world. This is due to the presence of some of the world's greatest and most extensive watersheds, including the Orinoco, Paraná, Tocantins, São Francisco, and Grijalva-Usumacinta systems. But even these mighty rivers are dwarfed by the Amazon River Basin. This unparalleled sanctuary of biodiversity in northern and central South America covers more than 6 million square kilometers (2.3 million square miles) and

boasts 15 percent of the total annual flow of all rivers on the planet. Its discharge by volume is over four times greater than that of Africa's Congo River, which has the world's second highest volume, and its annual outflow is ten times that of the Mississippi River.

The combined flow of the Amazon and its sister river systems are complemented by significant groundwater aquifers that account for almost 30 percent of the drinking water consumed in Latin America. In addition, species-rich wetlands are so abundant across tropical South America that it is sometimes referred to as "the continent of water." Together, these resources give Latin America and the Caribbean approximately one-third of the total world supply of renewable water resources (South America alone accounts for nearly 30 percent of total world runoff), even though it accounts for only about 15 percent of the planet's total land area. Moreover, this bounty is used by only 8.5 percent of the world population (World Resources Institute 2001). This dynamic exists because, as in other parts of the world, populations are not necessarily concentrated in the areas of greatest freshwater supply.

Considerable variations in supply exist within the region, however. For example, Brazil alone contains nearly 40 percent of the freshwater resources in the entire Latin America/Caribbean region, thanks to the immense Amazon river system that sprawls across its northern reaches. By contrast, three other drainage regions—the Gulf of Mexico Basin, the South Atlantic Basin, and the Rio de la Plata Basin—contain only 10 percent of the region's total freshwater resources, even though they account for one-quarter of Latin America's land area and hold 40 percent of the regional population. Other spots that are vulnerable to (or already suffering from) freshwater shortages include segments of the Andean plateau, the desert plateaus of Patagonia, and several Caribbean island states, most notably Barbados and Haiti (Shiklomanov 1999; World Water Council 2000). Notable differences in water availability also exist within some countries. For example, 85 percent of Argentina's freshwater resources are concentrated in about 30 percent of the country's total land area (UN Economic Commission for Latin America and the Caribbean and UN Environment Programme 2001).

Availability of Water Resources across the Region

At the beginning of the twenty-first century, the World Health Organization and UNICEF estimated that about 85 percent of the Latin America/Caribbean population enjoyed reliable access to freshwater, while sanitation services were in place for about 78 percent of the populace. But city dwellers are much more likely to receive such benefits than are the families of farmers and other rural inhabitants; an estimated 87 percent of the urban population in Latin

Residents of Villa El Salvador, a slum district of Lima, Peru, have no running water. GUSTAVO
GILABERT/CORBIS SABA

America has sanitation coverage, compared with 49 percent of the rural population. Similarly, approximately 93 percent of the urban population enjoys
safe drinking water, while only 62 percent of the rural population is covered
(the lowest-ranked country in the region is Haiti, where fewer than half of the
people have access to safe drinking water or basic sanitation services). All told,
about 78 million people in Latin America lack access to improved water supply, and 117 million people endure without basic sanitation services. The vast
majority of deprived people in both of these categories are found in South
America (World Health Organization and UN Children's Fund 2000).

Although urban centers have been more successful than rural villages in
providing these services, many cities are locked in an unsustainable pattern of
water consumption, the primary characteristics of which are escalating per
capita use and dwindling water flows and water tables. "Urban centers that developed in relatively arid areas have grown beyond the point where adequate
supplies can be tapped from local or even regional sources. Many of the
coastal cities in Peru (including Lima), La Rioja and Catamarca in Argentina
and various cities in northern Mexico are among the many cities with severe
constraints on expanding freshwater supplies" (Hardoy et al. 2001).

In Mexico, groundwater accounts for about one-third of the total freshwater supply and approximately two-thirds of its urban drinking water (UN
Environment Programme 2000). But households, ranchers, farmers, and

Table 6.1 Latin America and the Caribbean: Water Supply and Sanitation Coverage by Country, Area, or Territory, 1990 and 2000

Country, Area, or Territory	Year	% Total Water Supply Coverage	% Total Sanitation Coverage
Anguilla	1990	—	—
	2000	60	99
Antigua and Barbuda	1990	—	—
	2000	91	96
Argentina	1990	—	—
	2000	79	85
Aruba	1990	—	—
	2000	100	—
Bahamas	1990	—	—
	2000	96	93
Barbados	1990	100	100
	2000	100	100
Belize	1990	—	—
	2000	76	42
Bolivia	1990	74	55
	2000	79	66
Brazil	1990	82	72
	2000	87	77
British Virgin Islands	1990	—	—
	2000	98	100
Cayman Islands	1990	—	—
	2000	—	—
Chile	1990	90	97
	2000	94	97
Colombia	1990	87	82
	2000	91	85
Costa Rica	1990	—	—
	2000	98	96
Cuba	1990	—	—
	2000	85	95
Dominica	1990	—	—
	2000	97	—
Dominican Republic	1990	78	60
	2000	79	71
Ecuador	1990	—	—
	2000	71	59
El Salvador	1990	—	—
	2000	74	83
Falkland Islands (Islas Malvinas)	1990	—	—
	2000	—	—
French Guiana	1990	—	—
	2000	84	79
Grenada	1990	—	—
	2000	94	97
Guadeloupe	1990	—	—
	2000	94	61

(continues)

(continued)

Guatemala	1990	78	77
	2000	92	85
Guyana	1990	—	—
	2000	94	87
Haiti	1990	46	25
	2000	46	28
Honduras	1990	84	—
	2000	90	77
Jamaica	1990	—	—
	2000	71	84
Martinique	1990	—	—
	2000	—	—
Mexico	1990	83	69
	2000	86	73
Montserrat	1990	100	100
	2000	100	100
Netherlands Antilles	1990	—	—
	2000	—	—
Nicaragua	1990	70	76
	2000	79	84
Panama	1990	—	—
	2000	87	94
Paraguay	1990	63	89
	2000	79	95
Peru	1990	72	64
	2000	77	76
Puerto Rica	1990	—	—
	2000	—	—
Saint Kitts and Nevis	1990	—	—
	2000	98	96
Saint Lucia	1990	—	—
	2000	98	—
Saint Vincent and the Grenadines	1990	—	—
	2000	93	96
Suriname	1990	—	—
	2000	95	83
Trinidad and Tobago	1990	—	—
	2000	86	88
Turks and Caicos Islands	1990	—	—
	2000	100	96
United States and Virgin Islands	1990	—	—
	2000	—	—
Uruguay	1990	—	—
	2000	98	95
Venezuela	1990	—	—
	2000	84	74

SOURCE: World Health Organization. 2000. *Global Water Supply and Sanitation Assessment 2000 Report.*

factories are all extracting water from these aquifers at a pace that far exceeds natural replenishment rates. Some aquifers have been completely exhausted, while others have diminished so precipitously that remaining stores are deep in the earth, where quality is sometimes poor and retrieval prohibitively expensive. In addition, pollution of groundwater supplies has rendered some aquifers unusable. Across the country as a whole, it is believed that 15 to 20 percent of the main aquifers are already seriously overexploited (UN Economic Commission for Latin America and the Caribbean and UN Environment Programme 2001).

The problem of unsustainable consumption is particularly acute in Mexico City, the largest city in the world. Despite moderate average annual rainfall and the presence of large aquifers that provide more than half of the water for the capital and the wider metropolitan area, the sheer number of people inhabiting this region has overwhelmed regional water resources and prompted a string of increasingly desperate water diversion measures. Today, the city draws huge volumes of water via aquaducts from the Lerma Valley (60 kilometers [37 miles] away) and from Cutzamala (150 kilometers [93 miles] away) even as its reckless depletion of underground deposits has caused some surface areas to sink, damaging buildings, roadways, water pipe networks, and other infrastructure. The city also relies on an enormously complicated drainage system to take waste water out of the closed basin in which the city sits. Yet despite the spiraling maintenance and construction costs associated with these water projects—which are multiplying in size along with robust population growth and steady per capita consumption increases—local, state, and federal officials have made little effort to increase the efficiency of water use or encourage water conservation (Connolly 1999).

Elsewhere, some countries and municipalities have made tangible strides in improving access to safe water and basic sanitation services. Some Caribbean nations (Antigua and Barbuda, the Bahamas, and Barbados) are pursuing desalination technology as a way of compensating for uncertain rainfall levels, while other countries in Central and South America are tentatively exploring tariffs and pricing adjustments that could more accurately reflect the true value of water—and hence spur water conservation (UN Economic Commission for Latin America and the Caribbean 2000). But if the region hopes to meet its stated goal of halving the proportion of citizens without access to improved water supply and sanitation by 2015 (a goal formally adopted by the 2002 World Summit on Sustainable Development [WSSD]), much more dramatic steps will need to be taken. Degradation of existing water supplies is a serious issue that is reducing the region's bank of safe water, and much of the region is vulnerable to natural disasters that can obliterate existing water and sanitation services. In 1998, for example, Hurricane Mitch virtually destroyed the water distribution system in Honduras, producing water shortages for about 4.5 million people (75 percent of the population).

Finally, achieving reductions in the number of people without access to safe drinking water or basic sanitation means triumphing in an era of rapid overall population growth. By 2015, the region will have to meet the water supply needs of approximately 123 million additional people in urban areas and 23 million additional people in rural communities if it hopes to meet the WSSD goal. The task is even more daunting in the area of sanitation services, as cutting the number of people without sanitation in half by 2015 will necessitate expanding services to another 131 million urban dwellers and 32 million rural residents (World Health Organization and UN Children's Fund 2000).

Growing Competition
for Limited Resources

Across the globe, the twentieth century was an era of unprecedented growth in extraction and consumption of water, as demand from households, industry and commercial sectors, and especially agriculture climbed rapidly. By some estimates, global extraction of water increased by a factor of six over the course of the century, rising to nearly 4,000 square kilometers (1,540 square miles) per year (about one-fifth of the normal flow of the world's rivers) (Shiklomanov 1999). This galloping rate of growth in consumption even eclipses the world's population growth rate, which expanded dramatically over the same time period, from 1.5 billion to 6 billion people.

Even by these standards, extraction and consumption of water rose remarkably fast across the Latin American and Caribbean region during the twentieth century. With water readily available in most locales—which in turn contributed to a general sense that the resource was inexhaustible and ultimately impervious to human manipulation—the growing nations of Central and South America diverted massive quantities of water for irrigation, livestock, households, and factories. In Central America, water extraction increased tenfold over the course of the twentieth century, while South America was drawing eleven times the amount of water at the end of the century it was at its beginning (ibid.; UN Economic Commission for Latin America and the Caribbean and UN Environment Programme 2001). Moreover, the region's appetite for water seems unlikely to diminish any time soon given current populations trends. Indeed, steady increases in water extraction and consumption are projected over the next quarter-century for virtually all geographic regions and end-use sectors (UN Environment Programme 2002).

Currently, agriculture is the single greatest consumer of water in the region. Approximately 18 million hectares of land are fed by irrigation schemes across Latin America, and the practice accounts for 56 percent of total water withdrawals in the Caribbean and 78 percent of all withdrawals in Central America (ibid.). At present, agricultural use of water for irrigation also accounts for between 69 and 75 percent of total water consumption in South America—down from 95 percent of total consumption half a century ago, but still by far the single largest end-destination for water in the region (UN Economic Commission for Latin America and the Caribbean and UN Environment Programme 2001). The industry sector is another big consumer of water resources in Latin America, with 80 percent of total regional demand in this area attributable to Argentina and Brazil alone. Demand is rising in this sector, as well as among domestic households, where per capita and overall withdrawals continue to climb. In some instances, competing demands for limited water resources within countries—and between countries—have intensified to the point that they have sparked conflict. Many analysts predict that these conflicts will become more heated in the coming decades.

New Water Management Models Emerging

In recognition of the problems confronting the region vis-à-vis its freshwater resources—unsustainable rates of surface and groundwater extraction, growing conflicts between various users, pollution, ecosystem degradation—Latin America is increasingly moving beyond its traditional sectoral approach to freshwater management and adopting more enlightened management models that recognize the transboundary character of major river basins and aquifers.

This transition has not been a wholly painless one. "Many of the bodies set up [to implement multiple water use management models at the river basin level] have disappeared or have failed to make progress with integrated water management because of interinstitutional rivalries, conflicts with regional authorities, lack of the necessary funding, coordination and legal [authority] basis and confusion about their role, which creates the potential for competition with other authorities and sectors, or because they have had a complex relationship of administrative or financial dependence" (ibid.).

But despite these setbacks, the region has made evident progress in creating and supporting regionwide initiatives for conservation and sustainable use of freshwater. In South America, for example, Argentina, Brazil, Paraguay, and Uruguay are utilizing funds distributed by a wide assortment of international donor agencies to develop a sustainable management program for the Guarani Aquifer System, one of the world's largest aquifers (about 1.2 million square kilometers (460,000 square miles)), but also one that is currently being drawn down at an unsustainable rate (UN Environment Programme 2002). Elsewhere in South America, Ecuador and Peru have established joint management programs to administer and care for cross-border watersheds such as the Catamayo-Chiro and Puyango-Tumbes rivers. In Central America, meanwhile, Nicaragua and Costa Rica are working together to establish a management scheme that recognizes the transboundary nature of the San Juan River's basin and coastal zone (UN Economic Commission for Latin America and the Caribbean and UN Environment Programme 2001). And in 2002, Mexico and the United States reached agreement on a series of water conservation and allocation measures for the Rio Grande River, a border river whose resources—vital to farmers in both countries—have been the subject of considerable legal wrangling and political maneuvering in recent years.

Freshwater Pollution and Degradation Issues

In addition to declining water availability in cities and other locales experiencing rapid population and economic growth, the chief difficulties facing Latin American nations in the realm of freshwater stewardship include: eroding water quality caused by wide-scale pollution from untreated sewage and industrial and mining operations; deforestation and other forms of land clearing that cause erosion and siltation and disrupt ecosystems; and eutrophication and other unwelcome ecosystem changes stemming from excessive use of agricultural fertilizers and pesticides. These problems, which impact human communities and complex ecosystems of wild flora and fauna alike, are further exacerbated by anemic regulatory institutions and environmental laws that have failed to keep pace with threats.

Degradation of freshwater resources across the Latin America/Caribbean region has become much more significant over the last three to four decades, as population growth and migration patterns (of both people and industries) have placed rising pressure on rivers, wetlands, and aquifers that had previously been lightly exploited. Indeed, all of Latin America's major river systems have been scarred to some degree by the implacable advance of human activities, with predictable impacts on the terrestrial and aquatic species they support. South America's Orinoco River Basin, for instance, contains a rich diversity of habitat types and freshwater fish, including several endemic species. But endangered species such as the Orinoco crocodile are overhunted, and large areas of the basin have been cleared for agriculture, timber, and ranching, causing pollution and siltation (Revenga et al. 2003; World Wide Fund for Nature 2003).

The Paraná River and its tributaries, meanwhile, feature many fish species found nowhere else, but population pressures abound across the watershed. Water quality has been eroded by untreated sewage dumped from urban centers and pesticide runoff from farming operations. The basin as a whole has lost an estimated 500,000 square kilometers (190,000 square miles) of forest to timber cutters, farmers, and ranchers, which has left many feeder streams and rivers vulnerable to erosion and sedimentation. Elsewhere, timber extraction and gold and bauxite mining are taking a heavy toll on the rivers that drain South America's mountainous Guyana Shield, and freshwater lakes such as those that dot the High Andes are increasingly threatened by runoff of sediments and contaminants from mining, agriculture, livestock grazing, and overfishing. To the north, water quality and ecosystem integrity in the lakes nestled in Mexico's Sierra Madre range have been damaged by unsustainable withdrawals for irrigation and pollution generated by nearby factories, towns, and farms (ibid.). In Colombia, the Medellin and Bogotá rivers have been so badly contaminated that virtually no life exists in their depths (Castro 1995). And some remote rivers in parts of Central America have even been soiled by the toxic wastes generated by clandestine cocaine laboratories.

As important as these river and lake systems are for biodiversity and human sustainment, however, the health of the Amazon River Basin naturally attracts the most attention. After all, the waters of Amazonia are the linchpin of the region's ecological health, and a cornerstone of virtually all major economic sectors, including agriculture, energy, fisheries, transportation, and trade. But the Amazon watershed has undergone considerable alteration in the last half-century, with timber and mining operations, ranching and farming activities, pipeline projects, highways, hydroelectric projects, railroads, and explosive population growth all wreaking major changes on the region's rivers and tropical forests. Many experts believe that these developments, which are generally sanctioned on economic development grounds by the governments of Brazil and other countries sharing the basin, are devastating large swaths of the biodiversity-rich region. Scientists warn that continued inattention to conservation and sustainable stewardship ideals could ultimately result in the demise of the world's largest river system and tropical forest.

Finally, rapid population growth and attendant economic expansion is fundamentally transforming the species mix contained within riverine ecosystems in the Amazon and elsewhere. "Use of new technologies and tools by both the local people and the commercial fishermen is hastening the decline of some species," explained one analysis. "With increased participation in the market economy, more attention is devoted to saleable species. The breakdown of traditional beliefs, myths, and lore that served to protect aquatic fauna and their habitats is causing the inhabitants to reevaluate their resource base, often leading to accelerating harvests. The long-term trend does not seem promising. Species composition is becoming streamlined because those species requiring specialized habitats, having limited initial stock, and undergoing selected removal to supply market demands are reduced or eliminated" (Nishizawa and Uitto 1995).

Major Sources of Water
Pollution in Latin America

Of the numerous human activities that have a deleterious impact on freshwater quality and ecosystem integrity in Latin America, three warrant special mention: deposition of untreated sewage and other waste produced by cities and villages into waterways; consumption and contamination of water resources by farming and ranching interests; and water pollution stemming from mining activities.

WASTE AND INDUSTRIAL EFFLUENTS

Deposition of untreated sewage and industrial wastes into rivers, lakes, and streams is a major problem across much of the region. In the late 1990s, only about 13 percent of Latin America's collected sewage received any kind of treatment, though some countries have a much better record in this regard than others. For example, Barbados reports that 100 percent of its liquid waste receives some form of treatment, while Mexico manages to treat only 22 percent of its waste; countries such as Argentina, Venezuela, and Colombia report that 10 percent or less of their waste receives treatment (Pan American Health Organization 1998). This means that across much of Latin America, vast quantities of human waste from households as well as animal waste from tanneries, slaughterhouses, and meat-packing plants are dumped into waterways, where they ruin aquatic ecosystems and seep into aquifers, polluting valuable water resources with coliform bacteria and other health threats (ibid.).

Infrastructure for sewage treatment is particularly lacking in South America, though several large cities are developing sanitation projects with the assistance of international agencies such as the World Bank and the Inter-American Development Bank. But even as these isolated operations come on line, they will only partially stem the deluge of pollution that is generated by human settlements and industries and deposited into river systems. The impact of this defilement is often evident hundreds of miles downstream. Indeed, the discharge of millions of tons of liquid waste into waterways injures aquatic and marine ecosystems alike, for these polluted rivers ultimately empty their toxic loads into the fragile fishing waters of the Pacific and Atlantic coasts. And the decline of waterways is putting people in both urban and rural settings under increasing pressure to draw on polluted rivers and streams for their most basic water needs.

South America's Wondrous Pantanal

The Pantanal swamp in South America STEPHANIE MAZE/CORBIS

The Pantanal is the world's largest freshwater wetland system. It is difficult to tabulate the exact boundaries of the Pantanal, given the diversity of wetland definitions and difficulty of delineating wetland borders. But it extends over an estimated 170,000 square kilometers (65,000 square miles) of central-western Brazil, eastern Bolivia, and northeastern Paraguay—an area larger than the state of Florida.

Every year, this immense landlocked river delta receives floodwaters that last for months, a life-sustaining "flood pulse" that provides breeding and feeding habitat to a spectacular abundance of exotic plants and animals (Swarts 2001). Indeed, many experts believe that the Pantanal may contain the greatest concentration of fauna in the Americas. Yet as a former director of Brazil's national park system once noted:

"[P]eople outside Brazil know only the Amazon. . . . It's a shame because the Pantanal is a very important ecological place" (Banks 1991).

As the twenty-first century opens, much of the Pantanal remains in a relatively pristine state. Large swaths of tropical forest and vegetation within its confines thrive as they have for millennia, and its waters flow largely unfettered by dams and other diversions of human design. Human settlements are mostly small and widely scattered as well, giving animals plenty of room to tramp and dart beneath the region's sprawling green canopy. However, signs of human encroachment are gradually accumulating, and conservationists are urging regional governments to institute meaningful conservation and sustainable use measures now rather

(continues)

than wait until development pressures grow more acute, as they almost undoubtedly will."Unless the Pantanal's conservation is handled correctly, it will become just another system at risk, joining numerous other ecosystems around the world," declared Frederick Swarts, secretary-general for the World Conference on Preservation and Sustainable Development in the Pantanal (Swarts 2001).

One cause for concern is steady population and development growth in the Upper Paraguay River Basin, the heart of the Pantanal system. This is one of the more socioeconomically deprived areas of central South America, with poor health and education services, inferior communications and transportation infrastructure, and widespread impoverishment. Many of these people are unfortunately—but understandably—willing to engage in destructive exploitation of the Pantanal's resources if it will bring about improvements in their standards of living. Already, the region is facing increasing challenges in the realm of water pollution.

Many of the pollutants that now lace areas of the Pantanal originate in the highlands outside of the Pantanal, where human settlements are rapidly expanding. One infamous case of this type is Cuiabá, the capital of the state of Mato Grosso in Brazil. Located squarely in the Cuiabá River watershed, the city is completely bereft of waste treatment facilities. As a result, the city simply dumps its waste into the Cuiabá River day after day, where it is carried downstream to the Paraguay River, the

single most important freshwater artery of the Pantanal. Overall, an estimated 2 million inhabitants of the Upper Paraguay River Basin deposit their waste into the Pantanal every day. This situation will almost certainly worsen in the years ahead, as the population of the basin is projected to double by 2025 (ibid.). Other major sources of water pollution in the region are mining operations, which dump mercury, toxic tailings, and other by-products into rivers and streams, and agrochemicals such as fertilizers, herbicides, and pesticides that filter into the wetland as a result of runoff.

The Pantanal is also experiencing increases in erosion and sedimentation, as previously undeveloped lands are cleared for logging, farming, ranching, road construction, and other purposes. "As with other problems in this remote region, there are a number of good federal and state laws to limit land clearing and control erosion, but enforcement lags. For example, laws prohibit landowners from clearing forests all the way to the riverbank, but the restrictions are often ignored" (ibid.).

Currently, the World Conference on Preservation and Sustainable Development in the Pantanal (WCPSDP) lists seven anthropogenic threats to the wetland: (1) deforestation and other forms of land clearance in the watershed; (2) poaching and overfishing of wildlife, including key predators; (3) discharge of untreated urban waste in the state of Mato Grosso and elsewhere; (4) contamination from fertilizers and other agrochemicals; (5) discharges of chemical pollutants, such as mercury used in gold mining

(continues)

operations; (6) poorly planned and invasive road construction; and (7) local dam and dike construction (World Conference 2003).

In addition, two regional "megaprojects" have been cited as potential threats to the ecological integrity and health of the Pantanal. One of these is the $2 billion Gasoducto Bolivia-Brazil, or "Gasbol," pipeline, which seeks to transport Bolivian natural gas to various corners of Brazil. The project has been widely hailed in some quarters for its economic stimulus value for both countries and its capacity to provide millions of Brazilians with access to inexpensive natural gas. But the pipeline, which is already partly operational, plows right through the southern Pantanal, and concerns have been raised about the cumulative ecological impact of construction and maintenance operations.

The second controversial development project is the proposed Paraguay-Paraná Waterway Project, commonly known as the Hidrovia Project. This scheme to dramatically alter the Paraguay River and Parana River corridors to make them navigable for large trade ships was originally conjured up by the leaders of Argentina, Bolivia, Brazil, Paraguay, and Uruguay in the late 1980s. Advocates of the plan say that straightening, widening, and deepening various portions of the Pantanal would reduce regional transport costs and provide year-round ports for inland regions, and they add that waterway construction and maintenance would constitute a major new source of employment for the region. But

opponents contend that the scheme would pack a host of major environment impacts, from dislocation and destruction of vital feeding and nursery habitats to unpredictable disruptions to hydrological regimes to increased incursions by logging and mining outfits into the Pantanal's interior.

Currently, the cost of the Hidrovia Project is seen as so prohibitive that it may never attract the necessary investment money to be brought into being, at least as originally envisioned. However, WCPSDP secretary-general Frederick Swarts points out that "this does not mean that hydrological projects on the Paraguay River and its tributaries will not occur piecemeal and still impact the Pantanal in a major way. . . . At this point, the Pantanal is a vibrant, amazing natural treasure. It clearly can have a bright future. However, a bright future will require proper science and good management. The Atlantic Forest once stretched for 5,000 kilometers along the coast of Brazil. It now extends to less than four percent of its original size" (Swarts 2001).

Sources:

Banks, V. 1991. *The Pantanal: Brazil's Forgotten Wilderness.* San Francisco: Sierra Club Books.

Swarts, Frederick A., ed. 2001. *The Pantanal: Understanding and Preserving the World's Largest Wetland.* St. Paul, MN: Paragon House.

World Conference on Preservation and Sustainable Development in the Pantanal. "About the Pantanal." Available at http://www.pantanal.org (accessed April 2003).

AGRICULTURAL FERTILIZERS, HERBICIDES, AND PESTICIDES

Agriculture is a dominant economic activity across the region, and far more land is used for ranching and crop cultivation than for any other purpose. As a result, prevailing agricultural practices are a potent factor in determining the ecological health of rivers, streams, and groundwater resources. Unfortunately, many countries currently display a heavy dependence on agrochemicals—fertilizers, herbicides, and pesticides—that have been directly implicated in the severe degradation of freshwater systems. For example, excessive use of fertilizers in agriculture has enhanced algal growth and eutrophication in lakes, dam reservoirs, and coastal lagoons. Similarly, rising levels of nitrates have been documented in major river systems and in aquifers (UN Environment Programme 2002).

Experts warn that preserving the ecological integrity and health of freshwater systems will be impossible if Latin America does not make fundamental changes to its farming sector. "Agricultural run-off is the largest source of ground and water pollution in the countryside," concluded one UN report. "The use of agrochemicals has risen disproportionately and it is estimated that the quantity of heavy metals, chemicals and hazardous residues doubles every 15 years. . . . Fertilizer consumption alone rose by some 42 percent between 1990 and 1998" (UN Economic Commission for Latin America and the Caribbean and UN Environment Programme 2001).

In addition, agricultural expansion has been the impetus for the clearance of trees and other native vegetation from hillsides and other erosion-prone areas. Rainfall and irrigation subsequently washes unprotected soil into river systems, where it silts up rivers and reservoirs, smothering spawning beds, altering waterway dynamics, and damaging mangroves, sea-grasses, coral reefs, and other species-rich coastal areas.

MINING OPERATIONS

Some of Latin America's most dramatic episodes of water pollution have been laid at the doorstep of its mining industry. Many nations in the region rely on mining for critical foreign capital and economic stimulus, so they have erected few regulatory barriers to discourage investment. But this has had disastrous consequences for rivers and other natural resources, especially since many mining operations in Central and South America are of marginal ores that require purification prior to transport. In many instances this initial refining is undertaken at the mine site through the use of substances such as mercury and cyanide that are subsequently dumped into leaky reservoirs or discharged directly into streams and rivers, poisoning the flora and fauna.

Few Latin American nations have been left unscathed by poorly regulated mining operations, though some have suffered more than others. In Bolivia, waste materials from mines have contaminated entire river systems. In Pacific Coast countries such as Peru and Chile, mining operations have pulverized mountainsides into rubble, denuded watersheds, caused massive erosion and siltation of rivers, and flushed millions of tons of polluted mine tailings into rivers and streams, which subsequently carry them to coastal outlets (Hinrichsen 1998). For example, two massive Peruvian copper mines near the Chilean border are responsible for pumping more than 73 million metric tons of mine debris and tailings into local rivers annually (ibid.). Mining operations have also been the culprits in a number of environmental disasters, including a 1996 fiasco on the Pilcomayo River, which is shared by Uruguay and Argentina. In that incident a tailings dam collapsed, releasing 400,000 tons of toxic waste, including arsenic and cyanide, into the river. The spill not only devastated downstream fisheries and wildlife but also resulted in deaths and widespread illness in downstream indigenous communities that were not informed of the accident.

Small-scale mining has also had significant negative consequences for Latin American nations. In Brazil, thousands of independent poor miners, known as *gariempeiros,* have damaged many rivers and streams with their indiscriminate use of mercury to separate gold from washed paydirt. Once the mercury is discarded into the water, it enters the aquatic food chain, accumulating in ever greater concentrations as it works up the chain from algae to minnows to carnivorous fish and fish-eating birds such as kingfishers and raptors. In many Brazilian rivers, fish now contain mercury at levels that are well above World Heath Organization guidelines for safe human consumption. Yet subsistence communities—indigenous and otherwise—often have little choice but to consume these tainted fish.

In recent years, a number of nations have reluctantly begun to confront the serious mining-related water pollution problems that they have ignored for years. But if Latin America hopes to reverse current trends, fundamental institutional changes will have to be made, including significant strengthening of regulatory monitoring and enforcement mechanisms. In addition, freshwater quality and supply issues will have to be integrated into a host of other policy areas. "In most countries, water resources continue to be managed on a sectoral basis with little integration either between sectors or with other environmental management procedures," explained the UN Environment Programme. "Such an approach ignores vital interactions with much wider ecosystems and other functions, and ecological services related to water" (UN Environment Programme 2002).

Weighing the Pros and Cons of Dams in Latin America

Hydroelectric dam projects have been embraced in many parts of Latin America, most notably in Brazil, which relies on hydroelectricity for 90 percent or more of its electricity generation needs. As the twentieth century drew to a close, Latin America accounted for about 21 percent of global hydroelectric energy consumption. Much of this total is generated by South America's nearly 900 large dams (those more than 15 meters [50 feet] high), of which more than 500 are located in water-rich Brazil.

Humankind's ability to harness the natural power of rivers for the industrial, commercial, and household sectors has long been praised as an environmentally preferable alternative to fossil fuel power generation, which generates a variety of pollutants including greenhouse gases implicated in global climate change. Indeed, some analysts cite global warming mitigation as a significant justification for large hydroelectric dams. And some dams have been designed in ways that help the region's all-important agriculture sector access and distribute irrigation water. Given these factors, pressure to make further investments in this technology is high in Brazil and numerous other countries. After all, rapidly growing populations are placing great pressure on existing energy sources, and South America in particular is laced with large rivers that have not yet been collared with hydroelectric dams.

But existing and proposed dam projects in Latin America and other parts of the world are encountering greater opposition than ever before, both on environmental and social grounds. Detractors contend that large dams inundate species-rich forests and grasslands, reduce wild biodiversity, pollute water, and degrade fishery resources by blocking paths of migratory species (which in turn diminishes food security for rural populations) (World Commission on Dams 1999). Particular attention has been paid to dams' alteration of downstream aquatic habitat, including ecologically fragile estuaries and coastal areas. "Aside from flooding upstream reaches by creating a reservoir, scientists now recognize the 'tourniquet' effect that dams have on living rivers," explained one study. "By blocking flow of water and sediment, dams effectively cut off rivers from their floodplains and downstream reaches. Reduced flow decreases the amount of water available for aquatic species. Dams also capture sediment, thus depriving the downstream reaches of natural sediment load, causing geomorphic changes downstream. Flora and fauna are affected by both the flooding of habitat upstream as well as the alteration of downstream habitat" (Levy 2002).

Critics also assert that poor and indigenous communities in Latin America are often forced to relocate or absorb severe socioeconomic damage to make way for dams and reservoirs. Finally, opponents claim that dam developments often trigger a cascade of undesirable social side effects. In Brazil, for instance, it has been charged that "numerous social and public health problems are . . . linked to hydroelectric development and, as such, to the urban transformation of Amazonia. Moreover, hydroelectric projects are often the first stage in more complex land distribution and development schemes that influence the region's spatial organization and settlement structure by attracting unemployed workers, displacing resident populations, and flooding highways and existing towns and villages" (Browder and Godfrey 1997).

Tucuruí and other Controversial Hydro Projects

Some dam projects have proven particularly controversial over the last three decades, an era in which Latin America's hydroelectric sector has surged upward in production capacity. For example, Brazil's Tucuruí Dam facility— armed with 4,000 megawatts of installed capacity when it opened in 1984 and currently subject to an upgrade that will eventually double its capacity—has been characterized as an environmental nightmare by critics (ibid.). "Social and environmental costs received virtually no consideration when the actual decisions [to build Tucuruí] were made," observed Philip M. Fearnside of the National Institute for Research in the Amazon (World Commission on Dams 1999).

Shrouded in secrecy from its inception, the Tucuruí Dam has drowned a large swath of species-rich tropical forest, blocked migrations of rare and commercially valuable fish, and been responsible for rising concentrations of pesticides and other pollutants in the waterway. The social costs of the project, which remains one of the world's largest tropical dams, included inundation of seventeen towns and villages, which displaced as many as 35,000 indigenous people. "Such traditional riverine populations, concentrated in channel settlements, are the most vulnerable to dislocation by hydroelectric development projects," noted one analysis. "Given the economic logic of their settlement location, based on the extraction of river resources (e.g., fish, turtles, manatees) and forest products (e.g., rubber latex and Brazil nuts) and the necessity of river transport, these 'traditional' peoples are among the first to be dislocated in the process of river impoundment. While many of those who actually received dislocation relief moved to other rural areas, most of the dislocated undoubtedly ended up in Para's burgeoning towns and cities, involuntarily contributing to the region's urbanization" (Browder and Godfrey 1997).

Finally, Tucuruí and other Latin American dams have been faulted for their ripple effects on regional economies and investment. "The subsidized alu-

Vast tracts of forest were condemned to rot underwater when the Tucuruí Dam was set up. HERVE
COLLART/CORBIS SYGMA

minum industry that consumes two-thirds of Tucuruí's power distorts the entire Brazilian energy economy and leads to tremendous impacts as other
dams . . . are built to supply power to cities that could have been supplied by
Tucuruí had the output of Tucuruí not been committed beforehand to smelt-
ing aluminum for export," charged Fearnside. "The wide-ranging social impacts of Tucuruí's role as a supplier of power to the aluminum industry
include the opportunity cost of not having used the nation's financial and natural resources in ways more beneficial to the local inhabitants" (World
Commission on Dams 1999).

Numerous other dams in Latin America have been castigated for their ecological and social impact as well. Brazil's Balbina Dam near Manaus, for example, has been characterized as one of the greatest public works fiascos ever
undertaken in the Amazon. The hydroelectric facility produces only about 5
percent of the energy that Tucuruí does, despite the fact that each of the dams
drowned about the same amount of biologically rich rain forest area—approximately 2,500 square kilometers (1,000 square miles) (Fearnside 1989). In
Brazil's northeastern ramparts, the Itaparica Dam on the São Francisco River
created a reservoir of 840 square kilometers (325 square miles) that submerged the lands of 15,000 small farm families (De Onis 1992). And the wild
character of Brazil's Parana River has been forever altered by the erection of

dams all up and down its shining length (twenty-three dams completed or under construction at the end of the twentieth century). To many environmentalists and human rights activists, these types of costs, which are associated with all large dam projects, are simply not worth the trade-off in lost and degraded habitat and human dislocation.

Smaller dams are not immune from criticism, either. For example, Guatemala's Chixoy Hydroelectric Project submerged a comparatively modest 14 square kilometers (5.4 square miles) of land when it was built in the late 1970s and early 1980s. But while the "ecological footprint" of this facility was smaller than those of larger dams, it still wreaked extensive environmental damage to local ecosystems. In addition to the forest lost to the reservoir, the Chixoy Dam has been implicated in alterations to fish and native wildlife communities, including local extinctions of the giant river otter and other threatened species; increased incidence of malaria and dengue fever in nearby human populations; and sedimentation buildup behind the dam, which shortens the lifespan of the dam and deprives downstream ecosystems of natural deposition loads (Levy 2002).

Today, Latin America remains engaged in a difficult struggle to reconcile its pressing energy needs and the tremendous hydroelectric potential of its rivers with the ecological implications of dams. In Amazonia, numerous dams have been proposed under the banner of economic growth and development, but they are opposed by activists intent on preserving the basin's ecological integrity and the cultures of its indigenous communities. In Chile, the first of a series of six large hydroelectric dams touted as a clean and economically vital energy source have already been planted in the Biobío River, but these same structures have also been vilified for shredding the watershed's ecosystem and displacing indigenous communities. In Colombia, opponents of the proposed Urrá Dam on the Sinú River say that it will destroy the culture of the indigenous Embera Katío people and other fisherfolk communities, but advocates call it a giant step forward in creating economic opportunity for the region. And in Belize, a proposed hydroelectric dam in the Macal River Valley has drawn praise from impoverished citizens eager to attract new energy-thirsty industries and condemnation from environmentalists who contend that the dam will destroy 35 kilometers (22 miles) of tropical rain forest teeming with biodiversity—including jaguars, tapirs, and a rare subspecies of scarlet macaw—and endanger the country's tourism sector, which is heavily dependent on native forests and wildlife. Similar debates over the wisdom of proposed hydroelectric projects are now being waged all across the Latin America/Caribbean region.

At this time, the obvious energy potential of hydroelectric power, combined with the legitimate desires of Latin American people to improve their station in life, often trumps all other considerations. According to some estimates, for instance, the waters of Brazil's Amazon River Basin have the potential to generate an incredible 100,000 megawatts of hydroelectric power, equivalent to 100 nuclear power stations (Bunyard 1987). It is extraordinarily difficult for the developing countries of Latin America to turn their backs on such resources. But dam opponents believe that enthusiasm for these projects usually stems from inadequate consideration and appreciation of the myriad—but not easily quantified—benefits that natural hydrological regimes provide to human communities and ecosystems alike. "The natural flow of rivers and wetlands is not a pathological condition that needs to be cured," declared one expert. "The benefits of maintaining natural, healthy ecosystems are many but are rarely measured in standard economic calculations" (Abramovitz 1999).

Sources:

Abramovitz, Janet N. 1996. *Imperiled Waters, Impoverished Future: The Decline of Freshwater Ecosystems.* Worldwatch Paper 128. Washington, DC: Worldwatch Institute.

———. 1999. "The Profound Shift toward an Environmentally Sustainable Economy." In *The Pantanal: Understanding and Preserving the World's Largest Wetland.* Edited by Frederick A. Swarts. St. Paul, MN: Paragon House.

Anton, D. J. 1993. *Thirsty Cities: Urban Environments and Water Supply in Latin America.* Ottawa: International Development Research Centre.

Browder, John O., and Brian J. Godfrey. 1997. *Rainforest Cities: Urbanization, Development, and Globalization of the Brazilian Amazon.* New York: Columbia University Press.

Bunyard, Peter. 1987. "The Significance of the Amazon Basin for Global Climate Equilibrium." *Ecologist* 17, no. 4/5.

Castro, Gonzalo. 1995. *A Freshwater Initiative for Latin America and the Caribbean.* Washington, DC: World Wildlife Fund.

Connolly, Priscilla. 1999. "Mexico City: Our Common Future?" *Environment and Urbanization* 11 (April).

De Onis, Juan. 1992. *The Green Cathedral: Sustainable Development of Amazonia.* New York: Oxford University Press.

Fearnside, Philip M. 1989. "Brazil's Balbina Dam: Environment versus the Legacy of the Pharaohs in Amazonia." *Environmental Management* 13, no. 4.

Global Water Partnership. 2000. *Water for the 21st Century: Vision to Action.* Stockholm: GWP.

Goodman, David, and Anthony Hall, eds. 1990. *The Future of Amazonia: Destruction or Sustainable Development.* New York: St. Martin's.

Goulding, Michael, Nigel J. H. Smith, and Dennis J. Mahar. 1996. *Floods of Fortune: Ecology and Economy along the Amazon.* New York: Columbia University Press.

Hardoy, Jorge E., Diana Mitlin, and David Satterthwaite. 2001. *Environmental Problems in an Urbanizing World: Finding Solutions for Cities in Africa, Asia, and Latin America.* London: Earthscan.

Hinrichsen, Don. 1998. *Coastal Waters of the World: Trends, Threats, and Strategies.* Washington, DC: Island.

Lemos de Sá, Rosa M. 1992. "A View of Hydroelectric Dams in the Amazon." *Tropical Conservation and Development Program Newsletter* 25 (April).

Levy, Karen. 2002. *Life Submerged: The Environmental Impacts of Guatemala's Chixoy Dam.* Berkeley, CA: International Rivers Network.

Nishizawa, Toshie, and Juha I. Uitto, eds. 1995. *The Fragile Tropics of Latin America: Sustainable Management of Changing Environments.* Tokyo: United Nations University Press.

Pan American Health Organization. 1998. *Health in the Americas.* Washington, DC: PAHO.

Revenga, Carmen, et al. 2003. *Watersheds of the World* (CD-ROM). Washington, DC: World Resources Institute.

Shiklomanov, Igor, coord. 1999. *World Water Resources at the Beginning of the 21st Century.* Paris: UN Educational, Scientific and Cultural Organization, International Hydrological Programme.

Smith, Nigel J. H. 2002. *Amazon Sweet Sea: Land, Life, and Water at the River's Mouth.* Austin: University of Texas Press.

UN Development Programme. 2002. *Central America and Panama: The State of the Region 2002.* New York: UNDP.

UN Economic Commission for Latin America and the Caribbean. 2000. *Water Utility Regulation: Issues and Options for Latin America and the Caribbean.* Santiago, Chile: UNECLAC.

UN Economic Commission for Latin America and the Caribbean and UN Environment Programme. 2001. "The Sustainability of Development in Latin America and the Caribbean: Challenges and Opportunities." Report prepared for World Summit on Sustainable Development, Rio de Janeiro, October 23–24.

UN Environment Programme. 2000. *GEO Latin America and the Caribbean Environment Outlook.* Mexico City: UNEP.

———. 2002. *Global Environment Outlook 3 (GEO-3).* London: UNEP and Earthscan.

UN Food and Agriculture Organization. 2002. *The State of Food and Agriculture 2002.* Rome: FAO.

Water Centre for the Humid Tropics of Latin America and the Caribbean (CATHALAC). 1999. *Vision on Water, Life and the Environment for the 21st Century— Central America and Caribbean.* Panama City, Panama: CATHALAC.

World Commission on Dams. 1999. "Second Regional Consultation of the WCD on Latin America, August 12–13, 1999, São Paulo, Brazil." Available at http://www.dams.org/kbase/consultations/latin (accessed April 2003).

World Health Organization and UN Children's Fund (UNICEF). 2000. *Global Water Supply and Sanitation Assessment 2000 Report.* Geneva and New York: WHO and UNICEF.

World Resources Institute. 2001. *World Resources Report, 2000–2001.* Washington, DC: WRI.

World Water Council. 2000. *Water in the Americas for the Twenty First Century, July 26–28, 2000, Final Report.* Montreal: World Water Council.

World Wide Fund for Nature. 2003. *Global 200 Ecoregions.* Available at http://www.panda.org/about_wwf/where_we_work/ecoregions/global200/ (accessed March 2003).

Oceans and
Coastal Areas

—C. Brad Faught

Latin America—the Caribbean and Central and South America—is a highly varied region of languages, peoples, social and political development, ecosystems, biodiversity, and climatic zones. From tropical beaches and rain forests in the north to polar cold in the south, Latin America encompasses a startlingly array of habitat, all of which is influenced by the presence of the Atlantic and the Pacific oceans.

The azure waters of the Caribbean, as well as elsewhere in Latin America, teem with aquatic life. Colorful fish abound, as do sharks and shellfish. Their presence has long attracted tourists, adventurers, and fishers whose activities create jobs and bring in foreign exchange, but the cost to the environment is high. Overfishing is a serious problem in the region, as is the ubiquitous presence of oil drilling platforms and tankers. Every day some 5 million barrels of oil are transported through the Caribbean, much of this cargo generated by regional oil production leaders Venezuela, Colombia, and Mexico. Frequent accidents in transport of this material discharge oil into the sea, and these contamination episodes are further exacerbated by oil leakage from drilling rigs as well as that coming from tankers in the form of wastes and bilge waters. The near-shore waters of most of the region's urban areas, meanwhile, are clogged with raw sewage and municipal garbage. This problem may well worsen in the years ahead because the growth of cities remains mostly unchecked, driven by an influx of people from the impoverished areas of the countryside.

Regional recognition of the proliferating threats to coastal and deep-water ecosystems is growing. However, efforts to protect Latin America's oceans and coastlines are hampered by powerful international economic interests, uneven local political development, and considerable discrepancies in the financial wherewithal of the various states that compose the region.

Marine Systems of Latin America

Just as the total land mass of Latin America encompasses a wide range of climatic conditions and ecosystems, so too do the marine waters of this corner of the world. Indeed, the character of the region's marine systems are wildly different, from the tropical and subtropical waters of the Caribbean and Central America to the temperate conditions found in South America, and even the subarctic conditions in the remote southernmost reaches of the continent.

Latin America's seas exhibit an abundance of physical and geographic features as well, including massive kelp forests and sea grass beds, coastal mangrove forests, coral reefs, coastal dunes and beaches, and hundreds of river deltas and estuaries teeming with life. All told, the region contains about 64,000 kilometers (40,000 miles) of coastline and another 16 million square kilometers (6.2 million square miles) of maritime territory. (Under the UN Convention on the Law of the Sea that came into force in 1994, all coastal nations have sovereign control over the waters and seafloor that lie up to 12 miles off their shores, as well as dominion over seas extending 200 miles from inhabitable land. The 200-mile zone is known as an Exclusive Economic Zone [EEZ], and it provides even the smallest Caribbean nation with sovereign rights to explore, exploit, conserve, and otherwise manage marine resources of considerable size.)

Mangrove forests line much of Latin America's shoreline, and concentrations are especially high in the region of the equator, where climate and ubiquitous deltas and coastal lagoons provide an ideal environment for them. These forests, which currently cover between 40,000 and 60,000 square kilometers (15,500 and 23,200 square miles) of Latin America and the Caribbean, are vital in the reproduction, development, and feeding of numerous marine species, including many of the most commercially valuable ones. In many areas, however, mangrove forests are being swept aside by development schemes. In the Caribbean, the most important coastal and marine ecosystems are coral reefs, "which are comparable to the tropical rain forests because of their high productivity and biodiversity" (UN Economic Commission for Latin America and the Caribbean 2001). But as in other parts of the world, water pollution and climatic changes have taken a toll on reef health and cast a shadow over their future. Numerous reefs in the Caribbean—including the 700-kilometer-long (435-mile-long) Meso-American Caribbean Reef System, the second largest barrier reef in the world—have suffered from bleaching events in recent years (Wilkinson 2000).

Fisheries Threatened by Overexploitation and Pollution

The Caribbean fishery is relatively small in global terms, accounting for just 0.2 percent of world production, but it is of vital importance regionally as a food source and economic activity (UN Food and Agriculture Organization 2002). Unlike seas to the north, where continental shelves such as the Grand Banks of Newfoundland historically have supported enormous fisheries, the Caribbean relies on the presence of coral reefs, sea-grass beds, and mangrove forests to provide the major breeding, feeding, and nursery areas for commercially valuable fish and shellfish stocks. Absent in the region too are the up-swellings of nutrient-rich subsurface water. Consequently, Caribbean seas are generally less nutritious than those found farther south and farther afield, such as in the Indian Ocean. Still, tuna, grouper, and conch—as well as many other species— are found in the Caribbean, although not in their former abundance.

The situation differs in South America, where the Humboldt Current that moves up the Pacific coast brings with it cold, nutrient-rich waters that serve to stimulate a vast fishery centered off the shores of Peru and Chile. Worldwide, only the fishery of the Pacific Northwest exceeds in volume that of the west coast of South America (ibid.). Sardines and mackerel compose the bulk of the catch. On the Atlantic side of the continent, Brazil dominates annual total catch figures.

In all areas of Latin America, though, intense pressure on natural sea stocks has meant that aquaculture and mariculture have become vital components of fish and seafood production. Shrimp farms in Honduras, for example, have soared, although overall aquaculture and mariculture have been hampered by outbreaks of disease, the vagaries of the market, and hurricanes and other natural disasters. In 1998, for example, Hurricane Hugo took a heavy toll on the fragile Honduran shrimp industry.

Marine Fisheries in the Waters of the Caribbean and Central America

Central America is dominated by the waters of the Gulf of Mexico and the Caribbean Sea, which together comprise over 4 million square kilometers (1.5 square miles). Some 200 million people live on or near the seashore, and each year the population swells by 100 million tourists who flock to the myriad resorts that hug the white sand beaches of the region. The population is overwhelmingly urban—in excess of 70 percent—and most of its major cities are located on the coasts. Many of the islands of the Caribbean have high population densities. Barbados, for example, has more than 500 people per square kilometer, while Antigua has about 300 people per square kilometer (World Resources Institute 2000). This trend shows no signs of altering its trajectory, meaning that human pressure on islands and coastlands will continue to increase. Already such pressure has resulted in consistent degradation of coastlines. Exacerbating the problem is inland urbanization. The relentless expansion of the region's cities and towns has resulted in considerable destruction of natural habitat and widespread soil erosion. Siltation of rivers has resulted, which in turn has done much to damage deltas and mangrove swamps that are vital fish spawning and nursing areas. Meanwhile, industrial production has pumped millions of tons of effluent into near-shore waters, a situation made that much worse by the toxins and the raw sewage that plague the rivers that empty into the sea.

Fisheries in Central America and the Caribbean are mostly smaller-scale commercial operations and artisanal in nature. Like many other regions else-where, overexploitation has resulted in systemic changes in fish stocks. In recent years, however, expansion has taken place in deep-sea fishing, which has meant a doubling in Caribbean marine production, while aquaculture production has been static (UN Food and Agriculture Organization 2002). The picture is similar in Central America, where marine production rose consistently over the last decade, peaking at more than 21 million tons—almost one-quarter of world production—in 1996. Within the region, greater marine production has been met with approbation by fishers, fish plant workers, and governments hard pressed to supply social services to largely impoverished populations. But an unwelcome development in recent years has been the increase in longline fishing in the deeper waters of the Caribbean and Central America by commercial fleets from Japan and South Korea especially. The plying of these waters by foreign trawlers is a source of local resentment and concern, but the governments of the states from which these ships emanate routinely disregard both formal protests and informal complaints.

Despite these difficulties, Caribbean and Central American governments increasingly are overcoming preexisting cleavages based on language and culture and working together to both preserve and improve their natural resources. Especially important in this work have been two organizations, the fifteen-member Caribbean Community and Common Market (CARICOM), and the Latin American Economic System (LAES), which is made up of twenty-eight member states. Both intergovernmental bodies are concerned principally with fisheries issues, including the maintenance and improvement of fish habitat. Together, they have conducted studies tracking annual catch levels; species depletion; and the health and extent of mangrove forests, sea-grass meadows, and coral reefs.

Important to the health of the Caribbean Sea and the Gulf of Mexico too is the tropical rain forest, the size of which has steadily diminished as a result of a combination of resource extraction and slash and burn subsistence cultivators. The loss of forest cover leads quickly to loss of topsoil. Damage to the watershed ensues, which has a cumulative impact on the viability of mangrove swamps and sea-grass beds.

Isla Trinitario slums in Guayaquil, Ecuador JEREMY HORNER/CORBIS

Marine Fisheries in the Waters of South America

Many of the features of the marine fishery of the Caribbean and Central America appear also in South America. The coastline is vast—some 30,000 kilometers (19,000 miles) in length—and intense pressure is brought to bear on much of it by steady urbanization, the denuding of watersheds, and the presence of ecologically damaging industrial effluents. Colombia excepted, coastal areas on the Pacific side of the continent are magnets for the impoverished and dispossessed of the interior. In Ecuador, for example, more than half of the country's populace lives along the coast. The country's largest city, Guayaquil, has a population of 3 million, having doubled in size in the last twenty years, and it unfortunately stands as a monument to the kinds of pressures rampant and unplanned urbanization can bring to bear on coastlines: destroyed mangrove swamps, raw sewage emptying into near-shore waters (in this case, the Golfo de Guayaquil), and mushrooming barrios containing few or no sanitation services.

To the south, the waters off Colombia and Ecuador are cold and nutrient rich and mingle with freshwater from tropical rivers emptying into the sea. In both countries, coastal fishing is mostly artisanal. The mangrove forests remain fairly extensive, and the Colombian Pacific coast, for example, is able to support approximately 12,000 artisanal fishers whose catch is for direct consumption or for sale in local markets (Sheppard 2000). The deep-water fishery off the South American west coast is rich, and production has held steady for the last five years. The fleets of Peru and Chile lead the way in marine production. Peru's coast extends in a fairly straight line for about 3,000 kilometers (1,900 miles), supporting a population of about 14 million people (UN Development Programme 2002). It is serrated by the mouths of fifty-three rivers that empty their freshwater loads into the fast-flowing waters of the Humboldt (or Peruvian) Current. The Humboldt moves northward from Antarctica, and within its regular up-swellings can be found an abundant biological diversity. More than 700 species of fishes compose the Peru marine system, with some 70 of these being commercially important. The Peruvian anchovy, Pacific sardine, jack mackerel, snake mackerel, and the South Pacific hake lead the way; prawns are the most valuable crustacean to Peru's economy.

The presence of the El Nino-Southern Oscillation (ENSO), an irregular climatic occurrence that results in warm, nutrient-poor waters rising to the surface, has played havoc with marine production lately, however. The Peruvian anchovy is especially sensitive to ENSO's effects, and in 1997–1998 production fell precipitously from about 8 million tons to just 6.47 tons. Since then, however, production has climbed back to its earlier level (UN Food and Agriculture Organization 2002).

The Humboldt Current visits the Chilean coast as well, and the seasonal up-swellings of nutrient-rich water are an important component of a robust coastal fishery that typically registers annual production of upward of 7 million tons (ibid.). Chile also relies heavily on anchovies, sardines, and mackerel, and tertiary production is centered on fishmeal. Artisanal activities account for only about 5 percent of Chile's fishery sector. ENSO's irregular occurrence has had the same sort of depressive impact on Chile's fishery as on that of Peru.

Chile shares the bottom of South America with Argentina. The Argentine coastline extends from the southern tip of the continent—Tierra del Fuego—to Buenos Aires, located partway up the Atlantic seaboard. The regional marine ecosystem is dominated by the Southeast South American continental shelf. Draining into this ecosystem are the waters of the Rio de la Plata Estuary system, a network that includes the Parana, Paraguay, and Uruguay rivers and ranks second in size in South America only to the Amazon.

Bolstered by this mix, the regional marine life is rich and diverse, and the ecosystems support an array of birds and mammals, especially the southern sea lion and southern elephant seal. The commercial fishery is large and growing in Argentina, with some 90 percent of the annual catch of approximately 1.5 million tons exported abroad (ibid.). The Argentine hake is the main commercial species, representing about 60 percent of the total annual catch.

Foreign fleets, especially trawlers from Poland, Taiwan, Japan, and Germany, have long been active in the area. The Falkland Islands War of 1982 between Argentina and the United Kingdom interrupted foreign fishing for a number of years, but internationally based ships are now plentiful again; they are exploiting Argentine hake, as well as southern blue whiting and Antarctic cod at maximum capacity levels.

Artisanal fishing in Argentina is practiced extensively along the coast to the north of Buenos Aires, and to the south near Rawson and Santa Cruz. It has a significant local impact by providing some 3,000 to 5,000 seasonal jobs a year. Southern king crab, stiletto shrimp, and scallops make up 80 percent of the artisanal catch (ibid.).

To the north of Argentina lies Brazil, the largest country in South America and the fifth largest in the world measured by land mass. Its coastline is over 9,000 kilometers (5,600 miles) in length and displays all manner of mangrove forests, cliffs, beaches, salt marshes, and coral reefs. Brazil's population is some 170 million, three-quarters of which live in urban areas. Its fishery accounts for most of the catch on the Atlantic side of South America—900,000 tons in 2000 (ibid.). The Brazilian fishery has reached its maximum exploitable limit, however, and the same sorts of problems that afflict its Latin American neighbors threaten the fishery's health.

Marine Resources
and the Threat of Pollution

Pollution of various kinds and from multiple sources is an ongoing challenge to all stakeholders in the Latin American marine fishery. In the Caribbean Basin, for example, less than 10 percent of sewage is treated. The situation is scarcely better in Central and South America. To untreated human waste are added industrial effluents and chemicals, which have fouled the near-shore fisheries of the more heavily populated and industrialized coastal strips of land. Pollution of this sort is especially devastating to the artisanal fishery, and there are a number of examples of communities of subsistence cultivators who have watched helplessly as their local fisheries are destroyed by the ravages of pollution.

Like other high-traffic ocean areas, the Caribbean Sea and the Gulf of Mexico are faced with the pollution generated by hundreds of cruise ships, fishing trawlers, and pleasure craft. But most serious of all is the pollution caused by oil tankers, spills, and drilling. Never was this peril seen more clearly than in June 1979 when an exploratory well located in the Campeche Sound blew out. For over nine months, oil gushed steadily into the Gulf of Mexico. By the time the well was finally capped in March 1980, almost one-half million tons of crude oil had fouled the water, fish, marine birds, and crustaceans of the Sound

Garbage and chemical waste covers a beach in Lima, Peru. HERVE COLLART/CORBIS SYGMA

(Hinrichsen 1998). The Campeche blowout was spectacular, but on a smaller scale damage to local ecosystems has been constant and severe throughout the waters of the Caribbean and Central America. As the region's main oil producers, Venezuela, Colombia, and Mexico cause most of the associated pollution. But tanker routes along both coasts of South America mean that the same type of problems exist for Argentina, Brazil, Chile, Peru, and Ecuador.

Pollution in the Caribbean and Central America

Oil production is a main pollutant in the region, and much scientific work has been done to map and model the impact of spills and blowouts. Since the 1979–1980 disaster in Campeche Sound there have been three more significant incidents in the Gulf of Mexico. However, Campeche accounts for around 80 percent of Mexico's crude oil production, so there is little likelihood of a substantial change in the fortunes of the shoreline of long stretches of the southern Gulf. Still, the Mexican government has recently completed a five-year National Development Plan that makes environmental protection an important feature of its economic development strategy. For the inshore fishery especially of any of the countries fronting on the Gulf of Mexico and the Caribbean Sea, measures such as these are promising. But as with all government regulations, implementation and enforcement are the keys to success (Sheppard 2000).

Proceeding south along the coasts of Belize and Nicaragua, the impact of shipping and industry decreases significantly. Nicaragua harbors the largest green turtle population in the Atlantic, and its extensive sea-grass beds have not been damaged as badly as those located in the high-traffic resort areas of the Caribbean. Nicaraguans who live near the Caribbean coastline are involved mainly in subsistence agriculture, and thus do not make as great a use of fertilizers and pesticides that can damage marine ecosystems when they are washed out to sea.

Nicaragua's relatively pristine coastal ecosystems mean that tourism is increasingly occupying the minds of government planners. They would like to take advantage of the desire of many people from North America and Europe to experience a tropical environment largely undamaged by industry, resource extraction, or shipping. This is not to say that Nicaragua has wholly escaped the problems that plague its Central American neighbors, however. The denuding of forestland and the consequent loss of topsoil, for example, are a serious concern in the country, symptomatic of rural impoverishment (UN Economic Commission for Latin America and the Caribbean 2001).

Elsewhere in Central America and the Caribbean, population growth is putting growing pressure on coastal environments. The region's wonderful variety of colorful fish and marine birds increasingly find themselves crowded out of their natural ranges by new tendrils of development and urbanization. Some coastal areas have escaped major habitat alteration, either because of their remote location or steps to provide them with formal protection from development. But even these areas face threats to their ecological integrity, as fast-moving currents bring wastes and pollution from elsewhere.

These worrisome trends are particularly perilous to the countries of the Caribbean because of their heavy economic dependence on tourism. "Tourism is the future of the Caribbean," stated one former president of the Caribbean Hotel Association. "But at the same time, we have to be very careful about our environment. Solid waste disposal is now a serious problem. Our waters are getting more polluted. Our reefs are dying. On a lot of islands the hotels are too close to the beaches. The sewage pollution is killing the reefs, which then causes beach erosion. If we are not careful, we will end up with loads of hotels, but no beaches and tourists" (Hinrichsen 1998).

In the future, the expansion of ecotourism—the fastest-growing niche of the international tourism sector—may do more to push environmental protection in the region than the most concerted regulatory and protection efforts of governments and advocacy organizations.

Meanwhile, coral reefs in the Caribbean Sea are under constant assault. Degradation occurs in various ways, from overfishing to hurricane-induced

164 LATIN AMERICA and the CARIBBEAN

destruction and erosion, to nutrient damage caused by the dumping of untreated sewage directly into near-shore waters. In Kingston, Jamaica, for example, approximately 40 million liters of raw municipal and industrial waste
are discharged daily into the harbor (ibid.). The loss of coral reefs is potentially devastating for fish and crustaceans because they act as feeding and
nursing grounds for a great number of species. Similarly, marine turtles such
as the green, the logger-head, and the leatherback are under intense pressure
to find suitable nesting grounds because so much of their required habitat—
beaches—has been appropriated by hundreds of regional resort properties
(UN Environment Programme 2002).

Industrial wastes are an ongoing problem across Central America and the
Caribbean. Increasing migration to cities and the concentration of industry
there has meant a relentless assault on the health of coastal waters. The toxins
discharged directly into rivers or oceans are many, but vary by location.
Heavy industry means substances such as lead and copper; logging and deforestation mean bleaching products and mercury; while mining carries with
it cadmium. In addition, the widespread use of pesticides has meant a direct
impact on the food chain because of their resistance to breakdown and their
persistence in embedding themselves in sediments and the food chain. Dead
fish scattered on all Caribbean beaches are testament to the impact of pesticide runoff.

Finally, shortfalls in solid waste disposal constitute another element in the
erosion of ecosystem integrity of coastal areas. Mountainous refuse dumps
have become a regular feature of overpopulated cities in developing countries
around the world, and Central America and the Caribbean are no exception.
On the islands and along the coastlines of the region, many sensitive and
species-rich ecological areas are pocked with unsightly garbage dumps. Their
presence causes a myriad of problems to local flora and fauna. From the ooz-
ing of toxic leachate to the presence of various nonbiodegradable compounds
to all manner of plastic goods, unregulated urban dumps blight their communities and are an underappreciated source of environmental degradation.

All told, the cumulative effect of marine pollution is having a consistently
deleterious impact on the waters and coastlines of the Caribbean and Central
America. Given the introduction of some new environmental and economic
regulations, there are reasons to hope that the situation will improve. But even
if real improvement does come, it may be too late for the Caribbean monk seal
and other sea-dependent species on the verge of extinction. Species eradica-
tion or reduction, together with coastline erosion, sea-grass bed diminishment, and coral reef degradation, paints a discouraging picture of the state of
the region's marine environment.

Pollution in South America

Unfortunately, the situation in South America is not markedly better than that found in the Caribbean and Central America. The sheer size of South America means that there are large swaths of territory effectively uninhabited by humans. But where human habitation does occur, its concentration results in a heavy impact. Indeed, relentless migration from inland areas to coastal urban centers has created a host of associated problems for the continent's oceans and coastal areas.

There are virtually no working sewage treatment plants in South America. As a result, most municipal and industrial wastes are dumped untreated into the Pacific or the Atlantic Ocean. Some improvement has been made in recent years with the building of urban sanitation plants with funds from USAID, the World Bank, and the UN Development Program, but there is much work to do in this regard (ibid.). A high rate of intestinal disorders is one result of so much untreated sewage, ranging anywhere from 40 to 60 percent of all illness across South America. Moreover, many harbors and near-shore waters have been rendered anoxic by this pollution and thus support no fish. In some areas, such as the heavily industrialized Santos Bay region of Brazil near the country's largest city, São Paolo, industrial and municipal discharges have severely compromised near-shore waters and degraded local ecosystems. Approximately 100,000 kilograms (110 tons) of pollutants such as phenol and various metals are discharged monthly into the Santos Estuary. And every year, the harbor is dredged and some 4,500,000 kilograms (5,000 tons) of sediment—replete with toxins—are removed and dumped farther out in the Atlantic, where their full ecological impact remains unknown (Sheppard 2000).

Water quality in South America is also at the mercy of a largely unregulated industrial and resource extraction base that readily dumps its untreated effluents and wastes into rivers, harbors, and other coastal areas. To chronicle the abuses is to itemize a litany of environmental woe: Ecuador discharges some 100 million cubic meters of wastewater into the Pacific yearly. In Peru and Chile, millions of tons of mine tailings are flushed directly into rivers that empty into the Pacific every year. Pesticide use—including the notoriously dangerous DDT—remains widespread, contaminating bays and inlets along both the Pacific and Atlantic coasts. All of these forces have a cumulative impact, especially when they come together. The Rio de la Plata Estuary, for example, is one of the most polluted in all of South America, with dead fish a recurring sight and undrinkable water a constant hazard (Hinrichsen 1998; World Resources Institute 2000).

Offshore shipping lanes in South America are less hazardous than those in the Caribbean and Central America because oil tanker traffic is considerably less, as is platform drilling. Still, container ship traffic is heavy between major cities, and these vessels contaminate the seas with wastewater discharges, residues from engine washing, and bilge dumping. The environmental performance of cruise ships has come under increased scrutiny as well in recent years. Rio de Janeiro is the cruise ship capital of South America, with more than 3,000 port landings per year, and this brand of tourism brings considerable economic benefits to numerous other coastal cities as well. But critics contend that the industry has not policed itself well in the realm of pollution, and proposals for greater regulation of waste treatment and disposal are being considered more seriously than in years past.

The health and vitality of South America's coastal waters have also been influenced by activities taking place hundreds of miles inland. South Americans continue to exploit their forests at an astounding rate, especially in the resource-rich Amazon Basin. From 1970 to 2000, for example, some 100 million hectares of verdant South American tropical forest disappeared in favor of farm and pastureland (World Resources Institute 2000). The consequences of deforestation for area rivers and coastal waters included widespread delta siltation and pollution through the toxic discharges of logging companies. And once farming begins on cleared land, other pollutants are added to the mix. Fertilizers and pesticides enter the rivers through normal runoff, and once they reach the rivermouth, they contribute to algal blooms and general eutrophication. In addition, the fouled rivers themselves surrender some of their capacity to facilitate spawning and fish migration.

The environmental picture in South America is a distressing one in numerous respects, but there are reasons to believe that the region can make inroads in addressing its pollution and unsustainable consumption problems. Indeed, virtually every country in the region has taken steps—albeit sometimes modest—to mitigate the environmental damage stemming from prevailing industrial and resource extraction practices.

Coastal Areas under Stress

Consistent human migration from inland regions to the coastal cities and towns of Latin America has produced many densely populated areas. This expansionary imperative is driven by the usual factors: more economic opportunities in urban areas (or at least the perception of such); the shrinking size of rural landholdings; drought or disaster in the home area; and destruction of local habitat or traditional livelihoods.

Most cities in the region are struggling mightily to absorb the legions of newcomers. Pressure on municipal services is usually overwhelming, and most cities are typified by a population distribution pattern in which wide swaths of slums without regular access to running water or basic sanitation services ring the original city core. There is no reason to think that this trend will subside. Medium-size and large cities grow at the fastest rate, which has driven the level of urbanization in Latin America and the Caribbean to its highest level ever: 65 to 70 percent of the total population, with population densities that are almost everywhere at record levels (UN Development Programme 2002).

For coastlines, the pressures of people and buildings and roads and infrastructure has meant the telescoping of erosion and destruction in certain areas. The loss of coral reefs, which are vital to marine food chains, is the main problem, but with it are associated problems such as sand removal and deepwater dredging and mining for minerals such as calcium carbonate, which reshapes the coastline and disturbs the ecosystem. Another consequence of coral reef degradation and loss is that it often leaves local inhabitants more vulnerable to storms.

In the Caribbean especially, many resorts and hotels have been established on mainland beaches located behind the natural breakwaters of coral reefs. Pollutants released by these facilities have taken a significant toll on reef health, with consequent declines in fish numbers and species (Wilkinson 2000). This is especially true of resorts that have been constructed quickly in recent years. Many of these have not incorporated high standards of waste disposal and sanitation into their designs (UN Environment Programme 2002).

All up and down the coastlines of Latin America, the scars of shortsighted development and exploitation can be seen. Since the early 1960s, for example, approximately half of the mangrove forests of Central and South America have been lost to some form of destruction. As regulators of coastal erosion, their loss is a critical indicator of the compromised state of coastlines. Elsewhere, the rapid expansion of resorts and hotels, housing developments, aquacultural enterprises, and extractive industries into previously pristine dune and beach ecosystems has ruined habitat for creatures including shellfish, raptors and other birds, and various species of endangered marine turtles. For example, the construction of Brazil's Highway 101 in 1970 caused an enormous amount of deforestation along the coast of southern Brazil, which in turn exacerbated mudslides and sediment loads at local rivermouths (Sheppard 2000).

The coastline of Latin America and the Caribbean will continue to undergo severe stress in the years ahead as constituent governments search for ways to provide for the demands of ever-expanding populations, hungry for a taste of the prosperity now so readily on display in this era of global commerce and telecommunications. In the main, most Caribbean and Latin American states need to incorporate much sounder coastal management programs in order to stem the tide of indiscriminate urban growth. Scientists have long identified the major problems, but finding the political will and the resources required to implement policies that will make possible both economic development and preserve imperiled ecosystems is the real challenge for governments.

The Potential Impact of Climate Change on Latin America

The most influential climatic event of the last ten years in Latin America and the Caribbean was the 1997–1998 El Nino-Southern Oscillation (ENSO). This phenomenon develops from a large-scale ocean-atmosphere fluctuation over the Pacific. ENSO can bring about a number of physical alterations, including a rise in water temperatures of as much as 6 degrees Celsius (11 degrees Fahrenheit). Temperature increases of this magnitude usually result in extensive damage to fish stocks and the mass mortality of larval fish species. Higher up the food chain, sea lion populations have been affected because of loss of food resources. As dramatic as ENSO's impact has been, however, scientists are as yet unsure of its long-term effects on species, habitats, and communities.

As demonstrable as ENSO's impact has been in recent years, the climatic event with the greatest potential impact is global climate change. Over the last several years, a scientific consensus has emerged that some airborne pollutants are transforming the planet's upper atmosphere so that it takes on greater insulating properties. This "greenhouse effect," in which the sun's heat is suppressed in the atmosphere by anthropogenic emissions of "greenhouse gases," is widely viewed as a potentially serious threat to ecosystems, economies, and social systems around the world, including those in Latin America and the Caribbean.

According to the Intergovernmental Panel on Climate Change (IPCC), the earth's accumulation of greenhouse gases will wreak major changes on natural ecosystems. For example, the greenhouse effect is expected to raise global average surface air temperatures by 1.4 to 5.8 degrees Celsius (2.5 to 10 degrees Fahrenheit) by the end of the twenty-first century if major reductions in greenhouse gas emissions are not made (Intergovernmental Panel on Climate Change 2001). Sea-level rise is inevitable in this situation, with consequent loss of coastal areas. For Latin America and the Caribbean, a 1-meter (40-inch) rise in the sea level by 2100 produced by the addition of massive amounts of polar melt-water to the world's oceans—a plausible scenario,

The town of Saint John's in Antigua, West Indies PAUL THOMPSON; EYE UBIQUITOUS/CORBIS

according to the IPCC—would be devastating. As has been noted earlier, the rate of urbanization along the region's coastlines has never been higher than it is today, and a rapid increase in the water level would imperil large parts of major cities such as Rio de Janeiro and Buenos Aires. Imperiled too would be beaches throughout the region and the resorts and infrastructure that go with them, as well as already diminished mangrove forests and other important habitat regimes.

As ENSO has shown, climate change would likely mean loss of fish stocks on a major scale. In the Caribbean all the islands would lose land to submersion, but the worst hit would be the tiny island states and territories such as St. Kitts and Nevis and Antigua, whose very existence as viable places for human habitation would likely end (ibid.). In the region's major cities, freshwater supplies would be compromised because of flooding of aquifers. Low-lying areas in Central America especially would suffer disproportionately as coral reefs would surrender their function as natural breakwaters. Precipitation rates would change, as would the pattern, severity, and frequency of storms. The latter point is of special importance in the hurricane belt of the southern Caribbean.

Measures Taken to Preserve and Protect Oceans and Coastal Areas

Economically, Latin America remains a developing region of the world, but within its boundaries can be found both great riches and abject poverty. There exist pockets of considerable wealth provided by oil and other resource extraction activities, industry, and agriculture, as well as terrible impoverishment, such as the manifest deprivations of the barrio, the region's visual signature to the rest of the world of extensive urban poverty. Entering the twenty-first century, the relative affluence of states and citizenries loom as a major factor in addressing growing concerns about the ecological state of the region's oceans and coastal areas.

Over the last quarter-century—and especially since the 1992 Earth Summit held in Rio de Janeiro, Brazil—Latin American awareness of environmental issues and their socioeconomic and quality-of-life implications has risen considerably. Today, popular and political support to protect and restore Latin America's natural treasures is stronger than ever before.

At the forefront of this spirit of renewal is the desire to improve the state of the region's oceans and coasts. Despite the fact that it is usually only ecological disasters that make the headlines, most Latin American countries have adopted guidelines, passed laws, and created government departments to manage and, in some cases, protect their waterways and coastlines. Examples of cross-border cooperation are proliferating as well. For example, the establishment of the Caribbean Environment Program (CEP) in 1976 was a watershed moment for that region. Created with the assistance of the UN Environment Programme and the UN Economic Commission for Latin America, the CEP now includes most Caribbean nations as signatories.

The CEP's mandate is to manage the Caribbean environment in such a way as to ensure "sustainable development," a phrase that began to be used routinely in government circles in the mid-1980s, around the same time that the CEP's ability to monitor the region became a reality. Early CEP triumphs included two international agreements designed to provide for a common front against rampant development and pollution. With these agreements—the Convention for the Protection and Development of the Marine Environment in the Wider Caribbean Region and the Protocol Concerning Cooperation in Combating Oil Spills in the Wider Caribbean Region—there exists now a strong legal basis for collective action. Politically, these initiatives have met with considerable popular support. As one UNEP official declared: "Environmental concerns are now part of each election in the region. In fact, the environment is one of the most important issues in the Caribbean" (Hinrichsen 1998).

Central and South America have moved in the same direction as their Caribbean neighbors in terms of increased public recognition of the importance of environmental issues to long-term socioeconomic prosperity. The effective implementation and enforcement of new environmental laws in most countries remain difficult, however. In large part the difficulty stems from the relative poverty of governments and the pressures put on them by large numbers of their people who are poor and dispossessed and who are attempting to eke out a living of any kind, often at the expense of the environment. Still, there have been a lot of successes, including the establishment of large protected-area networks, including major national parks and reserves; the adoption of land use planning regimes; and the creation of government ministries charged with the management and protection of natural resources and the environment. Environmental impact studies are also becoming more common for states throughout Latin America (Sheppard 2000). Of course, these environmental assessments are worthwhile only if they are unhindered by political and economic pressures and if their findings are given the weight that they deserve. By these measurements, results across the region have been mixed.

At the intergovernmental level in Central and South America, a number of steps have been taken to combat pollution of the contiguous oceans and to facilitate restoration of degraded coastlines. In 1981, Panama, Colombia, Ecuador, Peru, and Chile met and agreed on two pieces of collective action: the Convention for the Protection of the Marine Environment and Coastal Areas of the South-East Pacific, and an Agreement for Regional Cooperation to Combat Pollution of the South-East Pacific Due to Oil Hydrocarbons and Other Noxious Substances in Cases of Emergency. Additionally, most Latin American states are signatories to the Convention for the Prevention of Pollution from Ships (MARPOL), a pollution source of particular concern in the Caribbean and at major Central and South American port cities.

Coastal management in South America has been led by Brazil. Emanating from the establishment of the Secretariat for the Environment (SEMA) thirty years ago, the Brazilian government has undertaken a number of initiatives to protect the enormous length of coastline that falls under its control. In the process of doing so, twenty-nine conservation areas (a mix of national parks, national forests, environmental protection areas, and biological and ecological reserves) have been established, as well as the promulgation in 1988 of a National Plan of Coastal Management, followed seven years later by a more detailed National Program. In all cases, local participation is a key variable in successful management and preservation of the coastline, especially since conservation remains a low priority in many Brazilian state governments.

Environmental groups and societies have also become increasingly influential in a number of Latin American nations. These organizations often have mandates that are tied to a specific location, species, or waterway, but their outlook and activities tie them to heavyweight international conservation organizations such as the World Wildlife Fund and Greenpeace.

In some places, the efforts of policy makers, grassroots community groups, international environmental organizations, and scientists have paid tangible dividends, such as improved coastal water quality. But a daunting amount of restoration and conservation work remains to be done. In most of the major fishing zones, overexploitation continues to imperil the long-term health of fish stocks. Sea-lanes bustling with cruise ships, cargo vessels, and oil tankers continue to dump waste in fragile waters, despite new pollution regulations and improved enforcement measures. And deposition of untreated or partially treated waste and chemicals from agriculture, industry, and household sectors remains a huge problem in virtually every populated corner of the region. Moreover, the financial resources that most Latin American governments have at their disposal are much more finite than those enjoyed by North American and European governments. "The environment is under siege," lamented one UN Environment Programme report. "Unless both short- and long-term changes are instigated, sustainable development will remain a chimera" (UN Environment Programme 2002).

If Latin America is to be successful in its quest to protect and restore its oceans and coastal areas, the region's governments will have to continue to make a concerted effort to overcome the barriers that prevent environmental issues from taking precedence over those of a short-term economic nature. They will need the help of the international community in this regard, as debt repayment is an albatross around the necks of most of the states of Latin America. Indeed, the debt loads carried by most Central and South American countries are often cited as a major factor in their inability to create and fund initiatives and agencies to combat the pollution of their oceans and the degradation of their coastlines. Until this issue is resolved successfully, it is unlikely that Latin America will win the fight against environmental despoliation. Fiscal and human resources are required for the implementation and enforcement of environmental laws, and these are the very attributes impoverished countries lack the most.

In the meantime, the mangrove forests, the sea-grass beds, the coral reefs, the beaches, the fish and aquatic life, and the mammals that live in, on, or near Latin America's oceans and coastal areas will be hard pressed to resist incremental destruction at the hands of the region's growing populations. "Public outcries over the catastrophic spills of oil tankers, the fouling of beaches, and the killing of whales have prompted some promising actions," acknowledged one study of the world's oceans. "Yet these kinds of high-profile issues are not the largest problems. Less dramatic, but more pervasive and ultimately destructive, are the slow, persistent incursions of coastal habitat destruction, the relentless push to increase the global fish catch, and the dispersed pollutants that ultimately end up in the sea. Unless we make the oceans a substantive part of the global agenda for sustainable development and acknowledge and confront the threats that face them, the deteriorating state of the oceans will become an impediment to sustainable development rather than a resource" (Weber 1993).

Sources:

Berrill, Michael. 1997. *The Plundered Seas: Can the World's Fish Be Saved?* San Francisco: Sierra Club.

Browder, John O., and Brian J. Godfrey. 1997. *Rainforest Cities: Urbanization, Development and Globalization of the Brazilian Amazon.* New York: Columbia University Press.

Hardoy, Jorge E., Diana Mitlin, and David Satterthwaite. 2001. *Environmental Problems in an Urbanizing World: Finding Solutions for Cities in Africa, Asia, and Latin America.* London: Earthscan.

Hinrichsen, Don. 1998. *Coastal Waters of the World: Trends, Threats, and Strategies.* Washington, DC: Island.

Intergovernmental Panel on Climate Change. 2001. *Climate Change 2001: Mitigation, Impacts, Adaptation, and Vulnerability: Summaries for Policymakers.* Geneva: IPCC.

Jenkins, Rhys, ed. 2000. *Industry and Environment in Latin America.* London: Routledge.

O'Riordan, Tim, and Susanne Stoll-Kleeman, eds. 2002. *Biodiversity, Sustainability and Human Communities: Protecting beyond the Protected.* New York: Cambridge University Press.

Population Action International. 2000. *People in the Balance: Population and Natural Resources at the Turn of the Millennium.* Washington, DC: PAI.

Sheppard, Charles, ed. 2000. *Seas at the Millennium: An Environmental Evaluation.* 3 vols. Oxford: Pergamon.

United Nations and World Health Organization. 2002. *World Health Report 2002.* New York: UN and WHO.

UN Centre for Human Settlements. 2001. *The State of the World's Cities Report 2001.* Nairobi: UNCHS.

UN Development Programme. 2002. *Latin America and the Caribbean: Meeting the Millennium Poverty Reduction Targets in Latin America.* New York: UNDP.

UN Economic Commission for Latin America and the Caribbean. 2001. "The Sustainability of Development in Latin America and the Caribbean: Challenges and

Opportunities, 2001." Report prepared for World Summit on Sustainable Development, Rio de Janeiro, October 23–24.

UN Environment Programme. 2000. *GEO Latin America and the Caribbean Environment Outlook.* Mexico City: UNEP.

————. 2002. *Global Environment Outlook 3 (GEO-3).* London: UNEP and Earthscan.

UN Food and Agriculture Organization. 2001. *The State of the World's Forests 2001.* Rome: FAO.

————. 2002. *The State of World Fisheries and Aquaculture, 2002.* Rome: FAO.

Weber, Peter. 1993. *Abandoned Seas: Reversing the Decline of the Oceans.* Worldwatch Paper 116. Washington, DC: Worldwatch Institute.

Wilkinson, Clive, ed. 2000. *Status of Coral Reefs of the World: 2000.* Townsville: Australian Institute of Marine Science.

World Resources Institute. 2000. *World Resources 2000–2001: People and Ecosystems: The Fraying Web of Life.* Washington, DC: WRI.

8

Energy and Transportation

—RONALD YOUNG

Individual nations within Latin America have varying energy needs and re-sources, but on a regional basis, oil, natural gas, and hydroelectric power are the primary means by which the nations of Central America, South America, and the Caribbean satisfy the energy needs of their industrial, com-mercial, and household sectors. In South America, oil has long been domi-nant—in part because fossil fuels such as coal that are heavily utilized in other regions of the world are not present in large quantities, and in part be-cause of the growing hegemony of the automobile. In Central America, meanwhile, nations have tapped into the natural power of rushing rivers to generate about half of their electricity from hydroelectric schemes. But here, too, rising demand for gasoline to feed the tanks of proliferating automobiles and trucks—demand for which is driven by rapidly expanding populations and improvements in economic status—is perhaps the single most impor-tant energy consumption trend in terms of environmental impact. Indeed, rising rates of motor vehicle use are cited as the biggest factor in Latin America's declining urban air quality and its rising emissions of greenhouse gases responsible for global climate change.

Fossil Fuels and Their Environmental Impact
The environmental impact of fossil fuel dependence—locating, extracting, transporting, and consuming oil, coal, and natural gas—draws criticism from conservation groups, health organizations, and policy makers all over the world. Critics contend that exploration, extraction, and transport activi-ties associated with oil, coal, and natural gas take a heavy toll on the environ-ment. Specific problems cited include fragmentation and degradation of forests, grasslands, wetlands, and other species-rich habitats; soil erosion and

175

Figure 8.1 Composition of Final Energy Consumption Worldwide, 1973 and 1999

By Region, 1973

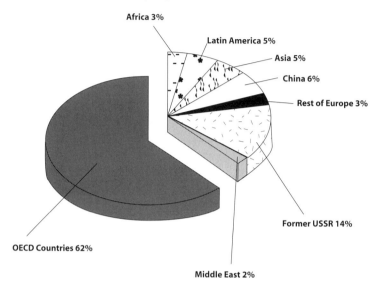

Africa 3%

Latin America 5%

Asia 5%

China 6%

Rest of Europe 3%

Former USSR 14%

OECD Countries 62%

Middle East 2%

By Region, 1999

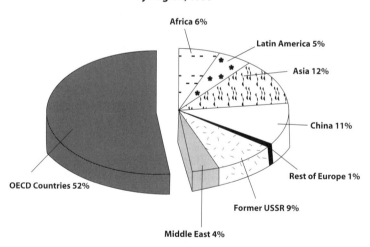

Africa 6%

Latin America 5%

Asia 12%

China 11%

Rest of Europe 1%

OECD Countries 52%

Former USSR 9%

Middle East 4%

SOURCE: The Sustainability of Development in Latin America and the Caribbean: Challenges and Opportunities (LC/G.2145 [CONF.90/3]), document presented at the Regional Preparatory Conference of Latin America and the Caribbean for the World Conference on Sustainable Development (Johannesburg, South Africa, 2002), Rio de Janeiro, Brazil, October 23–24, 2001 (http://www.rolac.unep.mx/foroalc/brasil2001/finales/CRPSusti.pdf), pp. 86.

NOTE: For a complete list of OECD member countries and their dates of entry, refer to appendix B on page 251.

degradation; localized problems with air quality; diminishment of freshwater quality in rivers, streams, lakes, coastal areas, and underground aquifers; and overall declines in the wilderness character of undeveloped areas. Consumption of oil and coal, meanwhile, is a major factor in air pollution and global climate change, popularly known as "global warming."

The varied environmental impacts of these practices are especially evident in Latin America and other developing regions of the world. In many Latin American countries, state control of natural resources is extensive, and the thirst for socioeconomic advancement often prompts the promulgation of environmentally damaging policies. In addition, while per capita energy consumption in Latin American countries is a fraction of what it is in North America and other economically developed regions of the world, the rapid population growth that is characteristic of many Central and South American nations is escalating pressure on existing energy reserves and the environment as a whole. From 1972 to 1999, for example, per capita energy consumption in Latin America increased from about 0.7 to 0.9 tons of oil equivalent, nearing the global average of 1.1 tons of oil equivalent (UN Environment Programme 2002).

The Oil Industry in Latin America

Latin America (including Mexico) holds 11.7 percent of the world's proven petroleum reserves, and it was responsible for about 8.6 percent of global oil consumption in 2001 (BP 2002). Venezuela, which was a founding member of the Organization of Petroleum Exporting Countries (OPEC), has the largest proven reserves in Latin America, with about 77 billion barrels in 2002. The sixth largest producer in the world, Venezuela sends nearly half of its oil to the United States.

Venezuela nationalized its oil industry in 1976. Today, the state-owned Petróleos de Venezuela, S.A. (PDVSA), is the largest oil company in Latin America and among the largest companies in the world. The company develops Venezuela's petroleum, petrochemical, and coal industries. It is also involved in the retail sale of petroleum products such as gasoline; maintains INTEVEP, a research and development center; and owns its own tanker fleet and a large refinery system. The company has the capacity to refine 1.3 million barrels per day (b/d) in Venezuela, including the Paraguaná refining center, one of the largest in the world. PDVSA also owns or leases refineries in Curacao, the United States, and Europe (Energy Information Administration 2002; Karl 1997; Tugwell 1975).

In 1989 the Venezuelan government began to allow a degree of foreign investment in the country's oil industry. That trend was halted, however, after the election of Hugo Chávez as president in 1998. In 1999, a constitutional amendment banned the privatization of PDVSA. A new hydrocarbons law in 2001 also raised royalty rates from 16 to 30 percent and established that PDVSA must own at least 51 percent of any new exploration and production projects (Energy Information Administration 2002). In 2002 and 2003, the nation's oil operations were shaken by political instability. Opponents of President Chavez sought to oust him from office, accusing him of steering Venezuela's economy into recession with leftist policies and seeking excessive power under the guise of a "social revolution." Chavez supporters, on the other hand, contend that the president's efforts to end socioeconomic inequality in Venezuela are badly needed. In January 2003 opponents of the Chavez government organized a massive national work stoppage that crippled the state-owned oil industry, source of half of the government's total income. During the course of the two-month strike, output from PDVSA dropped from 3.2 million barrels a day to 200,000 barrels a day, costing the country an estimated $6 billion. But the strike crumbled in March 2003, and Venezuela quickly set about bringing its oil production output up to prestrike levels.

Mexico is the other major oil producer in Latin America, possessing about 30 billion barrels of proven reserves in 2002. Oil is a major source of government revenue in the country, accounting for about 40 percent of government income. Like Venezuela, Mexico's major export market is the United States. Indeed, it is the second largest supplier to the U.S. market after Saudi Arabia. Mexico also sells significant amounts of petroleum to the Netherlands Antilles, Spain, and Japan. Although Mexico is not a member of OPEC, it often sets its prices and production levels in line with those of the oil cartel (Energy Information Administration 2002; Wirth 1985). As in Venezuela, the Mexican oil industry is run by a state-owned company. Known as Petróleos Méxicanos (PEMEX), it is the sixth largest oil company in the world.

In the early twentieth century, Mexico held a large part of the world's known oil reserves. Most production was in the hands of foreign oil companies, mainly from the United States and Great Britain. During the 1930s, these foreign companies frequently fell into disputes with workers over wages and other issues, and one disagreement eventually worked its way to Mexico's Supreme Court. The court ruled in favor of the employees, but the oil companies ignored the ruling. In response, Mexican president Lázaro Cárdenas nationalized the oil industry.

PEMEX is popular among the Mexican people, as it represents the country's independence and sovereignty. PEMEX has a monopoly over exploration and production of all hydrocarbons, a right guaranteed in the country's constitution. In addition to its exploration and production activities, PEMEX also has six oil refineries in Mexico. However, these facilities are insufficient to re-fine all of Mexico's oil. PEMEX is attempting to modernize its existing refiner-ies, and it anticipates building additional facilities to keep pace with the country's production capacity. But at this time, much of Mexico's oil is refined outside of the country—primarily in the United States. In fact, because of its lack of refining capacity, Mexico must import about one-fourth of its gasoline to meet demand (Energy Information Administration 2002)

Most of Mexico's oil comes from Campeche Bay in the Gulf of Mexico, with another one-fourth of its known reserves located in the Chicontepec region of Veracruz state. PEMEX has yet to fully develop this region on account of cost and the limitations of existing technology at their disposal. But it continues to study various development scenarios and has pondered enlisting the aid of foreign interests through service contracts. The region could prove to be one of the world's largest reserves, with some estimates placing the amount of oil at 70 billion barrels (ibid.).

Brazil also possesses significant proven oil reserves of approximately 8 billion barrels, and it produces approximately 1 million barrels a day. De-spite its ample reserves and production, however, Brazil's large population and its growing commercial and industrial appetites force it to import about 40 percent of its oil, mainly from Argentina, Venezuela, and Saudi Arabia. Petrobras, a 51 percent government-owned company, has a monopoly over the oil industry in Brazil. An international leader in deep-water offshore drilling, more than half of Petrobras's oil comes from the offshore Campos Basin southeast of Rio de Janeiro. Petrobras is also the country's leading oil re-finer, owning eleven of Brazil's thirteen facilities (ibid.).

Argentina is Latin America's fourth-largest producer and third-largest ex-porter. In 2000, Argentina had about 2.8 billion barrels of proven reserves. The country produces about 800,000 barrels a day and consumes about 500,000 barrels a day, exporting the remaining output to thirsty neighbors such as Chile, Bolivia, Uruguay, and Brazil. The Neuquen Basin, located in central Argentina, is home to about half of the country's known hydrocarbon reserves. The country is seen as having relatively little potential for future ex-ploration, and production from existing reserves has declined modestly after peaking in 1998. Since then, political and economic conditions have adversely affected the oil industry. For example, in 2002, government economic policies included a cap on oil exports and a 20 percent tax on oil exports (ibid.).

Argentina's largest producer is Repsol-YPF. In 1999, Spain's Repsol, a major refiner and marketer of oil, bought the Argentine government–owned *Yacimientos Petroliferos Fiscales* (YPF) for $13.5 billion, creating one of the world's largest oil and gas companies. With its purchase of YPF, Repsol's oil reserves more than quadrupled in size. Repsol-YPF also maintains an extensive network of gas stations in Argentina and is the country's largest oil refiner (ibid.).

Oil and the Environment
in Latin America

The oil industry's prevailing modes of operation in Latin America have caused a number of environmental problems and controversies. For example, the industry's history in Venezuela, Latin America's biggest oil producer, has been marked by repeated episodes of environmental pollution and alleged damage to indigenous peoples and their livelihoods. In 1997, for example, the government awarded concessions to reactivate oil fields along the Orinoco River in the Delta Amacuro, home to a community of some 25,000 indigenous inhabitants known as the Warao. The Warao and environmental groups have claimed that oil development in the region will harm the environment and the culture of the indigenous people.

Pollution from oil and other waste traced to the oil industry is also a major issue in Venezuela's Lake Maracaibo. The lake is the largest in South America and has been a major oil-producing basin since the 1920s, but today its waters have been fouled by waste dumped by oil tankers and oil leaks from the industry's pipeline network. Leaks from old wells—supposedly inactive and sealed—also damage the lake's many mangroves, which are essential habitat for a wide range of flora and fauna. Perhaps the worst single disaster on the lake came in 1997, when the Greek-registered ship *Nissos Amorgos* ran aground and spilled 25,000 barrels of oil into Lake Maracaibo. Overall estimates place the cost of cleaning the lake at more than $1 billion annually for ten years (Alexander's Gas and Oil Connections 2002).

Venezuela is hardly unique in its struggle to balance economic prosperity with ecological protection. Indeed, environmental damage associated with oil exploration, extraction, transport, and production has been reported in every Latin American country in which such activity takes place. Incidents span the decades as well, with some of the worst pollution events occurring offshore. The region's largest peacetime oil spill, for example, occurred on June 3, 1979, in the Gulf of Mexico, when an offshore oil rig dumped some 140 million gallons of oil in the sea (ibid.). More than twenty years later, in January 2000, a pipeline ruptured off the shore of Rio de Janeiro, Brazil, spilling more than 300,000 gallons of oil into Guanabara Bay. One year later, explosions erupted on the world's largest oil rig off the coast of Brazil, killing eleven workers. After five days of attempts to salvage the forty-story platform, the rig sank into

An oil-drilling rig in the middle of Lake Maracaibo, Venezuela STEVE STARR/CORBIS

the ocean, spilling 9,500 barrels of oil into the open sea and contaminating vital habitat of the spectacled petrel, a threatened species of seabird (ibid.).

The Natural Gas Industry in Latin America

Parts of Latin America contain significant natural gas reserves, with major reserves located in Venezuela, Mexico, Bolivia, and Argentina. But its overall supply is modest compared with that of other parts of the globe. All told, Latin America (including Mexico) has only 5.1 percent of the world's proved reserves, and it accounted for only 5.4 percent of global consumption in 2001 (BP 2002).

Venezuela has the largest reserves and is the second largest producer, after Mexico. Traditionally, Venezuela has concentrated on exploiting its large petroleum reserves, leaving significant offshore deposits of natural gas (discovered in the late 1970s) untapped. The country now hopes to exploit these natural gas reserves, however, especially for export to the U.S. market. Venezuela cannot use all of its potential natural gas production domestically, so it hopes to export about 70 percent of its production (Wu 1995).

Venezuela's first major natural gas plan was known as the Cristobal Colon Project. But this initiative, which involved foreign investment from companies such as Shell and Exxon, has been put on hold. In 2002, the country announced it would move ahead with a new plan called the Mariscal Sucre project. The project would involve the building of a $2.7 billion natural gas plant that would open in 2007. The state-owned PDVSA would own 60 percent of the project, while foreign companies including Shell and Mitsubishi would provide most of the rest of the financing for the project (Energy Information Administration 2002).

Mexico has the second largest reserves and produces more natural gas than any country in the region. Mexico has been actively investing in its natural gas market since the mid-1990s, eager to reduce its reliance on expensive oil fuel and to rein in its emissions of pollutants associated with oil and coal consumption. To this end, the country has been constructing new gas-fired power plants and converting older plants from oil and coal to natural gas. The government has also been encouraging the use of gas in industry and in homes.

All of Mexico's gas is produced by the PEMEX. However, in 1995, the Mexican government opened the transportation, storage, and distribution of natural gas to private investment. Private firms can also participate in the import and export of natural gas. This growing demand has outpaced production, and Mexico increasingly must import natural gas, mainly from the United States (ibid.; Wu 1995).

Argentina traditionally has been third in both reserves and production. However, in 1999 it surpassed Venezuela to become the second largest producer in the region. At the same time, discoveries in Bolivia may place that country's reserves ahead of Argentina. Natural gas is the most important energy source in Argentina, which has the longest history of natural gas production in South America (the state gas transmission and distribution company Gas del Estado was formed in 1946 and major exploitation of natural gas resources began in the 1960s). In 1992, natural gas production in Argentina was privatized and transferred to ten private consortia. Today, Argentina exports significant amounts of natural gas, mainly to Chile and Brazil. The recent economic crisis in the country has hurt the industry, with many companies reporting significant losses in 2002 because of a devaluation of the currency and other government policies (ibid.).

Bolivia, one of Latin America's poorest countries, has become a natural gas "hub" in South America. Although Bolivia has been involved in the extraction and production of natural gas since the 1960s, the discovery of significant new gas reserves in the late 1990s has placed the country squarely in the region's energy spotlight. Proven reserves grew more than five times between 1999 and 2002, while estimates of unproven reserves give Bolivia the second largest natural gas supply in South America, behind only Venezuela. Bolivia has a small domestic market and consumes only about 20 percent of the natural gas it currently produces, so a dramatic increase in natural gas exports would be a tremendous economic boon to the nation and its people (Energy Information Administration 2002; Alexander's Gas and Oil Connections 2002).

Since 1998, most of Bolivia's gas exports have gone to Brazil, although exports to Argentina resumed in 2002. In 1999, a pipeline connecting Bolivia with Brazil became operational. This pipeline was the largest private-sector infrastructure project in South America, costing more than $2 billion and covering more than 3,200 kilometers (2,000 miles). It brings Bolivian natural gas to São Paulo and Porto Alegre in Brazil. Although Brazil is Bolivia's main trading partner, demand in Brazil for Bolivian gas has not been as high as originally hoped for. Thus Bolivia plans to promote exports to other countries, as seen in a plan to build a pipeline to Paraguay (ibid.).

Bolivia also has hopes of exporting natural gas to the U.S. market, and in 2001 several companies formed a consortium known as Pacific LNG. The goal of the new consortium is to send natural gas by pipeline to a port on the Pacific Ocean. Bolivia, however, is a land-locked country. A pipeline route would thus necessitate crossing the Andes and negotiating agreements with neighboring countries. Bolivia would prefer to send its natural gas through Chile, as it is politically stable. However, relations between Bolivia and Chile have been poor since the War of the Pacific in the late nineteenth century. In 1978, the two countries broke relations, and in July 2002, Bolivians took to the streets to protest the plan to ship gas through Chile (ibid.).

Bolivia's ambitions to expand its natural gas production and transport systems are also complicated by environmental concerns. For example, proposed expansions of the country's natural gas pipeline system would slice through Bolivia's rich, dry Chaco forests and the many indigenous communities living there. Both the Guarani and Weenhayek people have registered complaints against the construction of gas pipelines, citing the damage that such expansion could wreak on local water supplies and habitat harboring animals upon which the indigenous communities depend for their livelihoods. Opponents also cite the cultural impact of these expansion schemes, noting that indigenous peoples would become more dependent on wage labor and the market economy, while thousands of new workers would come into their lands (ibid.).

Hydroelectric Power in Latin America

Hydroelectric power plays a major role in a number of Latin American countries. The region as a whole (including Mexico) accounted for more than 21 percent of the world's total hydroelectric consumption, and 28 percent of total energy consumption. In North America, by contrast, hydroelectric power accounted for only 8 percent of total consumption (BP 2002; Energy Information Administration 2002).

Blessed with four great river systems—the Amazon, the Paraná/Paraguay, the Tocantins, and the São Francisco—Brazil produces the most hydroelectric energy in the region. All told, the country has a hydroelectric capacity of about 58,000 megawatts, making it one of the leading producers of hydroelectric power in the world, second only to Canada in the late 1990s. In addition, much of Brazil's hydroelectric potential is still unexploited, as numerous rivers with significant water volumes have not yet been harnessed for production.

Brazil's current reliance on hydroelectric power—this technology accounts for more than half of the country's total energy production and more than 90 percent of Brazil's electricity—has its roots in the 1950s, when Brazil began building numerous large hydroelectric plants and transmission systems. Among these facilities is the Itaipú hydroelectric power plant, the largest in the world. The plant was built between 1975 and 1991 as a joint venture between Brazil and Paraguay on the Paraná River. Construction of the plant was a monumental undertaking, as workers had to remove 50 million tons of earth and rock and shift the course of the world's seventh largest river. After its completion, the American Society of Civil Engineers named Itaipú one of the "Seven Wonders of the Modern World." Today, Itaipú provides 25 percent of the energy supply in Brazil and about 80 percent of Paraguay's electrical energy (Energy Information Administration 2002; Wu 1995).

Itaipú Dam on the Paraná River in Brazil COREL

Historically, Brazil's hydroelectric power has been reliable, as hydrological conditions have generally been favorable and low supply has been rare. However, in 2001, Brazil faced a major energy crisis attributable in part to its reliance on hydroelectric power. Severe drought gripped many parts of the country, and by June 2001, reservoirs at many hydroelectric plants fell to critical levels. Others factors also contributed to the crisis. Demand for electricity had been growing by about 5 percent each year since 1990, especially in the industries of Brazil's southeast and central states.

Desperate to avert blackouts, Brazilian authorities took emergency measures to cut consumption and diversify supply sources. Industries and business were told to reduce consumption by 15 to 25 percent and to suspend all new expansion requiring electrical connections. Households consuming more than 100 kilowatt-hours had to reduce their consumption by 20 percent or face three- to six-day cuts in their supply. In some states, officials ordered four-day work weeks and new "holidays" in order to reduce industrial consumption. The government energy rationing program ran from June 2001 to March 2002 and enabled the country to weather the crisis without resorting to rolling blackouts (Energy Information Administration 2002).

Although the Brazilian government has indicated a willingness to invest in other energy production sources, it still plans on increasing hydroelectric power in the country. This strategy has been criticized in a number of areas.

Economic problems include long delays in construction and major cost over-runs that have greatly contributed to Brazil's debt. Construction of hydroelec-tric plants can also disrupt rural communities (often poor or indigenous in character) that reap little benefit from development. Finally, while hydroelec-tric power's attractiveness as a clean source of energy should not be underesti-mated, concerns about its other environmental impacts—deforestation, destruction of wildlife habitats, and harm to aquatic biodiversity—have in-tensified in recent decades (ibid.; Gleick 2000).

Several other Latin American countries also use significant amounts of hy-droelectric power. Venezuela is the second leading hydroelectric producer in the region, generating approximately 62 percent of its electricity from this sector annually. Most of Venezuela's hydroelectric power is produced in the Orinoco River basin, the second largest in South America after the Amazon, and the third largest in the world. The state-owned Corporación Venezolana de Guyana (CVG) owns and operates the Guri Dam/Raul Leoní hydroelectric facility on the Caroní River, a tributary of the Orinoco. With a generating ca-pacity of 10,055 megawatts, this facility is the second largest hydroelectric plant in the world. CVG also owns the country's second largest complex, the three Macagua plants downstream from Guri on the Caroní, and it is build-ing two additional facilities on the Caroní. When this expansion is com-pleted, the facilities on the Caroní River will be one of the world's leading power-generating cascades, at more than 17,000-megawatt capacity (Energy Information Administration 2002).

The third major producer of hydroelectric power in Latin America is Paraguay, which has no known oil reserves. Paraguay is the co-owner of two of the world's largest plants; it owns and operates the Itaipú facility with Brazil and the Yacyreta plant with Argentina. Itaipú supplies more than 90 percent of Paraguay's relatively small demand for electricity. (Paraguay actually exports about 90 percent of the power it generates from hydro and other sources.) Paraguay and Brazil equally divide the power generated at the Itaipú plant, ac-cording to the terms of the 1973 Treaty of Itaipú.

The rest of the country's electricity comes from the Yacyreta plant on the southern border with Argentina. Paraguay also shares the power from this plant equally with Argentina. The two countries are also planning a new 3,000-megawatt facility called Corpus Cristi on the Paraná River, upstream from Yacyreta. However, announcement of this development has sparked strong op-position from local community and environmental groups (ibid.; Wu 1995).

Nuclear Energy in Latin America

The use of nuclear energy is not widespread in Latin America, which ac-counted for only 1.1 percent of worldwide nuclear energy consumption in

2001 (BP 2002). Nuclear power has never been a significant alternative in the region for several reasons. Limited uranium supplies, shortages of investment capital, and potential environmental damage from the nuclear fuel cycle have been major deterrents. Concerns about nuclear accidents and long-term storage of nuclear waste have also contributed to wariness about the wisdom of reliance on this energy source. As a result, at the close of the twentieth century only three Latin American countries—Argentina, Brazil, and Mexico—had nuclear power-generating capacity.

Argentina opened its first nuclear facility in 1974. This reactor was the first nuclear plant in Latin America and only the second in the developing world after India. A number of factors led Argentina to embark on its nuclear program. First and foremost, the country was eager to increase its energy security through energy sources other than oil, upon which it was very dependent. In addition, unlike most other Latin American countries, Argentina possessed abundant deposits of uranium. The nuclear program also dovetailed nicely with Argentina's overall emphasis on industrialization. Finally, geopolitics played a role in the Argentines' decision to build nuclear reactors, as the country competed with Brazil and Chile for regional supremacy.

The program has been managed by the Argentine navy through the Comisión Nacional de Energia Atomica (CNEA), which was formed in 1950 and has run efficiently with little government interference. By 1980, 1.3 percent of Argentina's energy production was supplied by nuclear plants, and by 1991 the figure reached about 3 percent. Argentina has two operational nuclear plants, the 350-megawatt Atucha I and the 650-megawatt Embalse plant, which now supply about 9 percent of the country's electricity. However, the country's nuclear program was significantly slowed in the 1990s by economic problems and budget cuts. Several planned reactors were canceled. The country spent $2.7 billion working on the Atucha II plant, which is nearly complete. However, construction has been halted because of a lack of funding. Some estimates place the amount of funds needed for completion at about $800 million. There has also been some discussion of privatizing the nuclear industry, but those plans have been shelved, at least temporarily (Energy Information Administration 2002; Wu 1995).

Brazil's first nuclear power plant began operations in 1985, but its second facility did not open until fifteen years later. The new nuclear power plant has helped alleviate the country's growing energy problems, although its production capacity was not great enough for Brazil to avert its 2001 energy shortage. A third nuclear plant is scheduled to open in 2006 (Energy Information Administration 2002). Mexico was the last Latin American country to initiate a program of nuclear power generation, opening its only plant in 1989. Known as Laguna Verde, the facility is located in the state of Veracruz and has two units, each capable of producing 674 megawatts (ibid.).

The Coal Industry in Latin America

Coal has traditionally not been a major source of energy in Latin America, and today it accounts for only about 5 percent of the region's energy consumption. Only 2.3 percent of the world's proved coal reserves are found in Latin America (including Mexico); as a result, the region was responsible for only 1.3 percent of global coal consumption in 2001 (BP 2002).

Armed with an estimated 7 billion short tons of coal reserves, Colombia is currently the leading coal producer in Latin America. These reserves include the Cerrejon Zona Norte mine, the largest coal mining operation in Latin America and the largest open pit coal mine in the world. Most of Colombia's electricity, however, comes from hydroelectric power, so it generally exports about 90 percent of its coal production to the United States, Europe, and other Latin American countries (International Energy Agency 2002; Energy Information Administration 2002).

Brazil has the greatest quantity of known coal reserves in Latin America (nearly 12 billion short tons) and is the region's biggest consumer of the fossil fuel, accounting for about two-thirds of the total Latin American demand (BP 2002). The Brazilian National Department of Mineral Production estimates that the country uses more than 17 million tons annually, with the steel industry accounting for as much as 75 percent of the nation's total coal consumption. This heavy reliance on coal for steel operations has made Brazil the U.S.'s second largest market for coal exports (ibid.).

Renewable Energy Resources in Latin America

A number of Latin American countries have begun to utilize renewable energy resources on a limited basis. In particular, some countries are increasingly using off-grid renewable resources to provide electricity to residents of remote, rural locations. There are some 75 million people in Latin America who do not have access to electricity because they live in places not reached by their country's electricity grid. In response, governments in countries such as Brazil and Argentina have established federal programs to provide electricity to these citizens. For example, in Brazil, the government began the National Program for Energy Development of States (PRODEEM) in 1998. It invested $25 billion in renewable energy resources, especially photovoltaic technology. The government funded hundreds of community projects that would reach about 200 rural residents each. In Argentina, the government and the World Bank sponsored a $120 million project to provide renewable energy to 70,000 rural households. The project concentrated on the use of both photovoltaic and wind power. The Argentine government also passed legislation that requires utility companies to buy wind power—which is an emerging focus of investment in the region—when it is available (International Energy Agency 2002.)

Other countries are also starting to examine the possibilities of using renewable energy resources. In Bolivia, solar power is used in some isolated mountain villages, where 2,000 photovoltaic systems are in place. In Riberalta, a town of 60,000 near the Brazilian border, nutshells are used to produce energy. The Colombian government has encouraged the use of wind power through tax breaks. In Honduras, the Inter-American Development Bank claims that 40 percent of the population is without electricity. In response, it has approved a $5 million loan to study the use of photovoltaic and solar systems in the country. If successful, the project will expand to provide renewable energy to 100 villages. In Costa Rica, the government has taken an ambitious approach, mandating that by 2025, all of its energy must come from renewable sources (ibid.). Toward this end, it has joined other countries in the region such as Jamaica and Barbados in making significant investments in wind energy and other renewable technologies.

Subsidies in the
Latin American Energy Sector

As in many parts of the developing world, Latin American countries often utilize energy subsidies. However, such subsidies can have a number of negative effects. By maintaining prices below actual cost, government subsidies encourage increased energy consumption. This greater consumption can lead to lower economic efficiency, environmental problems, and a drain on government budgets. Although subsidies can have some short-term benefits, in the long term the removal of subsidies can have a number of positive effects. Governments can improve social welfare by using funds for social programs rather than subsidies. Analysts also cite the removal of subsidies as a key to decreasing energy consumption—which would in turn lower local and global pollution levels and reduce the rate at which natural resources are depleted. Finally, removing subsidies encourages development of technologies that allow for sustainable development (International Energy Agency 1999).

Venezuela is one example of a Latin American country where the government heavily subsidizes most sources of energy and fuel. Government-imposed price controls have traditionally kept prices below their actual cost, which in turn influences energy consumption and emissions in Venezuela.

The International Energy Agency has estimated that in the Venezuelan case, energy consumption is about 25 percent higher than it would be if there were no subsidies. The IEA also claims that emissions of carbon dioxide—the main greenhouse gas responsible for global climate change—would be 26 percent lower if the government were to remove its energy subsidies. Subsidization rates are highest for coal (although it is used in small amounts), natural gas, and electricity. Oil products are also subsidized, but at lower rates. Most savings would come from lower natural gas consumption in power generation and industry.

For their part, Venezuelan governments have often claimed that they would like to restructure the system of subsidies. However, the potential political and social consequences are high, especially in the case of gasoline and electricity. The political volatility of the issue was seen in 1989, when the government raised gasoline prices, which in turn led to an increase in public transportation prices, causing rioting and looting in the capital city of Caracas that left more that 300 people dead (ibid.).

Liberalization and Privatization of the Energy Industry

During the 1990s, the governments of many Latin American countries sought to reform energy markets in their countries. Argentina and Chile were among the pioneers in implementing these changes, while energy-rich countries such as Mexico and Venezuela were slower to implement reforms. These reforms took different paths in the various countries of the region. In some cases, energy markets became completely private, while in other cases governments allowed limited private participation in public energy companies (World Energy Council 2001).

A number of factors led to the liberalization and privatization of the energy sector in the region. Low reliability of power systems, lack of investments in areas such as distribution and billing, older generation facilities, and unsound subsidies all contributed to the changes. In most cases, the government had been the sole provider of energy through agencies that enjoyed various degrees of autonomy. Now, both foreign and domestic private investors have a say in Latin American energy markets. This change has had some positive results. Overall, access to both electricity and gas has increased in many countries. For example, in Argentina, about 55 percent of the population had access to electricity before privatization; after reforms were put in place, this percentage rapidly rose to 85 percent. A similar reaction unfolded in Peru, where availability grew from 47 percent to 75 percent of households.

In addition to improved access to energy sources, private investment has often spurred the use of more advanced technology, improvements in areas such as metering, billing, collection, and line maintenance, and reductions in illegal connections. Liberalization has also been credited with reducing corruption and introducing more modern management practices. These changes have enabled countries to improve reliability and quality of energy services and improve their overall public image (ibid.).

At the same time, however, there have been negative consequences associated with energy market liberalization schemes. In some cases, lower prices act to discourage investment, and unemployment in the energy sector has grown. And while there has been some improvement in environmental standards, compliance has been uneven. In general, the changes have done little to help the most socioeconomically marginal sectors of Latin American society (ibid.).

Transportation and the Environment in Latin America

The transport sector in every Latin American country is unique, with its own peculiar traits shaped by geography, economic development, and political history. Indeed, the means of primary transport vary from region to region, with states in the Caribbean and Central America much more heavily dependent on marine shipping than those of South America, where railroad networks are more extensive. But in all of these regions, motor-vehicle traffic dominates the transportation landscape. It accounts for the lion's share of goods and passenger transport across Latin America, consumes prodigious amounts of oil, and serves as the impetus for all sorts of new construction—roadways being the most obvious example—that fragment or degrade natural areas.

Latin American countries face a number of pressing transportation issues, particularly in the region's many large cities. As in many parts of the world, a growing reliance on private automobiles is evident across Central and South America. As the number of vehicles grows, traffic congestion becomes a more significant problem. Furthermore, higher per capita motor vehicle ownership rates contribute to a decline in public transportation demand and quality of service. Combined with the fact that many cities in Latin America are large and sprawling, the journey to work for many urban inhabitants has become both long and expensive. In Mexico City, for example, the World Bank reports that 20 percent of commuters spend more than three hours each day traveling to and from work, while 10 percent require more than five hours to make this journey (World Bank 2002). All of these trends are contributing to worsening air pollution levels in nearly every country.

The urban poor, in particular, are affected by this situation. In many large Latin American cities, the poor are forced to live on the fringes of the city in order to be able to afford land or housing. These poor areas are located as much as 30 to 40 kilometers (20 to 25 miles) from employment centers. In addition, some squatter settlements in cities such as Rio de Janeiro or Caracas are not serviced by any form of urban transportation. Such inaccessibility to transportation by the urban poor leads to various forms of social exclusion, including high rates of unemployment, poor access to education and health care, and general impoverishment (ibid.).

Safety and security are increasingly becoming major concerns for the users of urban transportation in Latin American cities. Frequent accidents, service breakdowns, and disquieting incidents of crime have eroded public confidence in public transportation, which has further intensified reliance on private vehicles. Again, the poor suffer the most, as they often have no alternative to using the sometimes dangerous public transportation system. In Caracas, Venezuela, the World Bank has reported that if commuters miss the last safe trip at night, they will stay overnight at their workplace rather than risk making the perilous journey home on public systems. Women, especially, are often deterred from traveling at night, forcing them to withdraw from education programs or jobs.

In response to these critical problems, some countries such as Mexico, Brazil, and Argentina have implemented traffic safety programs that have had tangible positive results. For example, in Brasília, the government launched a "Peace within Traffic" safety program in 1995. Within two years, the traffic death rate fell from 11 to 6.6 per thousand accidents (ibid.). But "with very few exceptions, rapid growth in demand for motorized transport has swamped transport [infrastructure] capacity in the cities of the developing world," including those of Latin America (National Research Council 1996).

A Revolution in Bus Transit Systems?

The cause of improving transportation systems and making them less environmentally destructive, however, is not a hopeless one. Success stories in this realm dot the region, from Bogotá, Colombia—where successful programs to restrain vehicle ownership, encourage walking and biking, and enhance bus transit have all been implemented—to Chile, which has privatized its transportation system with rewarding results. In the early 1990s, Chile launched an ambitious and sophisticated program to privatize roadways, freight railways, and other transportation infrastructure elements. "Today, all the main highways in Chile are built, financed, and operated by private companies. In the future, smaller roadways and even urban streets may be privatized as well. Freight railways or the right to use the tracks have been sold to private operators, resulting in greatly increased business on the affected lines. The overall effect has been far greater investment in transportation facilities than could have been provided by cash-strapped government agencies" (Sperling and Clausen 2002).

Increased investment in bus transit—a venerable but still viable mode of public transport—has also been cited as a key to improving transport systems in Central and South America and the Caribbean (Fulton et al. 2002; ibid.). Most conventional bus systems currently operating in Latin America are floundering, beset by inadequate investment, shortcomings in municipal planning, and inconsistent levels of service quality. This poor performance has contributed to a significant decline in the share of passengers who ride buses in Latin American cities. For example, in São Paulo, South America's largest city, the share of passengers riding buses fell from 51 percent in 1977 to about 25 percent in 1997. In Mexico City, the proportion fell from 42 percent in 1986 to just 8 percent by 1995. Throughout most of Latin America, people enjoying increasing levels of economic prosperity have instead turned to private forms of transportation, swayed by their comfort, convenience, and social status (International Energy Agency 2002).

In recent years, however, improving existing bus systems—the primary mode of public transportation in Latin American urban settings—has been a major focus of environmentalists, policy makers, and urban planners alike. Certainly, the benefits of an efficient and popular bus system would be significant, including reduced traffic congestion, improved mobility for all socioeconomic groups, and lower pollution levels in Latin American cities (Sperling and Salon 2002; Fulton et al. 2002).

Mindful of these benefits—and their likely positive impact on economic development—Latin American cities have taken the lead in implementing a system sometimes known as bus rapid transit (BRT). Advocates of BRT systems state that they have the potential to revolutionize bus systems by increasing average speeds, reliability, convenience, and capacity. Proponents assert that these improvements will lead to higher ridership rates, providing profits for the companies involved and a host of social and environmental benefits for the larger community (International Energy Agency 2002; Fulton et al. 2002).

BRT systems, also known as busways, give priority to the rapid movement of buses as an alternative to rail systems used for rapid transit. BRT systems can compete with light rail systems in terms of passenger capacity, although subways can move many more passengers. BRTs are also much cheaper to construct and operate than any rail-based systems. In addition, the systems have the flexibility to adjust to changing urban infrastructure, and they can be built incrementally (International Energy Agency 2002).

The "tube" bus shelters are the pride and joy of Brazil's urban transport system. HERVE COLLART/CORBIS SYGMA

Bus Rapid Transit in Curitiba, Brazil

Perhaps the best known and most successful BRT project in the world is the one in place in Curitiba, Brazil. City officials developed the system in the late 1970s to give mass transit priority over private vehicles. Curitiba utilizes all of the main aspects of BRT systems, including exclusive busways, traffic signal prioritization, and rapid boarding systems. By 2000, the city had some 1,900 buses that carried riders on 14,000 daily trips that covered more than 316,000 kilometers (195,000 miles). The system carries about 1.9 million passengers each day, similar to the number of some subway systems. Curitiba's BRT system has an overall customer satisfaction rating of 89 percent, and urban planners and politicians from around the world visit the city to learn from its experience (ibid.; World Bank 2002).

The system's integrated tariff uses a single fare that allows trip and transfers throughout the system. The fare is high for Brazil, although government and business subsidies help. The system also has express lanes that connect Curitiba with a number of nearby cities, and it is supplemented with 270 kilometers (167 miles) of feeder routes. In addition to the BRT system itself, the city has emphasized a land-use development plan that is integrated with the transportation system. Such an approach maximizes the BRT system by utilizing high-density commercial and residential areas around the bus stations. The success of the Curitiba system has led to attempts to copy it in other Brazilian cities, such as São Paulo, Belo Horizonte, Recife, and Porto Alegre (ibid.).

The Transmilenio BRT Project in Bogotá, Colombia

Politicians and planners in Bogotá, Colombia, have also designed a BRT system, known as Transmilenio. The Transmilenio project is part of a comprehensive strategy to restrict automobiles and promote nonmotorized transportation in the city and surrounding environs. A well-publicized master plan has gained the system widespread support among the city's populace, which is fed up with the city's perennially severe traffic congestion. Bogotá residents even voted to make their city car-free—except for taxis—during the morning and evening rush hour by 2015. This ambitious plan was struck down by Colombia's Supreme Court, but it certainly is indicative of public discontent with the city's traffic situation.

The Transmilenio BRT service began in December 2000. By May 2001, the system was carrying some 360,000 passengers every weekday. During peak travel times, the system can transport 42,000 riders every hour. As with other BRT systems, Transmilenio utilizes exclusive busways on the central lanes of Bogotá's major arterial roads in concert with feeder bus lines and dedicated stations, located in the median of major roads about every 500 meters (1,600 feet). The initial system used 162 buses traveling over 20 kilometers (12 miles) of exclusive lanes equipped with 32 boarding stations. The system uses diesel buses with a capacity of 160 that provide both local and express service, and it is designed to provide easy access for pedestrians and bicyclists (ibid.).

Private consortia of local transport companies operate the buses after winning competitive concession contracts. All revenue is deposited into a trust fund from which operators are paid according to the terms of their contract. The overall system is managed by a new public company called Transmilenio, S.A., which is funded by 3 percent of the total ticket sales. The system receives no direct government subsidies, although it is partly funded by a fuel tax in Bogotá. Thus far, the system has generated enough revenue to make it profitable for the participating private companies (ibid.).

The Transmilenio project seems to be a success by almost any measuring stick. It has dramatically reduced bus fatalities, improved system performance, and reduced emissions of some pollutants by as much as 40 percent. It is also in the early stages of a fifteen-year expansion project that will, if the plan comes to fruition, expand the BRT to include twenty-two transportation corridors covering more than 388 kilometers (240 miles). Planners envision that by 2015, 85 percent of the city's population will live within 500 meters (1,600 feet) of a Transmilenio station (ibid.).

Transportation and the Environment in São Paulo, Brazil

São Paulo is the largest city in Brazil and in South America. The city has experienced rapid economic development and population growth since the 1960s, making it one of the world's biggest metropolitan areas, with more than 16 million inhabitants. The city's growth has been accompanied by numerous problems, however, including serious air and water pollution.

In the last quarter-century of the twentieth century alone, the population of the city grew by more than 6 million. During this same period, the number of private automobiles tripled, while the number of buses increased only by 25 percent (Fulton et al. 2002).

Population growth and attendant increases in motor vehicle ownership have saddled the city with traffic congestion of truly epic proportions. Residents of São Paulo make some 30 million trips daily, of which about 20 million are made on some form of motorized transport. Most of these trips are made via private car, truck, or motorcycle, a pattern that is degrading air and water quality at an alarming rate. In the early 1990s, about half of the city's smog came from factories and half came from motor vehicles. By 2002, about 90 percent of these emissions came from motor vehicles. Today, São Paulo ranks as one of the world's ten most polluted cities, bedeviled by high levels of carbon monoxide, ozone, particulates, and other contaminants spewing from automobile tailpipes. The decline in air quality has in turn led to higher incidences of respiratory and cardiovascular diseases, and even greater mortality rates. Nonetheless, few inhabitants want to utilize the city's bus system, which is overcrowded (because of an inadequate vehicle fleet), provides generally poor service, and is not wholly integrated with suburban train networks (International Energy Agency 2002).

This situation has placed increased pressure on the government to solve the problem of traffic congestion and pollution. Some improvements have been achieved, as the government has established emissions standards for new vehicles and required improvements in fuel quality. However, enforcement is often lax.

Another initiative of recent vintage is the Integrated Urban Transport Plan (PITU), implemented in February 2000 by the Secretary of State for Metropolitan Transport (STM). This plan has ambitious goals, including increased investment in bus and rail transit, reductions in bus pollutant emissions by 40 percent, reductions in noise pollution, and a targeted 8 percent reduction in transport fuel consumption (ibid.). It also seeks to address the city's long-time dependence on older diesel-burning buses. Many of these buses are poorly maintained and use a low-grade, high-sulfur-content diesel fuel. All told, diesel engines in trucks and buses contribute more than half of the airborne particulate matter in São Paulo's major road corridors. The PITU plan calls for investment in newer bus models with cleaner-burning engines and urges increased use of cleaner fuels. For its part, Petrobras has indicated a willingness to upgrade the quality of the fuel it produces, but it claims that such a change will require an investment of approximately $1.2 billion (ibid.).

At the national level, meanwhile, Brazil is exploring major investments in ethanol as a substitute for gasoline. Unhappy with high world oil prices, Brazil began to produce ethanol from sugar cane in the 1970s. The program made significant inroads across the country, as about 40 percent of the automobiles in Brazil used the fuel, while others used an ethanol/gas blend. In the 1980s, however, gasoline prices dropped. This development, combined with ethanol's weak distribution system and a major strike by sugar cane workers, badly damaged the ethanol program. Today, less than 1 percent of Brazilian automobiles use the fuel (ibid.).

Currently, the Empresa Metropolitana de Transportes Urbanas de São Paulo, S.A. (EMTU/SP) is involved in a program with the UN Development Program (UNDP) and the Global Environmental Facility to develop and use fuel-cell buses in São Paulo. Under the program's current timetable, it will start with three buses that will operate for four years, then eventually expand until a fleet of 2,000 buses is roaming the streets of São Paulo and other cities. Proponents acknowledge that the program will not be commercially viable at first, but they contend that it can become profitable over time, and that it could greatly aid urban efforts to combat air pollution (ibid.).

Urban Transportation and Pollution: The Mexico City Case

The Mexico City metropolitan area covers more than 2,000 square kilometers (770 square miles) in the Federal District and the State of Mexico. With a population of around 20 million, it is one of the largest urban agglomerations in the world. Unfortunately, the Mexican capital is the result of largely unplanned urban growth fueled by natural population growth and continued migration from the countryside. Perceived economic opportunities in the city along with decreasing agricultural employment in the rural areas have led hundreds of thousands of Mexicans to move to the capital annually. The city grows by around 5 percent per year, about twice the national average. Indeed, about one-fourth of Mexico's population lives in Mexico City, which occupies a mere one one-thousandth of the country's territory. The metropolitan area contains more than one-third of the country's industry and close to half of its jobs (Tulchin and Redman 1991).

Mexico City has numerous environmental concerns, but degraded air quality from the transport sector is among the highest priorities. Today, an estimated 60 percent of Mexico's automobiles are driven in Mexico City, a city located in a deep valley surrounded by a chain of mountains. The topography thus acts to trap much of the emissions generated by the city's cars, trucks, locomotives, and airplanes in the metropolitan area. At this point, the task of reversing declining air quality trends in Mexico City is a daunting one, requiring major new investments in public transit and replacement of old, high-polluting vehicles with more environmentally friendly models.

Sources:

Adler, Emanuel. 1988. "State Institutions, Ideology, and Autonomous Technological Development: Computers and Nuclear Energy in Argentina and Brazil." *Latin American Research Review* 23, no. 2: 59–90.

Alexander's Gas and Oil Connections. "Country Analyses" of Latin American Countries. 2002. Available at http://www.gasandoil.com/ (accessed March 2003).

BP. 2002. *BP Statistical Review of World Energy 2002.* London: Group Media and Publications.

Energy Information Administration, U.S. Department of Energy. 2000. *International Energy Annual, 2000.* Washington, DC: Energy Information Administration.

———. 2002. "Energy Overviews" of Latin American Countries. December. Available at http://www.eia.doe.gov (accessed March 2003).

Fulton, Lew, et al. 2002. *Bus Systems for the Future: Achieving Sustainable Transport Worldwide.* Paris: International Energy Agency.

Gleick, Peter H. 2000. *The World's Water, 2000–2001.* Washington, DC: Island.

Goodman, David, and Michael Redclift, eds. 1991. *Environment and Development in Latin America: The Politics of Sustainability.* Manchester and New York: Manchester University Press.

International Energy Agency. 1999. *World Energy Outlook, 1999 Insights: Looking at Energy Subsidies; Getting the Prices Right.* Paris: OECD.

———. 2002. *World Energy Outlook: 2002.* Paris: OECD.

Karl, Terry Lynn. 1997. *The Paradox of Plenty: Oil Booms and Petro-States.* Berkeley and Los Angeles: University of California Press.

National Research Council. 1996. *Transportation Options for Megacities of the Developing World.* Washington, DC: National Academy Press.

Nogueira, Uziel. 1989. "Latin America: The Energy Sector and the Foreign Debt Crisis." *Towson State Journal of International Affairs* 24, no. 1.

Pumphrey, David L., et al. 1991. *Energy Policy in the Western Hemisphere*. Washington, DC: Woodrow Wilson Center.

Rask, Kevin. 1995. "The Social Costs of Ethanol Production in Brazil: 1978–1987." *Economic Development and Cultural Change* 43, no. 3.

Salazar-Carrillo, Jorge, and Robert D. Cruz. 1994. *Oil and Development in Venezuela during the Twentieth Century*. Westport, CT: Praeger.

Sperling, Daniel, and Eileen Clausen. 2002. "The Developing World's Motorization Challenge." *Issues in Science and Technology* 19 (fall).

Sperling, Daniel, and Deborah Salon. 2002. "Transportation in Developing Countries: An Overview of Greenhouse Gas Reduction Strategies." Prepared for the Pew Center on Global Climate Change. Washington, DC. May.

Street, James H. 1982. "Coping with Energy Shocks in Latin America: Three Responses." *Latin American Research Review* 17, no. 3.

Teixera, Maria Gracinda C. 1996. *Energy Policy in Latin America: Social and Environmental Dimensions of Hydropower in Amazonia*. Brookfield, VT: Ashgate.

Tugwell, Franklin. 1975. *The Politics of Oil in Venezuela*. Stanford, CA: Stanford University Press.

Tulchin, Joseph, and Andrew Redman. 1991. *Economic Development and Environmental Protection in Latin America*. Boulder and London: Lynne Rienner.

UN Development Programme. 2000. *World Energy Assessment: Energy and the Challenge of Sustainability*. New York: UNDP.

UN Development Programme, UN Environment Programme, World Bank, and World Resources Institute. 2000. *World Resources 2000–2001: People and Ecosystems, The Fraying Web of Life*. Washington, DC: World Resources Institute.

UN Environment Programme. 2002. *Global Environment Outlook 3 (GEO-3)*. London: UNEP and Earthscan.

VonLazer, Arpad, and Michele McNabb. 1985. "Inter-American Energy Policy: Prospects and Constraints." *Journal of Interamerican Studies and World Affairs* 27, no. 1.

Wionczek, Miguel S., et al. 1988. *Energy Policy in Mexico: Problems and Prospects for the Future*. Boulder, CO: Westview.

Wirth, John D. 1985. *Latin American Oil Companies and the Politics of Energy*. Lincoln: University of Nebraska Press.

World Bank. 2002. *Cities on the Move: A World Bank Urban Transport Strategy Review*. Washington, DC: World Bank.

World Energy Council. 1993. *Energy for Tomorrow's World: The Realities, the Real Options, and the Agenda for Achievement*. New York: St. Martin's.

———. 2001. *Energy Markets in Transition: The Latin American and Caribbean Experience*. London: World Energy Council.

Wu, Kang. 1995. *Energy in Latin America: Production, Consumption, and Future Growth*. Westport, CT: Praeger.

Air Quality and the Atmosphere

In Latin America and the Caribbean, emissions of chemicals that degrade air quality and atmospheric conditions are a major concern. Regional variations in air quality are significant, however. In fast-growing urban centers, where most people live, environmental and public health agencies are grappling with rising emissions from automobiles, industrial operations, power plants, and other sources. In numerous cities, air quality is a pressing health concern—and the focus of a growing array of antipollution initiatives. In remote, lightly populated areas, meanwhile, air quality is usually high. But human incursions into wilderness areas for the purposes of mining and timbering are eroding air quality here as well. Indeed, the stunning rate of deforestation seen in the Amazon Basin and other forested areas has been cited as the main source of atmospheric emissions in the region, inasmuch as forest cover removal reduces carbon sequestration capacity and releases carbon into the atmosphere. Latin America's current pattern of unsustainable logging is thus contributing to global climate change, a phenomenon that has the potential to be enormously destructive to the region's ecological and economic resources.

Air Quality in Latin America and the Caribbean

Air pollution problems intensified in Central and South America and Caribbean states during the 1990s, as economic and population growth drove per capita and overall consumption patterns to new heights. As demand for automobiles, electricity, and manufactured goods has risen, so too have emissions generated in the use or production of these materials. Between 1990 and

1999, for example, regional emissions of carbon dioxide—the main "green-house gas" responsible for global climate change, commonly known as "global warming"—soared by 37 percent. Emissions of other pollutants registered similar disquieting increases across the region, with increases recorded for suspended particulate matter (up by 6.2 percent during the 1990s), sulfur dioxide (up by 22 percent), nitrogen oxides (up by 41 percent), hydrocarbons (up by 45 percent), and carbon monoxide (up by 28 percent) (UN Economic Commission for Latin America and the Caribbean and UN Environment Programme 2001).

The release of these pollutants into the air constitutes a major public health issue in many Latin American cities, where roughly three out of four people live. In Mexico City, for example, studies have repeatedly established a close correlation between urban air pollution and the acceleration of pulmonary diseases, aging processes in the lungs, and respiratory infections (World Health Organization 1999). In Ilo, Peru, home to one of the world's largest copper foundries, dark toxic clouds containing sulfur dioxide levels more than thirty times the concentrations recommended by WHO guidelines were recorded as recently as 1995 (Follegatti 1999). And the city of Cubatão, Brazil, has long been saddled with the sobriquet of the "Valley of Death" because of the deplorable levels of air and water pollution emitted by the numerous industrial plants entrenched there. During the 1980s, air pollution in the city

Table 9.1 Air Pollution (Gas and Particle Emissions, in Gigagrams)

Emissions of	1970	1980	1990	1999	Percentage Increase 1990–1999
Particles	110.98	144.82	188.48	200.15	6.2
Sulphur dioxide	1,873.13	3,035.27	3,452.38	4,194.98	22.0
Nitrogen oxides	2,668.27	4,747.87	5,761.81	8,123.50	41.0
Hydrocarbons	665.17	1,121.36	719.99	1,043.28	45.0
Carbon monoxide	10,334.12	17,460.23	21,555.02	27,693.19	28.0
Carbon dioxide	420,282.79	750,205.14	922,273.89	1,165,237.71	37.0

SOURCE: United Nations Environment Programme, 2001

The Cubatão petrochemical complex, nestled between the São Paulo escarpment and the Atlantic Ocean, is a notorious polluter in the region. TED SPIEGEL/CORBIS

was so thick and toxic that schoolchildren routinely went to local health facilities just to breathe medicated air (Lemos 1998).

In all three of the above-mentioned cities—Mexico City, Ilo, and Cubatão—air quality conditions have improved somewhat in recent years because of new emissions regulations and various antipollution initiatives. Nonetheless, air quality in these and most other Latin American cities remains poor. According to the UN Economic Commission for Latin America and the Caribbean, air pollution permanently affects the health of more than 80 million of the people in Central and South America and Caribbean nations. It has also been cited as the main cause of over 2.3 million cases a year of chronic breathing difficulties among children and of over 10,000 cases of chronic bronchitis among adults (UN Economic Commission for Latin America and the Caribbean and UN Environment Programme 2001). Moreover, the economic cost of treating health problems associated with air pollution is significant, especially for developing nations with limited means to provide social services. By one estimate, respiratory and other problems stemming from exposure to airborne pollutants result in the loss of roughly 65 million working days annually across Latin America (Romieu et al. 1990).

Latin America's booming transport sector is the single biggest culprit in the region's declining air quality. Ownership and use of gasoline-burning automobiles and other motor vehicles has escalated dramatically in most countries over the past three decades, propelled by rapid population growth, rising standards of living, and various economic and trade reforms that have dramatically boosted imports of used motor vehicles. In some cities, such as Buenos Aires and Mexico City, transport accounts for 70 percent or more of urban air pollution.

Many of the vehicles that rumble through these and other cities still operate on leaded fuel, producing lead concentrations far above World Health Organization safety guidelines. And while steps have been taken to phase out leaded gasoline in the region, the sheer number of new automobiles, trucks, motorcycles, and buses that are introduced to Latin American roadways every year make it difficult to realize net improvements in air quality. In Santiago, Chile, for example, the city's automobile fleet is on a pace to double in size every five years (UN Economic Commission for Latin America and the Caribbean and UN Environment Programme 2001).

Moreover, the expansion of the motor vehicle fleet in Santiago and other big cities is being driven by older used cars that are not outfitted with catalytic converters and other pollution-mitigation technology. In Mexico, automobiles produced since 1997 pollute up to 100 times less than one made before 1995. But two-thirds of the cars and trucks roaming the city's streets are more than ten years old ("Right to Drive," 2002).

Another major factor in Latin America's worsening air quality is growing emissions output from the industrial sector. Ascertaining the true level of industrial emissions in Latin America is a difficult task. Most countries have made only limited investments in pollution monitoring technology, and comprehensive reviews of pollution trends in the energy, transportation, and municipal sectors are the exception rather than the rule. Nonetheless, it is apparent that textile plants, manufacturing facilities, pulp mills, oil refineries, mining sites, and other industrial enterprises all bear some responsibility for declining air and atmospheric quality in the region. Some of these operations, unrestrained by meaningful regulations or enforcement mechanisms, are terribly destructive at the local level, spewing poison into nearby neighborhoods and degrading regional ecosystems.

The continued unfettered operation of these high-polluting enterprises in urban centers and industrial corridors reflects an institutional paralysis that has long gripped all too many environmental protection agencies in Latin America and the Caribbean. In Mexico, for instance, it has been charged that

pollution has become integrated into the Mexican economic and political system. There are many possible political motivations behind the tolerance of limited industrial inspection. Industrial regulation is unattractive because it threatens the viability of many small industries, the bedrock of the Mexican economy. Political and administrative weaknesses, especially in the face of economic temptations for corruption, are also evident factors. Regardless of the political motivations behind current regulatory failures, Mexico faces a stark reality. The air quality of the city is damaging the health of its people, the environment and, even the tourist industry. (Ristroph 2000)

On the positive side, evidence suggests that some Latin American countries have registered limited success in curbing industrial emissions in recent years. This is especially true of those states that have attracted significant investment from foreign firms, as these operations often bring greater integration of environmental considerations in their general operating practices. But most small and mid-sized factories in the region have made little or no investment in this area, and some large companies remain notorious polluters. Moreover, it has been speculated that air pollution problems associated with industrial development could be further exacerbated by deregulation and privatization of the power sector, which is taking place in some Latin American nations. For example, in countries such as Argentina, Brazil, and Colombia, deregulation and privatization could trigger reduced use of clean-burning hydroelectric power in favor of oil and coal, which generate carbon dioxide, sulfur dioxide, and other pollutants when consumed (UN Environment Programme 2000b).

Another significant source of air pollution is the agriculture sector, which has become increasingly mechanized and which disperses significant quantities of pesticides and herbicides into the air in certain locales. In some cases, these activities exert a significant impact on public health. For example, studies conducted in Colombia and Ecuador in the early 1990s revealed that more than 60 percent of agricultural workers involved in production for foreign markets reported symptoms of acute pesticide poisoning, while many other laborers experienced serious chronic health problems ranging from stillbirths and miscarriages to respiratory and neurological problems (UN Environment Programme 2002). Health problems associated with exposure to pesticides and herbicides have also been reported in communities that adjoin treated fields and pasturelands.

Other air pollution sources worthy of mention include forest fires (both wildfires and prescribed burning for land clearance purposes), which can severely compromise air quality at the local and regional level, and household consumption of biomass (wood and other organic matter). The latter serves as a major fuel resource for about 20 percent of the Latin American population, and it is the primary means by which many rural families cook their food and heat their homes. But consumption of wood and other biomass in indoor settings with poor air circulation exposes families—and especially women, who handle the majority of cooking and heating chores in Latin American households—to dangerous levels of air pollution. In Colombia and Mexico, it has been estimated that women using firewood and other biomass for cooking are up to seventy-five times more likely to contract chronic lung disease than the average resident of these countries (UN Development Programme, UN Environment Programme, World Bank, and World Resources Institute 1998; ibid.).

Some of Latin America's population centers, including megacities such as São Paulo, Rio de Janeiro, Buenos Aires, Santiago, and Mexico City, have made tangible progress in reducing air pollution by encouraging natural gas use in the energy sector, upgrading public transport options, tightening pollution standards for transport and industry sectors, investing in more environmentally friendly fuels, raising fuel economy standards, and improving international cooperation in addressing transboundary air pollution issues. Reforms of regulatory agencies—and especially their pollution monitoring and enforcement responsibilities—are also underway in a number of countries and municipalities. But in many Latin American countries, these measures may not be sufficient to squarely address growing population and economic pressures driving declining air quality. "By 2010, 85 percent of the population [in Latin America and the Caribbean] are expected to be living in urban areas," observed the UN Environment Programme, "and combating air pollution and preventing its negative health impacts will be a priority in every country" (UN Environment Programme 2002).

Latin America and the Ozone Layer

The ozone layer is located in the stratosphere, a region of the atmosphere that extends from 10 to 50 kilometers (6 to 30 miles) above the earth's surface. Ozone protects humans, animals, and plants from the full force of cancer-causing ultraviolet radiation emitted by the sun. The ozone layer's radiation filtering properties thus protect food crops, forests and vegetation, and plankton, all of which are integral parts of the food chain for humans, animals, and marine life, respectively.

In the 1980s, the international scientific community determined that this all-important component of the atmosphere was being eaten away by airborne chemicals generated by human activity. Specifically, researchers discovered that releases of chlorofluorocarbons (CFCs)—chemicals used as refrigerants and in aerosol sprays—were creating "holes" in the ozone layer, especially over the world's Antarctic and Arctic regions. The international community responded decisively to this emerging crisis, passing the 1987 Montreal Protocol on Substances that Deplete the Ozone Layer. This international treaty—the first geared explicitly toward protection of the global atmosphere—mandated a global phaseout in production and consumption of CFCs and other ozone-depleting substances (ODS).

Developed nations such as those in North America and Europe took the lead in eliminating the use of CFCs. Obligated to end all production of CFCs by 1995, these parties to the protocol also moved to phase out production of the pesticide methyl bromide, another chemical implicated in ozone depletion. In 1995 more than 100 nations agreed to phase out their manufacture and use of the pesticide.

By 1996, global consumption of CFCs had declined to 160,000 tons, about one-sixth the level of consumption of only one decade earlier. This reduction was due primarily to the efforts of industrialized nations. Further gains in this area, however, will have to come primarily from developing nations, which were given until 2010 to phase out CFC production under the terms of the Montreal Protocol.

Meeting the terms of the protocol looms as a formidable task for some developing nations. Across the world, production of ODS in developing countries more than doubled from 1986 to 1996, and consumption levels ticked upward by 10 percent as well. Latin America, however, seems better situated than some other regions to meet the challenge of eliminating CFCs. The UN Ozone Secretariat notes that in contrast to other developing regions, the Latin American and Caribbean region had reduced its total production of CFCs from 1986 levels by more than 20 percent by the late 1990s. And while Latin American production of CFCs still represented about 15 percent of world production in the late 1990s, countries such as Argentina and Chile—countries relatively close to the Antarctic ozone hole—have already developed policies and measures to reduce production and consumption of ODS. Elsewhere, Brazil halted its production of ODS in 1999, and Mexico—currently the main regional producer of CFCs and other ODS in the Latin American/Caribbean region—has passed a series of laws to end its dependence on CFCs and choke off the thriving black market trade in these ozone-depleting materials.

The international community's swift and decisive response to the threat of stratospheric ozone depletion may ultimately prove to be one of the world's great environmental triumphs of modern times. Scientists acknowledge that ozone depletion could reach historically high levels in the early 2000s, because long-lived CFCs emitted in earlier decades are continuing to rise into the stratosphere. But if the Montreal Protocol is fully implemented by signatories in the developing world, the ozone layer should begin a slow recovery, returning to normal levels by about 2050. Indeed, concentrations of CFCs are already declining in earth's lower atmosphere. But this welcome scenario will come to pass only if the nations of Latin America and other developing regions of the world deliver on their promise to end production and consumption of ozone-depleting substances. And the international community will also need to address environmental problems associated with some ODS alternatives that have emerged in recent years, including hydrochlorofluorocarbons (HCFCs) and hydrofluorocarbons (HFCs), two CFC substitutes that have been implicated as factors in global climate change (Anderson and Sarma 2003).

Climate Change
in Latin America

Airborne pollution has long been recognized as a potentially deadly threat to the earth's flora and fauna, including humans. In recent years, however, a scientific consensus has emerged that some of these same airborne pollutants are transforming the planet's atmosphere so that it takes on greater insulating properties. This "greenhouse effect," in which the sun's heat is trapped in the atmosphere under a growing blanket of emissions known as "greenhouse gases," poses a potentially major threat to world ecosystems and the people, animals, and plants that depend on these systems for their survival.

The main source of carbon dioxide—estimated to be responsible for about 60 percent of global warming attributable to human activities—and other greenhouse gases is the burning of fossil fuels. Lesser sources of greenhouse gases include methane emissions from livestock and landfills, nitrous oxides from agricultural fields, emissions of fluorinated gases from industry, emissions of carbon dioxide from volcanic activity, and releases of carbon dioxide from carbon-storing forests that are cut down.

According to the Intergovernmental Panel on Climate Change (IPCC), a group operating under the joint sponsorship of the United Nations and the World Meteorological Organization that ranks as the world's most authoritative investigator of global warming, evidence of climate change attributable to human activities is already proliferating around the planet, with rapid melting of polar ice caps and record-breaking temperatures the most noteworthy manifestations. According to the IPCC, nine of the world's ten hottest years in recorded history occurred between 1990 and 2000 (Intergovernmental Panel on Climate Change 2001b).

If left unchecked, the earth's accelerating retention of greenhouse gases in the atmosphere will fundamentally transform the planet and its natural ecosystems. Some of these changes may prove beneficial in certain respects to some regions (by transforming arid and semiarid areas into more productive farmland, for example), but many of the consequences are expected to be devastating for people, flora, and fauna around the world, especially in developing countries. The single greatest element in this transformation will be rising temperatures. The IPCC has forecast that the planet will warm by 1.4 to 5.8 degrees Celsius (2.5 to 10 degrees Fahrenheit) during the twenty-first century if major reductions in greenhouse gas emissions are not realized. The probable repercussions of this warming of the planet include increasingly severe and numerous storms, altered rain and snowfall patterns that will bring greater incidence of flooding and drought, inundation of islands and coastal areas from rising sea levels (precipitated by melting glaciers and polar ice caps), expansion of malaria and other tropical diseases into previously temperate zones, and possible mass extinctions of species of mammals, birds, reptiles, amphibians, fish, and plants (Intergovernmental Panel on Climate Change 2001a).

Scientists believe that the severity of many of these changes can be blunted if countries unite to take prompt actions now. To date, the main international responses to the climate change issue have been the 1992 UN Framework Convention on Climate Change (UNFCCC) and the 1997 Kyoto Protocol. The former convention resulted in a legally nonbinding, voluntary pledge from major developed nations to reduce their greenhouse gas emissions to 1990 levels by 2000. The latter is a UN-brokered agreement that established legally binding language for developed nations to reduce their emissions of greenhouse gases to at least 5 percent below 1990 emissions levels by 2012. The protocol enters into force when it has been ratified by at least fifty-five parties to the convention, including developed countries accounting for at least 55 percent of total carbon dioxide emissions in 1990. But the future of the Kyoto Protocol, which even supporters acknowledge is only a first step in addressing global climate change, is uncertain. The United States, which ranks as the world's leading producer of greenhouse gases, has decided not to ratify the treaty, citing economic hardship and the exclusion of developing countries. In addition, some nations that have ratified Kyoto are reporting problems in reaching emission reduction goals.

Latin America's Contribution to Global Warming

In Latin America, inventories of greenhouse gas emissions are incomplete for most countries. But analysis of existing data suggests that Latin America, which has about 8.5 percent of the global population, accounted for about 5.4 percent of world greenhouse gas emissions at the beginning of the twenty-first century. Mexico is the single largest producer of greenhouse gases in the region, at 356 million tons a year, and it and Brazil together account for approximately 53 percent of the greenhouse gas emissions generated in the Latin America/Caribbean region. Significantly, however, these two countries produce only about 12 percent of the greenhouse gases generated by the United States annually, even though their combined population is roughly equivalent to that of the United States (UN Economic Commission for Latin America and the Caribbean and UN Environment Programme 2001). Moreover, yearly per capita emissions of greenhouse gases in Latin America remained below the world average throughout the 1990s.

But while Latin America is not presently among the world's leading transgressors in generating greenhouse gas emissions, output trends suggest that this could change in future decades. For instance, massive livestock operations in parts of Argentina, Brazil, Chile, Mexico, and Uruguay are a notable element of overall increases in output of methane, a recognized contributor to climate change. In fact, Latin America accounts for about 10 percent of global methane emissions.

Latin America's rising loads of greenhouse gas emissions have been driven primarily by increased carbon dioxide production, however. From 1980 to 1998, regional emissions of carbon dioxide rose by about 65 percent (UN Environment Programme 2001). Some of this increase has been attributed to growth in the industrial, agriculture, and transport sectors, all of which remain heavily reliant on fossil fuel consumption for their operations. Indeed, carbon dioxide emissions from the burning of fossil fuels jumped by nearly 35 percent from 1980 to 1999, with annual increases of about 2.5 percent recorded from 1994 to 1999 (UN Economic Commission for Latin America and the Caribbean and UN Environment Programme 2001). But deforestation is believed to be the principal culprit in soaring emissions of carbon dioxide, especially in the Amazon River Basin. In Brazil, for instance, analyses suggest that deforestation accounts for almost twice as much carbon dioxide as the energy sector (Chandler 2002). Altogether, Latin America and the Caribbean account for nearly half of all greenhouse gas emissions attributable to land use changes (UN Environment Programme 2000b).

Potential Impact of
Global Climate Change

By almost any economic or environmental measurement, most Latin American and Caribbean states are poorly situated to respond to the potential climatic changes and severe weather events contained in global warming forecasts. This is especially true of Caribbean nations, which are likely to feel the effects of climate change more acutely than other parts of the region, despite their negligible role in the generation of greenhouse gases. For example, even modest rises in sea level have profound implications for the economies, social and political structures, and ecosystems of small Caribbean island states.

Of course, rising sea levels associated with global warming would also wreak major changes on heavily populated coastlines and coastal ecosystems of coastal South American nations—and especially Argentina, Chile, Uruguay, and Venezuela—and the entire Central American subregion, where both Atlantic and Pacific waters lap against most countries' shorelines.

Global climate change could produce another major blow to Latin America's economic, social, and environmental structures in the form of altered regional water precipitation cycles. Increased incidence of flooding and drought are both predicted, which would have repercussions for water quality, fisheries, crop cultivation, livestock herds, and hydroelectric power generation in nations throughout South and Central America. The Intergovernmental Panel on Climate Change also expresses "high confidence" that Latin America will experience: more frequent and intense tropical cyclones that will threaten life, property, and ecosystems; declining productivity from subsistence farming activities, especially in semiarid environments of Latin America; and significant loss of biodiversity. Other potential threats include the expansion of vector-borne infectious diseases such as malaria, dengue fever, and cholera, and widespread disruptions in social and economic services resulting from temporary or permanent damage to ports, highways, and commercial centers (Intergovernmental Panel on Climate Change 2000).

Addressing the
Threat of Climate Change

The developing nations and territories of Latin America and the Caribbean are not legally obligated to meet specific greenhouse gas reductions under the UNFCCC or the Kyoto Protocol. However, the region as a whole has taken tangible steps to show its support for the principles behind these pacts. Several Latin American and Caribbean nations have adopted GHG mitigation and global warming adaptation initiatives ranging from increased investments in mass transit and the gasoline substitute ethanol to development of renewable energy resources, such as investments in wind farms in places like Barbados, Costa Rica, and Jamaica (UN Environment Programme 2002). For example, one country that has rallied to the cause is Mexico. The first large oil-producing nation to ratify the Kyoto Protocol, Mexico is reducing deforestation rates (which contribute to releases of carbon into the atmosphere), emphasizing natural gas over oil and coal in its energy plans, and implementing measures to curb the emissions generated by automobiles and trucks in its urban centers. These efforts have already produced tangible benefits, such as a 5 percent reduction in the country's annual emissions growth during the 1990s (about 10 million tons of carbon per year) (Chandler 2002).

Finally, climate change experts have given considerable attention to the significant carbon-storage capacities of Latin American forests in recent years. As the UN Food and Agriculture Organization acknowledged in its *State of the World's Forests 2001* report

> [W]hile the most effective means to reduce atmospheric concentrations of carbon dioxide is the reduction of emissions from fossil fuel combustion, in terms of land use change and forestry the conservation of existing forest carbon stocks has technically the greatest potential for rapid mitigation of climate change. As the majority of carbon emissions from deforestation occur within a few years of forest clearance, reducing the rate of deforestation will produce a more immediate effect on global atmospheric carbon dioxide levels than will afforestation/reforestation measures, in which similar volumes of carbon may be removed from the atmosphere but over a much longer period.

Latin America's "Kyoto Forests"

Forests in Latin America and elsewhere absorb carbon from the atmosphere in the form of carbon dioxide—the greenhouse gas principally responsible for global warming—during the photosynthesis process. Indeed, healthy forests act as carbon reservoirs or "sinks," storing large amounts of carbon in trees, understory vegetation, and the forest floor. The overall potential sink capacity of the world's forests is considerable. The Intergovernmental Panel on Climate Change states that implementation of a feasible global forest program could store up to 15 percent of the carbon dioxide emissions generated from fossil fuel consumption around the world between 2000 and 2050 (and could absorb up to 25 percent of emissions if sustainable timbering models become the rule). This scenario is especially relevant to Latin American nations, since tropical forests alone could sequester about 80 percent of the above-mentioned carbon emissions (Goetze 1999; Rotter and Danish 2000).

Conversely, when tropical forests are cleared, fragmented, and degraded, they not only lose their sink capacity but they also release significant amounts of carbon into the atmosphere. In fact, the IPCC has estimated that 15 to 20 percent of the 7 billion tons of carbon released annually into the atmosphere as a result of human activities is directly attributable to the destruction and degradation of tropical forests. As noted earlier, Brazil and some other Latin

American countries actually release more greenhouse gases into the air from deforestation than fossil fuel consumption.

In recognition of the fact that forests can both generate and remove carbon dioxide from the atmosphere, depending on how the resource is managed and cared for, proposals to combat global warming through various "carbon forestry" projects have proliferated. But the wisdom of pursuing this course of action has emerged as a subject of fierce debate, especially in the context of a part of the Kyoto Protocol known as the Clean Development Mechanism (CDM).

The Clean Development Mechanism provides for project-based "emissions trading" between developed nations (which are legally bound to the Kyoto agreement) and developing nations (which are not). The stated goals of the CDM are to help developed countries comply with their binding emission targets, assist developing countries in achieving sustainable development goals, and contribute to the ultimate objective of the Kyoto convention—stabilization and reduction of atmospheric greenhouse gas concentrations (Goldemberg 1998). Under the CDM, private companies, utilities, and governments from industrialized nations will be able to invest in projects in developing countries that both reduce carbon emissions and contribute to sustainable development. The investor country will be rewarded for its participation with credit that is applied toward its Kyoto target.

Two types of forestry projects have been touted as suitable for CDM consideration. The first category is the "sink enhancement" project, which aims to increase a forest's capacity to absorb carbon. Tree plantations and afforestation/reforestation schemes to expand the area or density of damaged forests fit under this type. The second category is the "source emission reduction" project, which utilizes protected area designations and sustainable management concepts to safeguard natural forests from high-impact logging, mining, or land conversion and thus keep carbon sinks intact (World Conservation Union 2002).

But the vague language of the Kyoto Protocol has given rise to considerable disagreement over whether forestry and other land-use change projects are permissible under the Clean Development Mechanism. In addition, many observers feel that giving the green light to such projects under the auspices of Kyoto would impact the environment in a number of harmful ways. Proponents, however, claim that these projects could effectively fight climate change while also safeguarding tropical forests and the biological diversity contained therein. The divergence of opinion about this subject extends to the environmental community, where organizations such as Greenpeace and Friends of the Earth have come out firmly against the concept (Friends of the

Clearing the Air in Mexico City

Mexico City is one of the largest cities in the world. Home to more than 18 million people in its sprawling metropolitan area, this capital city is the economic, political, and social heart of the country. But the air quality in the city has long been notoriously foul, in part because the city sprawls across a valley floor ringed by mountains that restrict dispersal of pollutants, and in part because its factories, power plants, and burgeoning motor vehicle fleet spew enormous volumes of emissions into the air. Carbon monoxide, nitrous oxides, sulfur dioxide, tropospheric ozone, hydrocarbons, and suspended particulate matter (SPM)—all swirl about the heads of Mexico City's residents in levels that often exceed international safety guidelines. By 1999, Mexico City's air and water quality had become so poor that the World Resources Institute called it the unhealthiest city in the world for small children to live in.

The single greatest factor in Mexico City's poor air quality is its exploding transport sector. Certainly, emissions from industry, agriculture, and municipal sectors play a part in creating the smog and haze that commonly bedevil the city. But in the late 1990s it was estimated that the transport sector was responsible for fully 70 percent of air pollution emissions in Mexico City. In turn, most of this pollution stems from the city's automobiles, the number of which increased fourfold between 1970 and 1996 (Instituto Nacional de

Estadistica 1998; UN Environment Programme 2002).

During the 1990s, air pollution in Mexico City reached such critical levels that the government imposed a string of measures designed to reduce emissions—or at least reduce exposure of vulnerable children to their effects. These measures, many of them introduced under an Air Quality Program that ran from 1995 to 2000, included restrictions on outdoor activities during periods of particularly poor air quality; school and factory closures on high-pollution days; limitations on the use of private automobiles (especially older models that emit higher levels of pollutants) to certain times or days of the week; and introduction of catalytic converters and low-sulfur gasoline. In addition to tightening pollution standards for vehicles, authorities also took steps to relocate heavy industry on the city's outskirts, away from high-density commercial and residential areas, to increase power plant usage of clean-burning natural gas, and to finance air quality improvement initiatives through new taxes on gasoline.

These measures actually produced tangible results, and in a relatively short time frame. Mexico City's airborne concentrations of lead, sulfur dioxide, carbon monoxide, and nitrogen dioxide have all been reduced to levels that meet international safety norms on most days. Nonetheless, the city's air quality remains far inferior to that of

(continues)

A major street in the Miguel Hidalgo area of Mexico City is clogged with traffic and smog during the morning rush hour. STEPHANIE MAZE/CORBIS

most other cities, with high levels of ozone and fine particulate air pollution looming as areas of particular concern.

Cognizant of the need for further action to reduce health risks for Mexico City's citizens—and of the growing threat of emissions from expanding populations and economic activity—Mexico City has launched a new round of initiatives designed to make further inroads in its stubborn air pollution problem. Indeed, Mexico City is "set to become the first city with its own climate action programme. The ambitious 2002–2010 Valley of Mexico Metropolitan Area Air Quality Improvement Programme, nicknamed Proaire III, will set a global precedent if it succeeds in its aim to reduce health expenditures through air quality management" (Talli 2002).

This ambitious plan, which is to be administrated by a Metropolitan Environmental Commission composed of representatives from federal, regional, and city agencies, has a special focus on bringing down high levels of ozone and fine particulate air pollution, but it also contains a host of measures targeting other types of air pollution. Built on two smaller initiatives introduced in the 1990s (Proaire I and Proaire II), the Proaire III air quality management scheme relies on a blend of emission abatement measures, environmental education proposals, and citizen participation programs. Altogether, it calls for $12 billion to $15 billion of public and private investment in more than 80 individual projects that together aim to achieve reductions of 18 percent in suspended particulates

(continues)

produced from car fuel, 16 percent in sulfur dioxide, 26 percent in carbon monoxide, 43 percent in nitrogen dioxide, and 17 percent in hydrocarbons over the ten-year life of the program. Realization of these goals would constitute a major public health triumph, as Proaire III's authors believe that up to $4 billion worth of benefits could be saved every year in avoided deaths, illnesses, lost time at work, and associated expenses.

Many of the Proaire III initiatives specifically address emissions from the fast-growing transport sector, such as a project to replace the city's 30,000 high-polluting microbuses with a fleet of new buses with higher passenger capacity and the ability to use cleaner fuels. Similarly, the program aims to give owners of taxicabs —among the most notorious polluters of Mexico City's streets and neighborhoods— financial incentives to buy newer cars. Another plank in the program is a set of new regulations for high-polluting trucks that place greater restrictions on their use and hours of operation. The initiative also seeks to accelerate the city's transition away from coal and oil to natural gas in its industrial and energy sectors, and calls for changes in virtually every institutional sector, from adoption of more stringent local zoning regulations to greater emphasis on green space conservation.

The authors of the Proaire III program and its many proponents in Mexico City and around the world contend that if it is implemented correctly—and adequately funded—it can be a model for other cities that are grappling with sprawl, transport, and other growth issues. Advocates acknowledge, however, that it won't achieve its goals without steadfast political support and effective administrative performance.

Sources:

Ezcurra, Exequiel, et al., eds. 1999. *The Basin of Mexico: Critical Environmental Issues and Sustainability.* New York: United Nations.

Instituto Nacional de Estadística, Geografía e Informática. 1998. *Estadísticas del medio ambiente. Mexico, 1997.* Aguascalientes, Mexico: INEGI.

Simon, Joel. 1997. *Endangered Mexico: An Environment on the Edge.* San Francisco: Sierra Club Books.

Talli, Nauman. 2002. "Mexico City's Battle for Cleaner Air." *Contemporary Review* 281 (November).

UN Environment Programme. 2002. *Global Environment Outlook 3 (GEO-3).* London: UNEP and Earthscan.

Earth 1997) and other international environmental groups such as the Nature Conservancy have championed it as a valuable tool, especially in places like Latin America where potential "Kyoto forests" abound (Rotter and Danish 2000).

Opponents of inclusion of forestry projects in CDM cite several areas of concern. They claim that carbon forestry projects would too often tend toward schemes that are inconsistent with biodiversity protection. For example, they fear that timber interests would seize on the fact that young, growing forests absorb higher quantities of carbon than mature, old-growth forests as a justification to harvest the latter and replace them with monocultural plantations (Friends of the Earth 1997). Objections have also been raised that carbon forestry projects might simply shift logging and other activities that produce carbon releases to other ecologically fragile locations, a phenomenon known as "leakage." Detractors also assert that projects too often bypass the economic and social concerns of surrounding communities, and they point out that some developing countries have expressed deep concern that CDM project financing could ultimately result in the loss of other forms of development assistance. Finally, critics claim that carbon forestry projects obscure the essential need for countries around the world to reduce their consumption of fossil fuels responsible for climate change. "Even if massive forestation took place world-wide, this would only postpone the need to drastically reduce carbon emissions," charged one international environmental organization. "This is because the forest would only capture and store carbon during its years of growth. Once it reached equilibrium, although the forest would provide a long-term carbon store, overall it would cease to act as a carbon sink" (ibid.).

However, supporters of carbon forestry projects—both within and outside of the CDM framework—offer equally spirited defenses of the concept. "That it is possible to conceptualize a bad forestry project is not a reason to eliminate all forestry projects, especially given the important role of forestry activities in climate change," responded one Nature Conservancy official involved in the organization's Latin America program. "If the IPCC is correct in its calculations of the extent to which anthropogenic greenhouse gas emissions [need] to be reduced to prevent global climate risks, then it behooves all observers to encourage the development of sound projects that protect forests, promote sustainable forestry practices, and provide greenhouse gas mitigation benefits" (Rotter and Danish 2000).

Proponents of carbon forestry projects—whether they take the form of conservation initiatives or reforestation schemes—say that they can trigger a cascade of social and environmental benefits ranging from biodiversity and watershed protection to transfers of sustainable forest technology and encouragement of ecotourism and other nonextractive sources of income for local communities (ibid.). The UN Development Programme has weighed in with the perspective that forest conservation "offers the greatest confluence of climate and biodiversity benefits and presents significant emission reduction opportunities. . . . The optimistic scenario is one where developing countries take a different path and minimize or in some cases avoid the choking smog and accompanying human deaths, massive deforestation, and species loss that developed countries [have] experienced. Developing countries may find ways of sustainably using their biological resources so that livelihoods can be realized while maintaining resource productivity in terms of local and global climate, biological diversity, water purification, and myriad other services just beginning to be recognized " (Goldemberg 1998).

Advocates of carbon forestry projects also point to several existing programs in Latin America and the Caribbean as unmitigated successes in meeting biodiversity protection, GHG mitigation, and community outreach goals. The Rio Bravo Carbon Sequestration Project in Belize has been characterized as one that has enabled area communities to make an economically successful transition away from farming toward sustainable forest management. In Bolivia, Noel Kempff Mercade National Park is the site of the world's largest carbon forestry project. In this project, the Nature Conservancy joined in a partnership with three U.S. energy companies and the Fundación Amigos de la Naturaleza (FAN) to protect 1.5 million acres of forest from logging by acquired a logging concession and placing the land within newly drawn park boundaries. The arrangement safeguards species-rich tropical forest that is home to jaguars, giant river otters, and nine species of macaws, and preserves a resource capable of absorbing up to 26 million tons of carbon over the next thirty years (Nature Conservancy 1999).The agreement also stipulates that the timber company will implement sustainable forestry principles on its other existing concessions, and not use money received from the deal to acquire new concessions (ibid.). "This kind of success has attracted the attention of some potential major investors and of developing countries, particularly in Latin America, with huge forests but insufficient resources to protect them," stated the Union of Concerned Scientists. "With the right policies to motivate properly designed and implemented projects, countries can work together to pull off the triple play of fighting climate change, protecting tropical forests, and preserving biological diversity" (Goetze 1999).

Sources:

Anderson, Stephan, and K. Madhava Sarma. 2003. *Protecting the Ozone Layer: The United Nations History.* London: Earthscan.

Baumert, Kevin A., et al. 2002. *Building on the Kyoto Protocol: Options for Protecting the Climate.* Washington, DC: World Resources Institute.

Chandler, William, et al. 2002. *Climate Change Mitigation in Developing Countries: Brazil, China, India, Mexico, South Africa, and Turkey.* Washington, DC: Pew Center on Global Climate Change.

Downie, David. 1999. "The Power to Destroy: Understanding Stratospheric Ozone Politics as a Common Pool Resource Problem." In *Anarchy and the Environment: The International Relations of Common Pool Resources.* Edited by J. Samuel Barkin and George Shambaugh. Albany: State University of New York Press.

Ezcurra, Exequiel, et al., eds. 1999. *The Basin of Mexico: Critical Environmental Issues and Sustainability.* New York: United Nations.

Follegatti, Jose Luis Lopez. 1999. "Ilo: A City in Transformation." *Environment and Urbanization* 11, no. 2 (October).

Friends of the Earth. 1997. *Forests and Climate Change.* Washington, DC: Greenpeace.

Goetze, Darren. 1999. "Triple Play." *Nucleus* 21 (spring).

Goldemberg, José, ed. 1998. *Issues and Options: The Clean Development Mechanism.* Washington, DC: UN Development Programme.

Hardoy, Jorge E., Diana Mitlin, and David Satterthwaite. 2001. *Environmental Problems in an Urbanizing World: Finding Solutions for Cities in Africa, Asia, and Latin America.* London: Earthscan.

Intergovernmental Panel on Climate Change. 2000. *The Regional Impacts of Climate Change: An Assessment of Vulnerability.* Geneva: IPCC.

———. 2001a. *Climate Change 2001: Mitigation, Impacts, Adaptation, and Vulnerability: Summaries for Policymakers.* Geneva: IPCC.

———. 2001b. *Climate Change 2001: The Scientific Basis.* Geneva: IPCC.

Jenkins, Rhys, ed. 2000. *Industry and Environment in Latin America.* London: Routledge.

Lemos, Maria Carmen de Mello. 1998. "The Politics of Pollution Control in Brazil: State Actors and Social Movements Cleaning Up Cubatão." *World Development* 26.

National Research Council. 1996. *Transportation Options for Megacities of the Developing World.* Washington, DC: National Academy Press.

Nature Conservancy. 1999. *Climate Action: Noel Kempff Mercado National Park (Bolivia).* Washington, DC: Nature Conservancy.

Population Reference Bureau. 2002. *World Population Data Sheet 2002.* Available at http://www.prb.org/pdf/worldpopulationDS02_eng.pdf (accessed January 2003).

Preston, Julia. 1999. "A Fatal Case of Fatalism." *New York Times,* February 14.

"The Right to Drive or the Right to Breathe? Air Pollution in Latin America." 2002. *Economist* (March 9).

Ristroph, Elisabeth Barrett. 2000. "Law and Odour." *Alternatives* 26 (summer).

Romieu, Isabelle, Henyk Weitzenfeld, and Jacobo Finkelman. 1990. "Urban Air Pollution in Latin America and the Caribbean: Health Perspectives." *World Health Statistics Quarterly* 23.

Rotter, Jonathan, and Kyle Danish. 2000. "Forest Carbon and the Kyoto Protocol's Clean Development Mechanism." *Journal of Forestry* 98 (May).

Simon, Joel. 1997. *Endangered Mexico: An Environment on the Edge.* San Francisco: Sierra Club.

Sperling, Daniel, and Deborah Salon. 2002. "Transportation in Developing Countries: An Overview of Greenhouse Gas Reduction Strategies." Prepared for the Pew Center on Global Climate Change. Washington, DC: May.

Stockholm Environment Institute. 1999. *Atmospheric Environment Issues in Developing Countries.* Stockholm: SEI.

UN Development Programme. 2000. *World Energy Assessment: Energy and the Challenge of Sustainability.* New York: UNDP.

UN Development Programme, UN Environment Programme, World Bank, and World Resources Institute. 1998. *World Resources 1998–1999.* Washington, DC: World Resources Institute.

——. 2000. *World Resources 2000–2001: People and Ecosystems: The Fraying Web of Life.* Washington, DC: World Resources Institute.

UN Economic Commission for Latin America and the Caribbean and UN Environment Programme. 2001. "The Sustainability of Development in Latin America and the Caribbean: Challenges and Opportunities." Report prepared for World Summit on Sustainable Development, Rio de Janeiro, October 23–24.

UN Environment Programme. 1998. *Production and Consumption of Ozone Depleting Substances 1986–1996.* Nairobi, Kenya: UNEP Ozone Secretariat.

——. 1999. *Caribbean Environment Outlook.* Kingston, Jamiaca: UNEP.

——. 2000a. *Action on Ozone, 2000.* Nairobi: UNEP.

——. 2000b. *GEO Latin America and the Caribbean Environment Outlook.* Mexico City: UNEP.

——. 2001. *GEO: Environmental Statistics for Latin America and the Caribbean.* Mexico City: UNEP Regional Office for Latin America and the Caribbean.

——. 2002. *Global Environment Outlook 3 (GEO-3).* London: UNEP and Earthscan.

UN Food and Agriculture Organization. 2001. *State of the World's Forests 2001.* Rome: FAO.

World Conservation Union-IUCN and UN Environment Programme. 2002. *Carbon, Forests and People: Towards the Integrated Management of Carbon Sequestration, the Environment and Sustainable Livelihoods.* Gland, Switzerland: IUCN and UNEP.

World Energy Council. 2001. *Energy Markets in Transition: The Latin American and Caribbean Experience.* London: World Energy Council.

World Health Organization. 1999. *Air Quality Guidelines.* Geneva: WHO.

Environmental
Activism
—KATHRYN MILES

The environmental movement in Latin America has been forced to battle through years of political unrest, economic crisis, and neglect of natural resources. But while still in its infancy in many ways, the region's environmental community has embraced an ambitious conservation mandate in myriad environmental areas, from reducing air and water pollution to preserving biologically significant wild habitat.

Even the most optimistic conservationists working in the region concede that the battle to ensure a worthwhile environmental legacy for future generations is a daunting one. Indeed, prevailing socioeconomic and political trends in Latin America make it one of the most ecologically vulnerable regions on the globe. From Mexico's Baja California to Argentina's Cape Horn, the region's natural wealth is being harvested and liquidated at a dizzying rate to meet local, national, and global appetites for timber, minerals, food, and other goods. "For almost five centuries, the natural heritage of Latin America and the Caribbean has contributed to the development of the industrialized countries, which has consequently given rise to the increasingly accelerated deterioration being experienced in the region," declared one analysis. "The industrialized countries have therefore incurred an ecological debt to the developing world, which now involves the obligation to support the sustainable development of poor countries to prevent further deterioration in the delicate balance of the planet's environment" (UN Environment Programme 1992).

There are countless examples of this "ecological debt" in modern Latin America. But environmental degradation is neither a new nor wholly Western phenomenon. Indeed, significant alteration of the Latin American environment occurred prior to Western colonization. Mexico, for instance, has "suffered the greatest environmental alterations in history. When the Europeans arrived in Mexico in 1519, they found the region already greatly transformed by waterworks constructed for the *chinampa* agriculture, by deforestation in the north of the basin, and by faunal extinction. The rate of the environmental change, however, has increased continuously since then . . . [and] awareness of the problem by different social groups has increased accordingly" (Ezcurra 1999)

A similar rate of change has affected other countries and cultures in the region. In much of Central America, for instance, rapid changes in sociopolitical systems have taken place with little regard for their impact on the natural environment. The effects of this lack of protection—rapid deforestation, watershed degradation, loss of fertility in soils, habitat fragmentation, biodiversity loss, unsustainable harvesting of fisheries and other resources, and environmentally compromised coastal areas—are only now becoming fully realized.

But in spite of—and perhaps because of—these obstacles, a strong movement of protection and conservation has risen in modern Latin America. Each culture within the region has nurtured environmental advocacy groups that are working to ensure that the region's resources remain protected and vibrant in the twenty-first century. But although Latin American environmental activism has taken root in a broad spectrum of cultures, religions, and biospheres, common themes are evident across the region. From the fledgling forest conservation organizations of the nineteenth century to the first governmental organizations of the early twentieth century and, finally, the grassroots and international environmental groups of this century, countries in Latin America have followed a remarkably similar track in their quest to implement sustainable conservation models that will safeguard the region's land, air, and water resources.

The Nascent Movement: 1800s–1950

Like any colonized region, Latin America found itself battling something of a cultural war in the eighteenth and nineteenth centuries. Indigenous peoples had developed their own systems of utilizing and celebrating the natural world, but many of these systems were at odds with those of the European settlers. These early colonizers initially demonstrated little interest in preserving or protecting the natural world. The Spanish monarchs Charles III and Charles IV had encouraged the creation of botanical gardens and the study of the flora and fauna of Spanish colonies in the region, but there was little initial interest in preserving the unique environment of the colonies. With the arrival of Prussian naturalist Baron Alexander von Humboldt in the early 1800s, however, conservation found a place within much of the region.

The Rio de Janeiro Earth Summit

Children greet a mascot during the 1992 Earth Summit in Rio de Janeiro, Brazil. ROBERT MAASS/CORBIS

In June of 1992, Rio de Janeiro hosted more than 30,000 visitors from around the world, including heads of more than 175 states and delegates from over 1,000 environmental organizations, for the UN Earth Summit, the largest environmental conference ever held.

Planning for the conference began several years prior, as the United Nations formed a preparatory committee, known as the PrepCom. Both Deputy Foreign Minister Andres Rozental of Mexico and Ambassador Ricupero of Brazil served as planning delegates for PrepCom. The summit itself was moderated by Brazil's president Collor, and it allowed the country to undertake capital improvements and educate the world about Brazilian culture.

As the world watched, delegates accomplished what many had deemed impossible. Against international skepticism, high-ranking governmental officials worked tirelessly with the world's leading NGOs to pass five basic agreements on future environmental action. "Government officials and ministers in Rio had to conclude in two weeks, what hundreds of diplomats could not resolve over the past two years. What was expected to be a two-week gold-pen cum massive photo opportunity quickly evolved into the most critical negotiation session" (UN Environment Programme, n.d.).

The five principal agreements reached at the Rio Summit consisted of a convention on biological diversity, principles of forest management, a convention on climate change, the Rio

(continues)

declaration on environment and development, and Agenda 21, a plan for sustainable development around the world. The latter agreement was divided into four sections: Social and Economic Dimensions, Conservation and Management of Resources for Development, Strengthening the Role of Major Groups, and The Means of Implementation. Although these four planning areas are of obvious importance for all nations and regions, they held special meaning for the countries of Latin America, where environmental issues and socioeconomic development issues are closely intertwined. Many of the goals established by Agenda 21 spoke directly to the environmental problems of Latin America.

In many regards, the Rio summit provided the impetus needed to work toward solutions for these very problems. Nearly all Latin American countries published a Post-Rio Report, which detailed the summit's events and drew national media attention (Scherr et al. 1993). Additionally, individual countries made significant strides in their environmental campaigns. Cuba, for instance, established a Commission on Climate Change immediately following the convention; the first charge of that commission was studying the emission of greenhouse gases in the country. Similarly, Mexican president Salinas came home from the convention and created the National Biodiversity Use and Documentation Commission (CONABIO), an organization bringing together

scientists and politicians in the name of protecting biodiversity.

But these initiatives were just the beginning. Following the earth summit, Belize greatly augmented its protected-area system by creating additional national parks. In addition, it initiated a program of environmental studies in school curricula and conducted environmental workshops for the tourism sector (ibid.). Some of the most sweeping changes following the Rio Summit occurred in Ecuador. Following the return of their Earth Summit delegate, Diego Cordovez, the Ecuadorian government undertook several steps to preserve the commitments made in Rio. The first was to ratify the UN conventions on climate change and biodiversity. Other actions included the creation of a Programme for the Environment and programs that would involve NGOs in decisions about and policies for the environment.

The summit also allowed for the creation of additional multilateral initiatives. One particularly significant program is EcoLogic and the EcoLogic Development Fund. Created out of a mandate from environmental leaders at the summit, EcoLogic brought together representatives of the indigenous peoples of Latin America, environmental activists, and international scholars and scientists. Its objective is to empower local peoples to protect and sustain their ecosystems while promoting social justice. Since its creation, EcoLogic has aided in the protection of more than 1 million acres of rain forests and wetlands in Belize,

(continues)

Honduras, Guatemala, Mexico, and Costa Rica.

Sources:

Robinson, Nicholas A., ed. 1993. *Agenda 21: Earth's Action Plan.* New York: Oceania.

Scherr, S. Jacob, et al. 1993. *One Year after Rio.* New York: Natural Resources Defense Council.

UN Conference on Environment and Development. 1992. "Earth Summit: Press Summary of Agenda 21." New York: United Nations.

UN Environment Programme. "Earth Negotiations Bulletin." N.d. Available at http://www.unep.org/ unep/ partners/un/unced/home.htm

Von Humboldt—accompanied by the French botanist Aime-Jacques-Alexandre Goujoud Bonpland—explored much of the Amazon basin and Mexico. Although his initial aim was exploring and mapping areas previously unknown to Western Europe, his mission took a decidedly environmental turn when he discovered the natural splendor of the tropical climate. Through his work with native tribes in South America, von Humboldt learned of the medicinal properties of many of the plants in the region, and he successfully urged the European governments to begin protecting these resources (von Humboldt 1811).

Von Humboldt's warnings about the danger of deforesting the region were heard by a small group of wealthy white settlers, who took up the cause and advocated against the dramatic cutting practices in the region. But these advocates were mired in an intricate web of economic and social systems that made their cause a difficult one: "Although von Humboldt had given clear warnings about the negative consequences of deforesting the basin's slopes, the ruling classes had little knowledge of the ecological services of forests as efficient regulators of water flows. On the other hand, the non-sustainable exploitation of natural resources was blamed on the indigenous groups who logged the forests for wood and for coal. More attention was devoted in the nineteenth century to the damaging effects of the logging of old-growth forests by impoverished Indian villagers" (Ezcurra 1999).

Interested parties continued their struggle, however, and in Mexico they were joined by Miguel Ángel de Quevedo, known as "El Apóstol del Arbol" (The Apostle of Trees). De Quevedo was the president of the newly formed Junta Central de Bosques, a lobbying organization formed in the early 1900s. The junta, widely acknowledged as the first environmental organization in Latin America, was also one of its most successful: shortly after its formation, the junta became an official advisor to the Mexican government and effectively aided in the first protective measures aimed at Mexico's natural resources. Meanwhile, Quevedo became something of a folk hero as he sought to single-handedly reforest the Mexican basin. He created a giant nursery in Los Viveros de Coyoacán, and by 1914 the program was producing over 2 million trees a year. Quevedo was also integral to the creation of natural resource protection polices included in Mexico's 1917 constitution (ibid.).

This era also witnessed the creation of Mexico's national park system. The first national park, Desierto de los Leones, was created in 1917. Named by a group of Carmelite monks whose order dictated that they must have "una casa de Desierto" (a house in the wilderness), this area became an official national park after President Venustiano Carranza signed a decree allowing for the official protection of the forest. Carranza's successor, President Lázaro Cárdenas, continued his work protecting the Mexican landscape. Between 1936 and 1939 the Cárdenas government oversaw the creation of twenty national parks and protected places in the Mexican basin. But these proved to be little more than "paper parks," and their designation did little to stop the degradation of Mexico's protected places. In fact, the deterioration of the newly minted national parks began within months of their creation. In 1946, for example, one of Mexico's largest paper factories received permission to launch timber felling operations in forests contained within El Ajusco, and these operations continued for six years (ibid.).

Following Mexico's lead, other countries in Latin America began to create policy that would allow for the protection of their wild and scenic places. With the Convention on Nature Protection and Wildlife Preservation in the Western Hemisphere in 1940, countries in Latin America made formal their commitment to the nascent modern environmental movement by pledging to protect land through the creation of national parks and reserves. It was not until some years later, however, that the region saw this goal realized. Indeed, it would take the scientific movement of the 1950s and the emergence of community-based environmental activism shortly thereafter to ensure that Latin America would take decisive steps to protect vital habitat from exploitation.

Policies of Protection:
The Second Wave, 1950–1980
The preservation of Latin America's environment took on a decidedly scientific cast in the 1950s. In 1952 in Mexico, biologist Enrique Beltrán founded the Instituto Mexicano de Recursos Naturales Renovables (Mexican Institute for Renewable Resources), an organization that sought to control the use of resources and ensure their sustainability. Meanwhile, in Ecuador, a group of

Jaguars rank as Latin America's largest feline predator. TOM BRAKEFIELD/CORBIS

scientists working with UNESCO and the World Conservation Union created the Charles Darwin Foundation. The foundation, established in 1959, dedicated itself to conserving the Galápagos ecosystems through research and environmental education. Their headquarters, located at the newly established Galápagos National Park, offered scientists from around the world an opportunity to experience the Galápagos Archipelago much as Darwin had done 100 years prior. They also established educational opportunities for students in Latin America and visitors from around the world.

Similar work was undertaken by the World Wildlife Fund (now the World Wide Fund for Nature). Founded in the United States in 1961, the WWF quickly focused its attention on Latin America. Of the five projects undertaken during its first year, two were dedicated to Latin American concerns. Additionally, its largest project—an initiative to protect the giant grebe of Guatemala—was one of the largest programs undertaken by the WWF. That same year, the WWF helped Colombian conservationists establish a small nature reserve. Other international nongovernmental organizations (NGOs) became involved in Latin America conservation efforts around this time as well, including the International Council for Bird Preservation (ICBP) and the International Union for the Conservation of Nature-IUCN (now the World Conservation Union).

Much of the reason that the WWF chose to focus its early energies on Latin America was the scarcity of private groups and initiatives within the region. The presence of the WWF did much to raise the awareness of local inhabitants, and it paved the way for a dramatic rise in private participation. Several years later, the Audubon Society founded a branch in Belize. This conservation group worked not only to save Belize's diverse bird population but also the habitats in which they live.

These organizations were greatly aided by the U.S. Catholic Council of Bishops. In 1965 the U.S. Council of Bishops approved an annual collection of funds and services aimed at aiding pastoral projects in Latin America and the Caribbean. This support quickly bloomed into a more comprehensive environmental plan, which included the creation of an officially sanctioned "eco-justice" conference. The Catholic Church's willingness to engage Latin American governments and communities on conservation issues proved to be enormously important. As the overwhelmingly predominant religion in much of the region, Catholicism is the very foundation of most cultural belief systems. By instituting environmental action within the church, Catholic bishops legitimized environmental protection in many Latin American countries.

In the meantime, several regional governments signaled that environmental issues were emerging as a higher priority. Indeed, countries such as Costa Rica began taking active steps to undo some of the environmental injustices of the past. In 1961, Costa Rica established the "Instituto de Tierras y Colonización" to redistribute land among the working *campensinos*, who had been stripped of much of their land in the previous century. Similar land reform was undertaken in Honduras, though with limited success. In too many instances, the land that was transferred back into indigenous hands was only marginally suitable for farming and other purposes.

Work by countries like Costa Rica was aided by the United Nations, which passed a series of acts and conventions directed toward environmental matters in Latin America. Some of the acts passed at this time included the Agreement for the Establishment of a Latin American Forestry Research and Training Institute (1959), the Treaty for the Prohibition of Nuclear Weapons in Latin America (1967), the Convention on International Trade in Endangered Species of Wild Fauna and Flora (CITES) (1973), and the Treaty for Amazonian Co-operation (1978). These acts, which came with international support, bolstered the work of NGO organizations and individuals throughout Latin America. They also set a standard that rapidly changing governmental systems felt pressured to uphold.

The United Nations also worked to unite Latin American governments under the auspices of environmental protection. In 1971, the Economic Commission for Latin America and the Caribbean and the UN Environment Programme (UNEP) organized a conference in which linkages between low levels of development and environmental degradation were emphasized. Indeed, participants in the conference indicated that "the development problems of the region were perhaps more closely linked to those of the environment than in any other developing region in the world" (UN Economic Commission for Latin America and the Caribbean 1991). These conclusions did not go unheard in Latin America, and governmental and nongovernmental organizations alike used these findings as a launching point for their endeavors.

That same year, an agronomist named José Lutzemberger joined with a group of Brazilian professionals to form the Gaucho Association for the Protection of the Natural Environment (AGAPAN). This group represented one of the first organized environmental associations in Brazil's history; it was also the country's first fully nonprofit organization. Lutzemberger went on to become something of an environmental hero in Brazil. His book *The End of the Future: A Brazilian Ecological Manifesto* received great national and international attention, and in 1987 Lutzemberger became president of Brazil's

Gaia Foundation, an organization that emphasizes recycling and agricultural sustainability.

This was also the era of Brazil's legendary Rubber Tapper campaign. The massive harvesting of the Brazilian rain forest had left smaller sustainable farmers and collectors of forest by-products (nuts, bark, etc.) without a viable ecosystem to support their work or lifestyle. Led by Chico Mendes, a labor organizer and supporter of environmental justice, rubber tappers launched a series of standoffs designed to stop industry and large ranches from further encroaching upon the soil. The first of these standoffs was in 1976; it was followed by hundreds of similar acts over the next decade. Environmental historian Ramachandra Guha estimates that over the course of this ten-year campaign, rubber tappers managed to save 2 million acres of forest (Guha 2000).

Meanwhile, Mexico continued its trend of institutionalizing environmentalism through a series of acts that coupled private and governmental resources. In 1972, environmental and human rights activist Iván Restepo created the Centro de Ecodesarrollo (CECODES: Centre for Eco-development), an organization that seeks to inform citizens about environmental problems through a series of publications. Viewed as militant and overly leftist in its thinking by some, the Centro has not been without its controversy. The more moderate Instituto de Ecologia (Institute of Ecology), founded by Gonzalo Halffter in 1974, works more directly with government and mainstream organizations to achieve the goals of environmentalism. The Instituto's primary focus is that of environmental assessments, and their production of these documents was the first of its kind in Mexico.

Much of the environmental policy created in Mexico during the 1970s was the work of presidents Luis Echeverria and José López-Portillo, who served a combined twelve years, from 1970 to 1982. Plagued with ever-worsening air quality that had sparked international attention, Echeverria and his government committed time and resources to the study of emissions and environmental planning. In 1971, Echeverria proposed and passed the landmark Law on Environmental Protection, and his successor, López-Portillo, created the Subsecretariat of Environmental Improvement (Subsecreatria de Mejoramiento del Ambiente, or SMA).

Similar actions were undertaken elsewhere in Latin America as private and governmental groups sought creative ways to bring attention to environmental problems and ensure their solution. Guatemala signed the Convention Concerning the Protection of the World Cultural and Natural Heritage Act in 1979, and shortly thereafter the country placed one of its premier national parks, Tikal National Park, on the heritage list. Although the park had been in existence since 1955, this move represented a significant change in the plan for conservation in Latin America. "By joining together the concept of nature and culture, which had previously been regarded as separate or even opposing elements, the Convention permits a sound management of both the archeological heritage, which is the chief concern in this case, and the extremely valuable natural heritage of the area" (UN Economic Commission for Latin America and the Caribbean 1991).

This conception of the environment as natural heritage spurred other countries to take similar action. In Argentina in 1977, a group of scientists, teachers, and business people all committed to raising environmental awareness formed the Fundación Vida Silvestre Argentina (FVSA). The FVSA, an NGO, works to preserve the biodiversity of Argentina through a series of educational and land grant initiatives. What is unusual about the FVSA is its ability to act like a government when the actual government of Argentina fails to do so. To that end, the FVSA forms treaties with private industry, creates reserves and parks with its own funds, and publishes reports on the state of the environment in Argentina.

Working in concert with organizations like the FVSA, the World Wildlife Fund deepened its presence in Latin America during this decade. One of the largest WWF projects of this era was the Minimum Critical Size of Ecosystems Project in the Brazilian Amazon. This initiative brought together environmental activists and scholars from North and Latin America. Not only did this alliance alert environmentalists throughout North America to the problems of environmental degradation in Latin America, but it also allowed the two regions to begin sharing resources and information. Doing so undoubtedly set the stage for the explosion of environmental organizations and movements in Latin America that took place in the final two decades of the twentieth century.

The Modern Movement: 1980–Present

Environmental concerns reached unprecedented levels in Latin America during the last decades of the twentieth century. A dramatic increase in NGO organizations demonstrated the real concern about and commitment to the environment held by citizens of Latin American countries. Growing public awareness of environmental problems soon filtered into the political arena, and governments responded by enacting a multitude of environmental acts aimed at preserving the declining health of the region's forests, wetlands, rivers, farmlands, and coastal areas.

A study of late-twentieth-century Mexico does much to illuminate the more general environmental trends in the region. Beginning in 1981, Mexico witnessed a sort of conservation boom in both governmental and private

232 LATIN AMERICA and the CARIBBEAN

sectors. During the 1980s, a series of important new conservation groups emerged. In 1981, a group of environmentalists founded ProNatura, a conservation organization dedicated to education and lobbying. Other groups that formed around this period included the Pro-Mariposa Monarca (1980), the Mexican Ecologist Movement (1981), Biocenosis (1982), Alianza Ecologista Nacional/National Ecological Alliance (1984), and the Grupo de los Cien/Group of 100 (1985) (Simonian 1995). The latter organization, formed by poet Homero Arijdis, boasted members that included the most prominent Mexican artists and intellectuals of the era. Their participation in conservationism brought much needed publicity and stature to the movement (Ezcurra 1999).

Many of these organizations, including the influential Mexican Ecologist Movement (MEM) and the Ecological Association of Coyoacán, function in dual capacities as both neighborhood associations and political pressure organizations. The membership of most Mexican environmental groups—of which there were more than 1,000 in the late 1990s—is middle-class and educated, but few managed to reach any meaningful levels of national membership and thus focused primarily on local and regional issues (Simonian 1995).

Meanwhile, in the Mexican government, environmentalism found its footing in policy, largely as a result of the work of presidents Miguel de la Madrid and Carlos Salinas de Gortari. Under the leadership of these individuals, Mexico experienced what scholars have described as the "second generation" of environmentalism. During their tenure, environmental concerns became a much higher priority in policy decisions, and several governmental agencies exclusively devoted to the environment were created. New environmental regulations and programs were passed during this period as well (Ezcurra 1999).

Under the direction of one of these new agencies—the Secretaria de Desarrollo Urbano y Ecologia (SEDUE)—the Mexican government drafted and published an Environmental Protection Law in 1984. The law set higher standards for emissions and the use of natural resources, many of which had been established the previous year during a heated session of the Mexican senate. Unfortunately, these regulations have been poorly enforced in subsequent years.

Environmental activists also pressed for increased protection of valuable habitat, and in 1983, the Mexican government passed a law to protect land in El Pedregal de San Angel and, more specifically, to protect the flora and fauna indigenous to this lava field. Two years later, the government established the National Commission on Ecology (Comision Nacional de Ecologia). The commission was charged with the weighty task of evaluating environmental concerns in Mexico and establishing a list of priorities for dealing with these concerns. It was also given the responsibility of communicating with the rapidly expanding number of conservation organizations around the country.

Brazilian Environmental Activist Chico Mendes

The legendary Brazilian union organizer and environmental activist Francisco "Chico" Alves Mendes Filho was born on December 15, 1944, near the town of Xapuri in western Brazil. He was part of a large family of poor rubber tappers (workers who gather latex from rubber trees) employed by wealthy estate owners in the area. Even as a child, Mendes spent long days working deep in the Amazon rain forest to help support his family. He started out by collecting firewood and hauling water, and he later learned the craft of draining latex out of rubber trees. Encouraged by his father, he developed a deep appreciation for the natural world around him during his youth. "I became an ecologist long before I had ever heard the word," he once said.

Although the estate owners generally discouraged literacy in their employees, Mendes also learned to read as a boy. His father provided him with the basic background, and his education was furthered by Euclides Fernandes Tavora, a military officer from a wealthy Brazilian family. Tavora arrived in Xapuri under mysterious circumstances and soon took the bright young man under his wing. It turned out that Tavora had escaped from prison, where he was sent after taking part in a failed coup against Brazilian leader Getulio Vargas. Tavora informed his pupil that he had joined in the coup attempt because he was disgusted by the huge gap between rich and poor in Brazilian society. Mendes and his tutor entered into many political discussions that had a strong influence on the young man.

During the 1960s Mendes began teaching other rubber tappers to read. He also started writing letters to Brazilian authorities complaining about the unfair treatment they received at the hands of wealthy estate owners. In 1964 the government of Brazil was overthrown in a military coup. The newly installed government encouraged clearing of the rain forest for ranching and development. Although the rubber tappers and native Indians who lived in the Amazon rain forest paid the price for these policies—through flooding, soil erosion, and the spread of disease—all of the rewards went to the wealthy and powerful landowners. By the late 1960s Mendes launched his first efforts to organize the rubber tappers into a labor union in an attempt to increase their political power.

In 1975 the rubber tappers succeeded in forming their first union, and Mendes was elected to its leadership. The union followed the principles of nonviolent protest as it lobbied for funding to build schools and hospitals and launched demonstrations that protected an estimated 3 million acres of rain forest from clearing by ranchers. The wealthy ranchers were infuriated by the union's actions, however, and often took out their hostility on Mendes and other leaders. In 1980, for example, Mendes suffered a severe beating at the hands of thugs hired by the ranchers. Several months later, union president Wilson Pinheiro was murdered. Despite escalating tension between the union and the ranchers, the movement spread

(continues)

throughout the 1980s as the rubber tappers established schools and education programs. In 1985 the rubber tappers of the Amazon united under the banner of the *Conselho Nacional dos Seringueiros* (National Council of Rubber Tappers) and began working closely with the indigenous Indian communities of the region.

During the 1980s Mendes expanded the scope of his activities from union organizing to environmental activism. During this period, the cutting and burning of Brazilian rain forests had risen to a particularly rapacious level, and it was taking a devastating toll on the environment. In addition to destroying the habitat of various animal species and wrecking the lives of rural people, the government's policies also contributed to air pollution and global warming. The environmental problems associated with the destruction of the rain forest extended beyond South America and gave the rubber tappers and Indians additional ammunition in their fight to change Brazil's policies. Mendes began to attract attention from outside Brazil in his fight to publicize the damage to the rain forest. He made numerous public appearances during the 1980s while lobbying and raising funds to support his cause. He eventually joined forces with environmental groups in the United States to convince international banking organizations to cut funding for development projects that would damage the Amazon rain forest.

By 1987, Mendes was known around the world for his efforts to save the rain forest and protect the interests of rural Brazilians. He won awards from the United Nations and the Better World Society and gained a reputation as one of the great defenders of the

(continues)

The growth of the Mexican environmental movement was mirrored throughout Latin America, as each country and culture underwent a similar transformation and organization of its conservation efforts. What follows is a brief account of the highlights of the environmental actions and policies in Latin America at this time in several of Latin America's countries and regions. Taken in sum, these initiatives demonstrate a growing commitment to environmental concerns at all levels of life and culture. They also reveal the power of coalition and cooperation.

Modern Environmental Advocacy around Latin America

In the Caribbean, much of the environmental action of this era has centered around projects jointly administered between individual countries, conservation organizations, and the UN Environment Programme. In 1974, the UNEP established a Regional Seas office and charged that office with coordinating

natural world. But Mendes's high profile also made him the chief enemy of ranchers and others who stood to gain from Brazil's policies. He received many death threats over the years and knew that his life was in danger, but he insisted upon remaining with his people in isolated Xapuri. "My blood is the same blood as that of these people suffering here," he explained. "I can't run. There's something inside me that cannot leave here. This is the place where I will finish my mission."

On December 22, 1988, Chico Mendes was killed by a shotgun blast to the chest. Brazilian authorities soon traced responsibility for the crime to a prominent family of ranchers. Mendes's death sent shock waves through Brazil and the worldwide environmental community. Thousands of rubber tappers came from across the region to attend his funeral. Although some of his enemies believed that his death would make it easier for them to benefit from the destruction of the rain forest, it only inspired his followers to fight harder to continue his mission. Today, his legacy of environmental activism continues to be recognized in numerous ways, including through the Chico Mendes Extractive Reserve, a 2.4-million-acre tract of Amazon rain forest that has been protected in his name.

Sources:

Collinson, Helen, ed. 1997. *Green Guerrillas: Environmental Conflicts and Initiatives in Latin America and the Caribbean.* Montreal: Black Rose.

Mendes, Chico. 1989. *Fight for the Forest: Chico Mendes in His Own Words.* Detroit: Inland.

Shoumatoff, Alex. 1990. *The World Is Burning: Murder in the Rain Forest.* Boston: Little, Brown.

---

the conservation efforts of various nations in the region. In concert with the Economic Commission for Latin America and a number of other UN and regional groups, UNEP's Regional Seas program adopted sixty-six long-term environmental projects designed to address a multitude of regional problems, including vulnerability to oil spills, unmonitored marine pollution from human and industrial wastes, rapid deforestation and soil erosion, inadequate protected area systems, threats to various species of flora and fauna, a paucity of trained professionals in environmental management fields, and public ignorance of the Caribbean's critical ecological issues (Mosher 1986).

The UNEP also aided in the creation of CAP, the Caribbean Action Plan. This plan, established in 1981, was the culmination of an environmental summit attended by twenty-five of the twenty-seven countries and territories in the Caribbean. The first of its kind, CAP articulated specific strategies for preserving the natural resources of the Caribbean. The objectives of CAP covered a wide range of issues, and it quickly attained significant progress in some key areas. For example, the CAP dramatically improved oil spill contingency planning in the region (ibid.). CAP also provided for the support of outreach organizations, the most successful of which was the Caribbean Conservation Association. Headquartered in Barbados, the CCA is a large grassroots organization boasting a membership of sixteen Caribbean countries. "Following CAP's creation, the association published a regional environmental education directory of existing institutions, materials, and experts, which the U.N. Environment Programme financed until the CAP trust fund had enough money. The association also produced a series of radio programs and two workshops in 1984 for the media and educators" (ibid.).

Governments in South America acted in kind. The Venezuelan government renewed its commitment to environmental concerns in 1985, when President Jaime Lusinchi launched a conservation plan as part of his Independence Day speech. In this speech, Lusinchi emphasized that the country's natural resources were finite, and he urged the Venezuelan citizenry to manage resources more efficiently for the sake of future generations (UN Economic Commission for Latin America and the Caribbean 1991). In Chile, meanwhile, environmental activists and small-scale farmers garnered a victory for the environment in 1987, when residents of Chanaral, a small town of 10,000 inhabitants, brought successful legal action against the National Copper Corporation of Chile (CODELCO), the world's leading copper producing company (ibid.).

This suit was significant not only because it demonstrated that landowners and activists could successfully battle big industry in Latin America but also because it highlighted important environmental issues. Copper production is notorious for its creation of sulfur dioxide and particulate emissions, which results in air and water pollution. The farmers of Chanaral, aided by activists, rose up against the continued production of these pollutants, thereby bringing international attention to their plight and effectively altering environmental policies for the entire nation of Chile. Similar action was taken in Santiago, Chile, where public pressure over air quality compelled the newly elected democratic government to take action. What resulted was a clean air plan, published in 1990, that outlined a three-tiered system for reducing emissions.

Some of the greatest environment strides during this period were made in Brazil, the wealthiest and most developed of the Latin American countries. Brazil is also the location of one of the most fiercely contested environmental issues on the planet during the late twentieth century: the harvesting of the Amazonian rain forest. "During most of this century, deforestation in the Brazilian Amazon was a nationally led process resulting directly from patterns of state intervention in the region manifested in large-scale colonization and integration projects. In a few decades, the region was transformed from a completely forested and sparsely populated region into a region with a high urbanization rate and an important role in national production and income. This modernization was achieved at high social and environmental costs. At that time, the Brazilian government placed particular emphasis on asserting its sovereignty over Amazonia and protecting itself against external interference. In the early 1980s, the first environmentalists concerned about the preservation of the Amazonian rainforest met with strong resistance from the Brazilian government" (de Campos Mello 2001).

The cause of preserving the Amazon rain forest was also taken up by North American and European environmental groups and a host of celebrities, all of whom brought public attention to the cause and pressure on the Brazilian government to demonstrate progress in containing the destruction. Much of the essential grassroots work on the issue, however, was undertaken by Brazilian and South American environmental groups. Their efforts have been integral to the formal protection of selected sections of the rain forest over the years. But the future of the Amazonian forest—and the biodiversity contained therein—remain in doubt today, as timber companies, ranchers, and settlements venture ever deeper into the interior.

Galvanized in part by the furor over management of the country's forest resources—and in part by political changes taking place in the country—environmental organizations flourished all across Brazil in the 1980s. "With the return of the country to democracy, the ecological movement established itself as a permanent political actor, the environmental issue became a permanent political actor, and the environmental issue became a locus for the exercise of citizen rights" (ibid.). Hundreds of small, local organizations formed during this time, their membership hailing primarily from middle-class and professional backgrounds—people with "high enough incomes to concern themselves not only with day-to-day survival but also with the quality of life in a broader sense" (Kaimowitz 1997). Since their founding, most of these groups have been primarily concerned with local issues (protection of trees and parks, pollution from nearby factories) or regional campaigns (to protect specific ecosystems such as the Atlantic forests or the watersheds of Paraná), though many have also engaged in public education campaigns about larger themes such as the impact of agrochemicals on freshwater systems (ibid.; Van der Heigden 2001).

Gradually, the mandate of a number of these groups expanded to include social justice issues as well. This melding of civil rights and environmental activism reached a crisis point in December 1988, when the environmental activist Francisco Alves Mendes Filho, known to the world as Chico Mendes, was murdered in Xapuri, Acre. Mendes was one of the first Brazilian activists who brought together social justice and the environmental cause. He worked as a union leader for *seringueiros* and led the aforementioned Rubber Tapper strikes. The United Nations awarded Mendes the "Global 500 Award" in 1987 for his work with the seringueiros; with this award came greater publicity and public awareness, which may have played a part in his murder a year later. Mendes's work did not end with his death, however. To the contrary, his death spurred scores of people in Brazil and elsewhere to champion his dual social justice and environmental causes.

The case of Mendes, while significant in its own right, is also a useful emblem of the globalization of the entire Latin American trend toward conservation. Indeed, by 1990 the declining state of the Latin American environment had become a matter of mounting international concern. As a result, the face of Latin American environmentalism changed dramatically.

> At the beginning of the 1990s, public opinion in developed countries grew increasingly aware of the extent of environmental destruction, especially with respect to tropical forests. Media campaigns were launched to support the ongoing debate over environmental protection. Another important factor was the development of an alliance between Brazilian and the international NGOs allowing grassroots movements and national NGOs to bypass the national government. This formed a transnational social movement network with broad international support. (de Campos Mello 2001)

One of the more innovative initiatives that came out of this shift was the Debt for Nature Program. This program allows private conservation groups or developed countries to purchase the debt of struggling Latin American countries in exchange for conservation efforts in that country. The first of these swaps was successfully completed in July of 1987, when Bolivia signed a debt reduction agreement with Conservation International, a U.S. environmental organization. In exchange for the $650,000 debt purchased by Conservation International, the Bolivian government agreed to ensure the legal protection of an area surrounding its Beni Biological Station and the Yacuma Park, both of which are significant bastions of biodiversity (UN Economic Commission for Latin America and the Caribbean 1991). Immediately following this successful transaction, similar debt swaps occurred in Ecuador, Costa Rica, and the Dominican Republic. These transactions brought together international organizations such as the Nature Conservancy and World Wildlife Fund, and regional groups, such as the Missouri Botanical Gardens and the Puerto Rico Conservation Trust.

These international organizations established a lasting presence in Latin America, either through direct action or financing the activities of local environmental organizations. The Nature Conservancy, for instance, instituted a series of initiatives during the 1980s on behalf of the Latin American environment. These programs began in 1980, at which time the conservancy began an International Conservation Program, the aim of which was the identification of natural areas and conservation organizations in Latin America in need of technical and financial assistance. One area identified by the conservancy was the fledgling National Parks Foundation of Costa Rica. In 1982, the NC provided Costa Rica with a conservation advisor who worked in the region and helped to establish the foundation. Similar programs were launched by the Nature Conservancy in Mexico and Brazil shortly thereafter. One of the largest programs undertaken by the Nature Conservancy was its Parks in Peril program, founded in 1989. This program brought together international members of the conservancy, funding from the United States, and the cooperation of Latin American governments in the name of conservation. What resulted was an action plan for the protection of 50 million acres in Latin America and the Caribbean and the creation of a park stewardship program.

Other groups, most notably Conservation International, the World Wide Fund for Nature, and the World Conservation Union-IUCN, have contributed their expertise, energy, and funds to the cause of environmental preservation as well, with a special emphasis on protected area creation and management. "The influences from the developed world have certainly helped to make environmental issues more visible in Latin America," observed one analysis. "They have brought about specific policy reforms in areas such as livestock subsidies in the Amazon and pesticide regulations, and contributed to the creation of environmental ministries and agencies throughout the region" (Kaimowitz 1997). Still, these organizations have in the past sometimes been faulted for paying too little heed to poverty and other root causes of deforestation, water pollution, and other forms of environmental degradation (ibid.). In recent years, however, many of these NGOs have expanded their programs to incorporate economic and social considerations more fully into their environmental sustainability programs.

The cosmopolitan spirit of the environmental movement continued in the diplomatic realm as well. In October of 1990, the UN Environment Programme hosted the Seventh Ministerial Meeting on the Environment in Latin America and the Caribbean. At this time, representative countries adopted the Action Plan for the Environment in Latin America and the Caribbean. They also expressly agreed that the plan should be considered a "working document" both for the Regional Preparatory Meeting organized by the Economic Commission for Latin America and the Caribbean and for the UN Conference

Maria Elena Foronda Farro : Peru's Crusader for Sustainable Development

Maria Elena Foronda Farro was born around 1959 in Lima, Peru, but grew up in the poor industrial fishing port of Chimbote, located 400 kilometers (250 miles) north of the capital. Of Chimbote's 300,000 residents, half live in extreme poverty and lack access to clean drinking water and basic sanitation. Although Foronda lived in more fortunate circumstances, she gained a strong interest in helping the people of her community from her father, a union lawyer. She eventually decided to dedicate her life to the cause of social justice. Foronda earned a master's degree in sociology in Mexico, then returned to Chimbote to perform volunteer social work.

Foronda soon focused her attention on Chimbote's fishmeal industry. Peru is the world's leading producer of fishmeal, which consists of ground and processed fish parts used to make animal feed, fertilizers, and preservatives. Fishmeal is produced in large factories along the Peruvian coast, 70 percent of which are located in residential areas. Many of these factories use obsolete technology that allows untreated waste to pollute the surrounding air, water, and soil. In Chimbote, for example, liquid effluents containing industrial chemicals, fish remains, blood, and oils were dumped directly into drains and streams. In some cases, obstructed pipes caused the hazardous waste to back up into city streets, and poor children would wade into it to collect fish remains to sell in town.

Pollution from the fishmeal industry combined with the area's poverty to make Chimbote the third most contaminated city in Peru. This contamination was the source of major health problems among the population of Chimbote, including fungal skin diseases, severe allergies, respiratory ailments, and even the cholera outbreak of 1991–1993. As a result of these problems—many of which affected children and the elderly most severely—the life expectancy for Chimbote residents was a decade below the national average in Peru. "Although the port generates much wealth for a few," Foronda wrote in her research paper "Chimbote's Local Agenda 21," "the bulk of the population must put up with minimal wages as well as a continuous assault on their health and that of their children."

Compounding the environmental consequences of air and water pollution from its factories, the fishmeal industry was also responsible for degradation of Peru's coastal marine environment. The industry employed such destructive fishing practices as bottom-net dragging to catch the tons of fish used in fishmeal production. In addition, the factories discharged water used in production processes into the sea at near-boiling temperatures, which created dead zones along the Peruvian coast.

To address the many environmental and social problems facing Chimbote, Foronda formed partnerships between community groups, fishmeal companies, and the government. She led campaigns to educate local people about their right to environmental protections. She also encouraged the

(continues)

formation of Citizen Environmental Vigilance Committees to monitor the business practices of fishmeal companies and pressure them to adopt meaningful environmental and health safeguards. "It is the men and women of the shanty towns who have been working to defend and conserve the environment, forming the first committees for defense of the environment, recognizing their own rights as citizens, and undertaking direct action to regain control of their surroundings," she explained.

Foronda's work in behalf of the disenfranchised communities of Chimbote aroused the ire of Peru's fishmeal industry and some government officials. In 1994 she and her husband, Oscar Solomon Diaz Barboza, were falsely accused of being members of the Shining Path terrorist group and sentenced to twenty years in prison. Foronda, a longtime advocate of nonviolence, believed that her enemies brought the charges in order to silence her outspoken environmental activism. "In Peru, there is still a law under which an accusation from a 'repentant terrorist' is sufficient grounds for the arrest of any person, even in the absence of any evidence of guilt," she wrote in "Chimbote's Local Agenda 21." "The arrest of the leaders in Chimbote was not the first instance of this law being used to put a stop to ecological work in Peru and it will not be the last."

Foronda's arrest attracted the attention of the human-rights organization Amnesty International as well as environmental groups worldwide. Pressure from both local and international groups forced the government to release her after she had served thirteen months of her sentence. Foronda chose not to press charges for false arrest. Instead, she immediately resumed her work in behalf of the people and environment of Chimbote in order to take advantage of the international recognition and support she had gained while in prison.

Today, Foronda is the founder and director of Natura, one of Peru's leading environmental groups. Natura has worked with progressive fishmeal companies to develop production methods that are both environmentally responsible and profitable. Such projects have provided models that demonstrate how companies can save money in the long run by reducing toxic waste emissions and working with local communities. Foronda's efforts have been effective in reducing pollution levels and improving health standards in Chimbote and other coastal cities in Peru. In 2003 she received the prestigious Goldman Environmental Prize in recognition of her work.

Sources:

Foronda, Maria Elena. "Chimbote's Local Agenda 21: Initiatives to Support Its Development and Implementation." 1998. *Environment and Urbanization* 10, no. 2 (October).
"Goldman Prize Recipient Profile: Maria Elena Foronda Farro." *Goldman Environmental Prize*, 2003. Available at http://www.goldmanprize.org/recipients/recipientProfile.cfm?recipientID=127 (accessed April 18, 2003)

on Environment and Development. This work was also in preparation for the pivotal Earth Summit, hosted by Rio de Janeiro in 1992 (see sidebar, page 223). With the increasingly international flavor of the movement, however, came a new set of problems. These problems were felt particularly by Mexico, which became entangled in debates about the environmental impact of the North American Free Trade Agreement (NAFTA) that it had signed with neighboring United States and Canada. NAFTA and similar trade agreements had brought needed development to the Mexican economy, but it also brought new obstacles to conservation. Issues of economy and conservation came to a head in 1991, when Mexico and the United States fell into a dispute over the harvesting of tuna and dolphin off of shared waters. This dispute was heard by a General Agreement on Tariffs and Trade (GATT) dispute panel in 1991. The panel "upheld Mexican sovereignty and thereby rejected the extraterritorial expansion of U.S. law, which appeared to many environmentalists to be fundamentally flawed. The ensuing conflict between advocates of trade liberalization and environmentalists led to a policy process that sought to reconcile competing interests in the trade-environment debate" (Williams 2001).

Pressure from environmental groups in the United States and Mexico led to a series of new initiatives on the part of the Mexican government. In 1990, the national government responded to criticism concerning air quality by creating the Mexican Programme against Atmospheric Pollution, an initiative that included *Hoy no circula* (Don't drive today) measures requiring automobile owners to forgo using their cars one day each week (Ezcurra 1999). Two years later, the federal government sought to strengthen its resources by dividing and expanding its federal environmental administration. This division resulted in the creation of two autonomous offices: the National Institute of Ecology (Instituto Nacional de Ecologia or INE), responsible for regulating and monitoring the use of the environment and specific natural resources, and an Environmental Protection Attorney General (Procuraduria Federal de Proteccion al Ambiente, or PROFEPA), a new office in charge of law enforcement in environmental matters (ibid.).

Colombia undertook similar environmental reforms at this time. Responding to a rising public outcry concerning the declining state of the country's air, land, and water resources, the Colombian government created a bill of law dictating the management of environmental problems. Belize demonstrated its own ingenuity concerning matters of the environment. Working with USAID, a coalition of NGOs, governmental departments, and international environmental organizations created PACT, the National Protected Areas Conservation Trust Fund. Shortly thereafter, PACT passed the PACT Act, which allowed Belize to charge a conservation fee. This fee allowed Belize to capitalize on the exploding industry of ecotourism, which brought visitors from around the world to Latin America. Collected fees were placed in an environmental trust fund, the endowment of which is used to finance a variety of conservation measures. By implementing schemes such as PACT, Belize showed that Latin American countries in economic peril could create a mutually beneficial relationships with more affluent cultures while preserving their environment and educating the world about its beauties.

In spite of initiatives like these, however, quality of life continued to be a fundamental problem for people of the region and a priority of environmental groups as well. In the Dominican Republic, for instance, pollution levels reached a point of crisis for many citizens. Like Mexico, the Dominican Republic had contended with increasingly poor air and water quality as industrialization accelerated across the country. Environmental groups soon found themselves the locus for complaints regarding pollution. As one analyst explained: "Industrial pollution is a concern for Santiago residents. Barrio organizations have filed petitions to protest chemical effluents from fabric-washing plants. The president of a local environmental NGO calls his organization 'the department of environmental complaints for the city of Santiago'" (Lynch 2001).

Meanwhile, organizations not traditionally associated with the environmental movement—groups such as women's organizations, neighborhood boards, and church groups—began to focus their attention on the rapid degradation of the Dominican Republic's resources: "Women's groups and neighborhood associations have raised concerns about water contamination, air quality, noise, and garbage. Residents and workers in riverine barrios have implicated canneries and distilleries as major polluters, citing fish kills as evidence" (ibid.). The effort of these disparate and varied organizations did not go unnoticed. To the contrary, their tireless advocacy work has been credited as a factor in the emergence of a variety of local and national government initiatives designed to combat growing pollution problems.

The 1990s also witnessed renewed interest in the environment by Cuba. Prior to this decade, the study of environmental concerns in Cuba had been focused on issues of disease prevention and containment and early ideas of sustainable forestry. During the last years of the twentieth century, however, Cuba experienced a renaissance of environmentalism as state and private organizations increased their campaigns of conservation. Lynch suggests that there are three reasons for this dramatic change in Cuban environmentalism: "First, the Chernobyl accident offered Cuba a chance to reject the Soviet development model (one it never wholeheartedly embraced). It also offered an opportunity to advance the state of nuclear epidemiology and a reason to

A Greenpeace protest sign against the Atucha I nuclear plant in Argentina CARRION CARLOS/CORBIS SYGMA

integrate environmental analysis into urban planning at a time when the country could have been expected to choose nuclear energy as the path of least resistance toward energy self-sufficiency. Second, the economic crisis of the early 1990s afforded opportunities to develop and test low-input technologies. The scientific community responded with innovations in low-input agriculture, alternative energy, and low-energy forms of transportation and construction. Finally, the 1992 UN Conference on Environment and Development (UNCED) provided President Fidel Castro with the platform from which to initiate a process of environmental planning and stimulate the growth of an indigenous environmental movement. Cuba's Agenda 21 report helped to legitimate the urban environment as an arena for scientific control, solid waste management, and safe handling of radioactive waste. It also identifies women, youth, workers, peasants, and NGOs as key environmental change agents" (ibid.).

By 1996, the Cuban government had successfully mandated that all projects seeking governmental funding must include an environmental plan in their requests. Furthermore, these projects must include opportunities for public participation and education concerning matters of the environment. Initiatives such as these allowed Cuba to become a quiet leader in the institutionalization of environmentalism, particularly at the national level.

Elsewhere in Latin America, private organizations continue to push for greater policy reform. Environmental advocacy organizations from Mexico to

Argentina steadfastly lobby their governments for improvements in environmental stewardship, educate their fellow citizens about ecological issues, and battle to safeguard vital habitat and biodiversity. They also are increasingly blending environmental and social justice goals, for "given the extreme and massive poverty in Latin America, the possibility of linking environmental problems with the struggle for social justice is practically the only way to make environmental issues relevant to the bulk of the population" (Kaimowitz 1997).

International NGOs remain key allies in these efforts. Indeed, major environmental organizations such as World Wide Fund for Nature, the Nature Conservancy, Greenpeace, the Audubon Society, and other groups have established branch offices in numerous Latin American cities. Many of the ambitious campaigns launched by these and other NGOs have paid enormous dividends for future generations of Latin American people. In 2001, for example, the Nature Conservancy completed another successful debt swap, this time in exchange for the protection of 23,000 acres of vulnerable forest land in Belize's Maya Mountain Marine Corridor. One year later, a group of international organizations including the World Wildlife Fund, the Nature Conservancy, and Conservation International joined with the governments of the United States and Peru to protect more than 27 million acres within the Peruvian Amazon.

Sources:

Christen, Catherine, et al. 1998. "Latin American Environmentalism: Comparative Views." *Studies in Comparative International Development* 33, no. 2 (summer): 58–87.

de Campos Mello, Valérie. 2001. "Global Change and the Political Economy of Sustainable Development in Brazil." In *International Political Economy of the Environment.* Edited by Dimitris Stevis and Valerier Assetto. Boulder, CO: Lynne Rienner.

DeVoss, David. "Mexico's City Limits." 1986. In *Bordering on Trouble: Resources and Politics in Latin America.* Bethesda, MD: Adler and Adler.

Ezcurra, Exquiel, et al., eds. 1999. *The Basin of Mexico: Critical Environmental Issues and Sustainability.* New York: United Nations Press.

Guha, Ramachandra. 2000. *Environmentalism: A Global History.* New York: Longman.

Haynes, Jeff. 1986. "Power, Politics and Environmental Movements in the Third World." In *Bordering on Trouble: Resources and Politics in Latin America.* Bethesda, MD: Adler and Adler.

Kaimowitz, David. 1997. "Social Pressure for Environmental Reform in Latin America." In *Green Guerrillas: Environmental Conflicts and Initiatives in Latin America and the Caribbean.* Edited by Helen Collinson. Montreal: Black Rose.

Lynch, Barbara. 2001. "Development and Risk: Environmental Discourse and Danger in Dominican and Cuban Urban Watersheds." In *International Political Economy of the Environment.* Edited by Dimitris Stevis and Valerier Assetto. Boulder, CO: Lynne Rienner.

Maguire, Andrew, and Janet Welsh Brown, eds. 1986. *Bordering on Trouble: Resources and Politics in Latin America.* Bethesda, MD: Adler and Adler.

Mosher, Lawrence. 1986. "At Sea in the Caribbean?" In *Bordering on Trouble: Resources and Politics in Latin America.* Bethesda, MD: Adler and Adler.

Nature Conservancy website, available at http://www.tnc.org (accessed March 2003).

Simonian, Lane. 1995. *Defending the Land of the Jaguar: A History of Conservation in Mexico.* Austin: University of Texas Press.

Szulc, Tad. 1986. "Brazil's Amazonian Frontier." In *Bordering on Trouble: Resources and Politics in Latin America.* Bethesda, MD: Adler and Adler.

UN Economic Commission for Latin America and the Caribbean. 1991. *Sustainable Development: Changing Production Patterns, Social Equity and the Environment.* Santiago, Chile: ECLAC.

UN Environment Programme. 1992. *The Countries of Latin America and the Caribbean and the Action Plan for the Environment.* Lomas Virreyes, Mexico: UNEP.

Van der Heigden, Hein-Anton. 2001. "Environmental Movements, Ecological Modernisation and Political Opportunity Structures." In *International Political Economy of the Environment.* Edited by Dimitris Stevis and Valerier Assetto. Boulder, CO: Lynne Rienner.

Von Humboldt, Alexander. 1811. *Political Essay on the Kingdom of New Spain.* Translated by John Black. London: Longman, Hurst, Rees, Orme, and Brown.

Williams, Marc. 2001. "In Search of Global Standards: The Political Economy of Trade and the Environment." In *International Political Economy of the Environment.* Edited by Dimitris Stevis and Valerier Assetto. Boulder, CO: Lynne Rienner.

Williams, Marc, and Lucy Ford. 1999. "The World Trade Organisation, Social Movements and Global Environmental Management." In *Environmental Movements: Local, National, and Global.* Edited by Christopher Rootes. London: Frank Cass.

World Wildlife Fund website, available at http://www.wwf.org (accessed February 2003).

Appendix A

African-Eurasian Migratory Waterbird
Agreement (AEWA)
http://www.unep-wcmc.org/
AEWA/index2.html

Albertine Rift Conservation
Society (ARCOS)
http://www.unep-wcmc.org/arcos/

Association of Southeast
Asian Nations (ASEAN)
http://www.asean.org.id/

Biodiversity Planning Support
Programme (BPSP)
http://www.undp.org/bpsp/

BirdLife International (BI)
http://www.birdlife.net

Botanic Gardens Conservation
International (BGCI)
http://www.bgci.org.uk/

CAB International (CABI)
http://www.cabi.org/

Centre for International
Forestry Research (CIFOR)
http://www.cifor.org/

Circumpolar Protected Areas
Network (CPAN)
http://www.grida.no/caff/
cpanstratplan.htm

Commission for Environment
Cooperation (CEC) (North
American Agreement on
Environmental Cooperation)
http://www.cec.org/

Commission on Genetic Resources
for Food and Agriculture (CGRFA)
http://www.fao.org/ag/cgrfa/
default.htm

Commission for Sustainable
Development (CSD)
http://www.un.org/esa/sustdev/csd.htm

Committee on Trade and Environment
(CTE), World Trade Organization
http://www.wto.org/english/
tratop_e/envir_e/envir_e.htm

Conservation International (CI)
http://www.conservation.org/

Consultative Group on International
Agricultural Research (CGIAR)
http://www.cgiar.org/

Convention on Biological
Diversity (CBD)
http://www.biodiv.org/

Convention on International Trade in
Endangered Species of Wild Fauna
and Flora (CITES)
http://www.cites.org/

Convention on Migratory
  Species of Wild Animals (CMS)
  http://www.unep-wcmc.org/cms

European Centre for Nature
  Conservation (ECNC)
  http://www.ecnc.nl/

European Community (EC)
  http://europa.eu.int/

European Environment
  Agency (EEA)
  http://www.eea.eu.int/

Forest Stewardship Council (FSC)
  http://www.fscoax.org/index.html

Foundation for International
  Environmental Law and
  Development (FIELD)
  http://www.field.org.uk/

Global Assessment of Soil
  Degradation (GLASOD)
  http://www.gsf.de/UNEP/glasod.html

Global Biodiversity
  Information Facility (GBIF)
  http://www.gbif.org

Global Coral Reef
  Monitoring Network (GCRMN)
  http://coral.aoml.noaa.gov/gcrmn/

Global Forest Resources Assessment
  2000 (FRA 2000), UN Food and
  Agriculture Organization
  http://www.fao.org/forestry/fo/fra/
  index.jsp

Global International Waters Assessment
  (GIWA), UN Environment Programme
  http://www.giwa.net/

Global Invasive Species
  Programme (GISP)
  http://globalecology.stanford.edu/DGE/
  Gisp/index.html

Global Resource Information Database
  (GRID), UN Environment Programme
  http://www.grid.no

Inter-American Biodiversity
  Information Network (IABIN)
  http://www.iabin.org/

Intergovernmental Oceanographic
  Commission (IOC), UN Educational,
  Scientific, and Cultural Organization
  http://ioc.unesco.org/iocweb/

Intergovernmental Panel on
  Climate Change (IPCC)
  http://www.ipcc.ch/index.html

International Center for Agricultural
  Research in the Dry Areas (ICARDA)
  http://www.icarda.cgiar.org/

International Centre for Living Aquatic
  Resources Management (ICLARM)
  http://www.cgiar.org/iclarm/

International Centre for Research in
  Agroforestry (ICRAF)
  http://www.icraf.cgiar.org/

International Cooperative
  Biodiversity Groups (ICBG)
  http://www.nih.gov/fic/programs/icbg.
  html

International Coral Reef
  Action Network (ICRAN)
  http://www.icran.org

International Coral Reef
  Information Network (ICRIN)
  http://www.environnement.gouv.fr/
  icri/index.html

International Council for the
  Exploration of the Sea (ICES)
  http://www.ices.dk/

International Council for Science (ICSU)
  http://www.icsu.org/

International Food Policy Research
Institute (IFPRI)
http://www.ifpri.org/

International Forum on Forests (IFF),
Commission on Sustainable
Developement
http://www.un.org.esa/sustdev/
forests.htm

International Fund for
Agricultural Development (IFAD)
http://www.ifad.org/

International Geosphere-
Biosphere Programme (IGBP)
http://www.igbp.kva.se/

International Institute of
Tropical Agriculture (IITA)
http://www.iita.org

International Maritime
Organization (IMO)
http://www.imo.org/

International Rivers Network (IRN)
http://www.irn.org/

International Union of
Biological Sciences (IUBS)
http://www.iubs.org/

Man and the Biosphere Program (MAB),
UN Educational, Scientific, and
Cultural Organization
http://www.unesco.org/mab/index.htm

Marine Stewardship Council (MSC)
http://www.msc.org/

Organization of African Unity (OAU)
http://www.oau-oau.org/

Organization for
Economic Cooperation
and Development (OECD)
http://www.oecd.org/

Ozone Secretariat Homepage
http://www.unep.ch/ozone/

Pan-European Biological and Landscape
Diversity Strategy (PEBLDS)
http://www.strategyguide.org/

Program for the Conservation of
Arctic Flora and Fauna (CAFF),
Arctic Council
http://www.grida.no/caff/

Protocol Concerning Specially
Protected Areas and Wildlife (SPAW)
http://www.cep.unep.org/law/
cartnut.html

Ramsar Convention on Wetlands of
International Importance (RAMSAR)
http://www.ramsar.org/

South African Development
Community (SADC)
http://www.sadc.int/

South Pacific Regional
Environmental Programme (SPREP)
http://www.sprep.org.ws/

Species Survival Commission (SSC),
World Conservation Union
http://iucn.org/themes/ssc/index.htm

TRAFFIC (the joint wildlife trade
monitoring programme of World
Wide Fund for Nature and World
Conservation Union)
http://www.traffic.org

United Nations Centre for
Human Settlements (UNCHS)
http://www.unchs.org

United Nations
Children's Fund (UNICEF)
http://www.unicef.org

United Nations Conference on
Environment and Development
(UNCED), Rio de Janeiro, June 1992
http://www.un.org/esa/sustdev/
agenda21.htm

United Nations Conference on Trade
and Development (UNCTAD)
http://www.unctad.org/

United Nations Convention to Combat
  Desertification (UNCCD)
  http://www.unccd.int/main.php

United Nations Convention
  on the Law of the Sea (UNCLOS)
  http://www.un.org/Depts/los/
  index.htm

United Nations Development
  Programme (UNDP)
  http://www.undp.org/

United Nations Educational, Scientific,
  and Cultural Organization (UNESCO)
  http://www.unesco.org/

United Nations Environment
  Programme (UNEP)
  http://www.unep.org/

United Nations Food and
  Agriculture Organization (FAO)
  http://www.fao.org/

United Nations
  Forum on Forests (UNFF)
  http://www.un.org/esa/sustdev/
  forests.htm

United Nations Framework Convention
  on Climate Change (UNFCCC)
  http://www.unfccc.de/index.html

United Nations Industrial
  Development Organization (UNIDO)
  http://www.unido.org/

World Agricultural Information Centre
  (WAIC), UN Food and Agriculture
  Organization
  http://www.fao.org/waicent/search/
  default.htm

World Bank (WB)
  http://www.worldbank.org

World Commission
  on Dams (WCD)
  http://www.dams.org/

World Commission on Protected Areas
  (WCPA), World Conservation Union
  http://www.wcpa.iucn.org/

World Conservation
  Monitoring Centre (WCMC)
  http://www.unep-wcmc.org

World Conservation
  Union (IUCN)
  http://www.iucn.org/

World Health Organization (WHO)
  http://www.who.int

World Heritage Convention (WHC)
  http://www.unesco.org/whc/index.htm

World Resources Institute (WRI)
  http://www.wri.org/wri/

World Summit on Sustainable
  Development (WSSD),
  Johannesburg, South Africa,
  September 2002
  http://www.johannesburgsummit.org/

World Trade Organization (WTO)
  http://www.wto.org/

World Water Council (WWC)
  http://www.worldwatercouncil.org/

World Wide Fund
  for Nature (WWF)
  http://www.panda.org/

WorldWatch Institute
  http://www.worldwatch.org/

Appendix B
Organisation for Economic Co-Operation and Development (OECD) Member Countries and Their Dates of Entry

Australia: June 7, 1971

Austria: September 29, 1961

Belgium: September 13, 1961

Canada: April 10, 1961

Czech Republic: December 21, 1995

Denmark: May 30, 1961

Finland: January 28, 1969

France: August 7, 1961

Germany: Spetember 27, 1961

Greece: September 27, 1961

Hungary: May 7, 1996

Iceland: June 5, 1961

Ireland: August 17, 1961

Italy: March 29, 1962

Japan: April 28, 1964

Korea: December 12, 1996

Luxembourg: December 7, 1961

Mexico: May 18, 1994

Netherlands: November 13, 1961

New Zealand: May 29, 1973

Norway: July 4, 1961

Poland: November 22, 1996

Portugal: August 4, 1961

Slovak Republic: December 14, 2000

Spain: August 3, 1961

Sweden: September 28, 1961

Switzerland: September 28, 1961

Turkey: August 2, 1961

United Kingdom: May 2, 1961

United States: April 12, 1961

Index